W9-ABG-807

The Poetics of Protest

Literary Form and Political Implication
in the Victim-of-Society Novel

GEORGE GOODIN

Southern Illinois University Press

Carbondale and Edwardsville

Library of Congress Cataloging in Publication Data

Goodin, George.
The poetics of protest.

Bibliography: p.
Includes index.
1. Fiction—History and criticism. 2. Politics and
literature. 3. Literature and society. 4. Narration
(Rhetoric) I. Title.
PN3448.P6G66   1985   809.3'93520694   83-27179
ISBN 0-8093-1173-9

88   87   86   85   4   3   2   1

For
Mary, Margaret, Sam, Pete, Ruth, Thomas, Tony, and Kate

Contents

Preface

THIS book deals with the poetics and rhetoric of one kind of social protest novel in order to explore some old problems concerning the capabilities and limitations of literature as a means of political expression. Although old problems are likely to be perennial ones, I hope at least to reformulate the issues, to provide a different angle of attack on them, and to lower the level of abstraction at which they are discussed.

Assessing how well literary works can treat political reality must entail some extraliterary criticism, just as assessing how well political acts treat human reality calls for some extrapolitical criticism. For this reason, I do at times make basically political judgments, and I wish I could offer some label for my political beliefs, so that readers might stand warned of bias. Unfortunately, without giving the subject more space than it deserves, I can offer nothing very satisfactory. My leftist friends tell me that I am conservative, others that I am radical. All agree that I am neither objective nor realistic. That is true. Often, I find what marches under those banners to be shortsighted and hardhearted. Perhaps I have attended too many faculty meetings. At any rate, I hope that my somewhat latitudinarian idealism does not unduly disturb readers who are more knowledgeable, pragmatic, or coherent in their political views. Insofar as I have clarified literary matters, which I am primarily concerned to argue, readers should find it easier to use their own political standards.

I am grateful to the National Endowment for the Humanities and to Southern Illinois University at Carbondale for support received during the course of research for this book and to many friends and colleagues who answered my

ix

questions and endured my thinking aloud. Royal Gettmann of the University of Illinois, Charles Elkins of Florida International University, Ray Mazurek of Pennsylvania State University, and Robert Griffin of SIU were kind enough to read the manuscript and to make many helpful comments. Alan Cohn, of the Humanities Library of SIU, helped greatly in locating relevant works and in calling many of them to my attention. I want to thank Nancy Gillespie, Scott Perlenfein, and Nancy Bowden for their considerable help and know-how in preparing the manuscript. My wife read and proofread many drafts, for which I am very grateful, despite her once telling me that she particularly liked the quotations.

The Poetics of Protest

1

Introduction: A Problem in Composition

> When a man suffers himself, it is called misery; when
> he suffers in the suffering of another, it is called pity.
> But how can the unreal sufferings of the stage possibly
> move pity? The spectator is not moved to aid the suf-
> ferer but merely to be sorry for him.
>
> —Augustine

IN 1794 William Godwin published *The Adventures of Caleb Williams*. In a brief preface withdrawn at the time "in compliance with the alarms of booksellers," he explained the purpose of the novel.

It is now known to philosophers, that the spirit and character of the government intrudes itself into every rank of society. But this is a truth, highly worthy to be communicated, to persons, whom books of philosophy and science are never likely to reach. Accordingly it was proposed, in the invention of the following work, to comprehend, as far as the progressive nature of a single story would allow, a general review of the modes of domestic and unrecorded despotism, by which man becomes the destroyer of man.[1]

In using the novel to criticize institutions by showing the suffering they can cause, Godwin was not alone. In the era of the French Revolution many novels protested social injustice by showing man destroyed by man.

At least as early as Diderot's *Nun*, first published in 1780, such novels had appeared. They still do, as Ken Kesey's *One Flew over the Cuckoo's Nest* indicates. The English Industrial Revolution gave rise to many, such as Gaskell's *Mary Barton* and Kingsley's *Alton Locke*. Continental Europe produced during the nineteenth century von Kleist's *Michael Kohlhaas*, Hugo's *Les Misérables*, and Zola's *L'Assommoir* and *Germinal*. The American depression brought about more: Dos Passos' *USA*, Steinbeck's *Grapes of Wrath*, Hemingway's *To Have and Have Not*, and Faulkner's *Wild Palms* and *Light in August*. During the same period Greene's *Power and the Glory*, Malraux's *Days of Wrath*, and Silone's *Bread and Wine* occupied themselves with the rise of totalitarianism. In the so-called Third World, James Ngugi's *Grain of Wheat*, Alan Paton's *Cry, the Beloved Country*, Carlos Fuentes' *Death of Artemio Cruz*, and Mariano Azuela's *Underdogs* have presented the effects of colonialism and its aftermath. These and many other novels, widely separated geographically and historically, form a distinct group among the many literary works devoted to social and political themes.

Wilbur L. Cross describes this group in its earliest form and supplies a name from that commonly given to its hero.

A tyrant or villain was selected from the upper class, who, hedged about by law and custom, wreaks a motiveless hatred on the sensitive and cultured hero, who, though born free, is not born to wealth and a title. The gentleman after a career of crime may or may not come to a disgraceful end. That was optional. The hero, after years of drudgery and abject labor, after perhaps being compelled to play the violin or to write poetry to keep from starving, either is crushed, or by a revolution of fortune gains comparative ease. The best examples of this distinctively "victim-of-society" story are Godwin's *Caleb Williams* (1794) and Elizabeth Inchbald's *Nature and Art* (1796).[2]

Malcolm Cowley makes a similar description of a later manifestation, which he calls the "art novel."

There are two essential characters, two antagonists, the Poet and the World. The Poet—who may also be a painter, a violinist, an inventor, an architect or a Centaur—is generally to be identified with the author of the novel, or at least with the novelist's ideal picture of himself. He tries to assert his individuality in despite of the World, which is stupid, unmanageable and usually victorious. Sometimes the Poet triumphs, but the art novelists seem to realize, as a type, that the sort of hero they describe is likely to be defeated in the sort of society he must face.[3]

In reviewing the fiction of Dos Passos from *Three Soldiers* to *1919*, Cowley notes that he broadened the social protest of his early art novels by turning to the suffering of those who were not artists. In doing so, he reversed the process which probably produced the art novel in the first place, for Harry Levin has attributed a narrowing of social protest in the novel to Flaubert, in remarking that he "transposed the revolt of the individual against society into a personal quarrel between the artist and the bourgeoisie."[4] However this may be, Cowley's art novel closely resembles Cross's victim-of-society novel. What their accounts have in common makes it evident that this group of novels is similar in more than purpose. In each the protagonist suffers unjustly because of an antagonist allied to entrenched social power.

Like other groups of literary works, these novels could be studied for many different reasons. A historical study could relate them to the many changing social, political, and literary conditions which gave rise to them, and perhaps try to gauge their impact on public events. A thematic study could treat the general but also particular understanding of social injustice which literary treatment makes possible. A genre study could establish their constants and variables, relate them synchronically and diachronically to other literary forms, and determine whether they do indeed make up a genre. Although these considerations cannot be ignored I want to concentrate on others. The similarities of purpose and action in these novels provide a very good opportunity for studying the implementation of purpose in literature—for studying literary works in terms of their poetics and rhetoric. They bring into focus some of the compositional problems caused by the resistance which literature offers to extraliterary purposes. They permit, since these purposes are largely political, a close examination of the compatibility of literary and political aims. Before getting into the problems created by their purpose, however, we need a better idea of the group we are dealing with.

I propose to follow Cross's example and to call this group victim-of-society novels. Although the term is cumbersome and presents some difficulties which I will have to address later, it has some currency, and its difficulties are no worse than those of other terms. To fully establish what it means will take the remainder of this book, but by looking now at what it does we can consider what sort of term it is and what sort of group it designates. It identifies a protagonist, a subject matter, and a basic action: victim, social injustice, and suffering. It thus resembles "picaresque novel," "*Bildungsroman*," and "detective novel," which function similarly. The groups designated by these terms differ from the mere subject matter groups so useful to librarians—political novels, religious novels, and so on—but they are open to similar objections. If construed broadly, they include almost any novel, and even if they are construed narrowly, many novels can be placed in more than one group.

Partly because of the first objection, I shall try to construe the victim-of-society novel rather narrowly and to avoid the imperialism of placing all or most novels within the scope of this study. I shall take the term to refer to a group formed by the intersection of social protest novels and novels of victimage. Thus, in addition to excluding all novels which are neither, it excludes all social protest novels in which the protagonist is not a victim in any significant sense: Disraeli's *Sybil*, Morris's *News from Nowhere*, and Tolstoy's *Resurrection*, for example. Similarly, it excludes all novels of victimage which are not primarily concerned with social protest, such as Richardson's *Clarissa* and James's *Wings of a Dove*.

Introduction

Since victim-of-society novels have the obvious purpose of presenting through the protagonist's suffering an injustice which is both social and remediable, there should be little need to argue the existence or centrality of such a purpose in the novels I shall treat. To be sure, presentations of unjust social institutions such as Dickens' Circumlocution Office have been interpreted as expressing the consoling absurdist doctrine that injustice is both omnipresent and omnipotent, but I shall not hesitate to treat them for their manifest purpose. Nevertheless, many novels do present protagonists who are victims not only of society but of nature, chance, the cosmos, and other adversaries which human beings can do little to oppose. Harry Levin makes the relevant distinction between two very different ways of presenting man: "Where Hugo, or even Dostoevsky, views him with humanitarian sympathy as the victim of society, Hardy views him as the plaything of nature, the victim of a cosmic joke. But, as Hardy suggests, there are two kinds of conflict: that between individuals and human institutions, and that between individuals and things inherent in the universe."[5] Although the very point argued by the writer of the victim-of-society novel is that too much injustice is perceived as a necessary consequence of the cosmos and too little as the arbitrary operation of human institutions, we cannot, when confronted with actual novels, always apply Levin's distinction with ease. There are many novels, such as Kafka's *Trial*, Camus' *Stranger*, and Chopin's *Awakening*, which deal with both kinds of conflict. Such novels and any other borderline cases I shall try to leave aside. In doing so, however, I do not at all want to deny or obscure the truth in the commonplace assertion that novels usually present conflicts between individuals and their social environments. Indeed the fact that, in an extremely broad sense, all or most novels may be victim-of-society novels seems to me not an embarrassment, but a guarantee that this study will have a relevance beyond its immediate concerns.

The second objection, that a single novel may belong to more than one group, I concede. It derives whatever force it has from the stubborn survival of the neoclassical theory that literary genres are like biological species, mutually exclusive groups to one and only one of which an individual may be said to belong. I find very interesting, even if unpersuasive, the modern search for mutually exclusive groups of literary works in the criticism of R. S. Crane, Sheldon Sacks, and others, but even Crane agrees with most other modern critics that the genre is not such a group. Tzvetan Todorov has suggested that if we conceive of literary works as "manifesting" rather than "belonging" to genre, we will find less strange the idea that one work can be assigned to more than one genre.[6] At any rate, calling a work a victim-of-society novel should not be taken as denying it a place in other groups or genres.

Only if we conceive genre itself in this way can the victim-of-society novel be a genre, but even so it may not be, because it differs in one very important respect from the detective novel, the picaresque, and the *Bildungsroman*. In a very influential formulation, Wellek and Warren have said, "Genre should be conceived, we think, as a grouping of literary works based, theoretically, upon both outer form (specific meter or structure) and also upon inner form (attitude, tone, purpose—more crudely, subject and audience)."[7] As we have seen, victim-of-society novels have a broad common purpose—protesting social injustice—and a common action—the protagonists suffer unjustly because of antagonists who can command the power of institutions. However, such a description, though adequate as the sort of first approximation with which the study of any group must begin, is hardly determinate enough to justify calling the victim-of-society novel a genre. Can it be made more determinate? Well, yes and no. What I shall show is that this group of novels contains several subgroups, each of which correlates a purpose and a structure definite enough to justify the claim that it is a subgenre. In the final analysis, I take any work to be a victim-of-society novel if it conforms to one of these subgroups, not on the basis of any very determinate description of the group as a whole. Therefore, the victim-of-society novel is a genre if it is appropriate to apply that term to a group made up entirely of related subgenres, and it may not be if no such inference is allowable. I shall leave this an open question because it cannot be resolved except through a long excursus on the criteria for genre. Even if I were up to that task, it would divert attention from the main problems with which this book deals.

By so openly manifesting their purpose, victim-of-society novels risk the charge of failing to achieve it, or misfiring. In speaking of *Caleb Williams*, Walter Scott moderated his praise by objecting

> on account of the moral proposed by the author, which, in direct opposition to that of the worthy chaplin of Newgate, seems to be, not that a man guilty of theft or murder is in some danger of being hanged, but that, by a strange concurrence of circumstances, he may be regularly conducted to the gallows for theft or murder which he has never committed. There is nothing instructive or consolatory in this proposition, when taken by itself; and if intended as a reproach upon the laws of this country, it is equally applicable to all human judicatures, whose judges can only decide according to evidence.[8]

Though little inclined to the moral proposed by the author in the first place, Scott had a point. To attack the legal system as a system, Godwin had to establish that it was more than accidentally unjust. Since he motivated its conviction of an innocent man by having Falkland frame Caleb Williams, the attack was deflected to Falkland. Nevertheless, Scott conceived the purpose and motivation of the novel too narrowly. Falkland is indeed attacked, but he himself is motivated to frame Williams by his exaggerated regard for honor. Because such a characteristic must originate socially, and the novel recounts its doing so, Godwin channels his social criticism through Falkland. The defect in the legal system proper, therefore, is not an accident or a necessary condition of all human judicature. It consists, at least, in the excessive influence of wealthy people on legal proceedings.

A more justifiable charge of misfiring can be seen in the letters Joseph Conrad wrote to John Galsworthy after reading the manuscript of the novel which became *Fraternity*. In the midst of writing *Under Western Eyes*, Conrad thought about Galsworthy's manuscript far into the night and eventually devoted to it three letters of criticism extremely sensitive to compositional problems in the victim-of-society novel. *Fraternity* attacks the English class system by presenting the interclass romance of Hilary, the protagonist, with a working-class girl whom he rejects in the end because of his upper-class instincts. As a means of realizing such a purpose, Hilary seemed defective to Conrad. Just as Scott did not find in Falkland's character a social criticism, Conrad saw Hilary as a "pathological case." He thought him inconsistent, because a class feeling strong enough to motivate ultimate rejection should have prevented his surrender to the girl's attractions in the first place. Seeking elsewhere his real motive, therefore, Conrad found it in his basic character, refinement. He thus felt compelled to explain the treatment of the girl as refined trifling, or flirting. When Hilary rejects her, "class is just the mask of impotence, and your attack misses its mark."[9]

According to Conrad, Galsworthy failed not only to hit the right target, but to suggest any grounds for hope that class injustice could be remedied.

> It is impossible to read a book like that without asking oneself,—what then? Are we to be sanitists or write checks, or are we to let casual girls embrace our knees till our, what shall I call it?—refined desire is completely satisfied, our humanity at the same time not being imperative enough and not elementary enough, I may say, to knock her mercifully on her head wards? Or is this,—I won't say tale,—is this vision of life and things, so admirably imagined, so felicitously and poetically presented, is it a mere declaration, not of the vanity of things (that would be a too optimistic view), but of the utter futility of existence? Pessimism can no further go (p. 78).

Only a few alternatives could have solved Galsworthy's problem. He could have taken one of Conrad's suggestions and simply kept Hilary out of sight more. He could have made Hilary unabashedly into a case of social pathology, as Godwin had made Falkland, but Conrad advised against this,

8

perhaps feeling it more congenial to his own temperament. Instead, Conrad suggested that Galsworthy present Hilary more positively: "If the thesis of the book is as I understand it, you should have presented to us a man really belonging to the class and with a noble instinct trying to assert his manhood against the heart-withering, brain-muddling convention—and then—had you so willed—knocked him down" (p. 81). It is fine criticism, which Galsworthy apparently ignored.

Accusations of misfire among victim-of-society novels are commonplace. For example, Ellison's *Invisible Man*, Malraux's *Man's Fate*, and Silone's *Bread and Wine* have all been charged with failing to achieve their social purposes. As we will see, many novels treated here have been similarly accused. Often, such accusations are broader. Irving Howe argues that political novels generally give nonpolitical solutions to political problems. David Caute finds that in committed literature "accidents are the rule rather than the exception." Sometimes these accusations envision no alternative for a writer except to adopt a different purpose altogether. James Baldwin claims, "The 'protest' novel, so far from being disturbing, is an accepted and comforting aspect of the American scene." Similar charges are yet more sweeping. Almost every literary form—including tragedy, comedy, romance, and realism—has been accused of an inherent generic bias favoring entrenched social power. All narrative, all literature, and all language have been characterized as biased toward *is* rather than *ought*. Leon Trotsky has seen in all art a bondage to the past which he calls "passive conservatism."[10]

Regardless of the scope of the argument, those who see misfires in victim-of-society novels essentially charge that the writer tries to present a conflict between man and human institutions, but actually presents one between man and the universe, or nature. This entails two different but related issues. The first concerns the targeting of the protest, which I shall call for convenience the clarity problem. The second, which I shall call the hope problem, concerns implications as to the task of remedying the sort of injustice presented. Although not the only problems, these are the main ones, and this book is largely concerned with how novelists address them.

Like other committed literature, victim-of-society novels raise the old question of compatibility between literary and political aims: how much does literary form constrain political expression? However, they do so in fairly specifiable ways, permitting us at times to see political aims in the act of becoming literary. How the problems of clarity and hope present themselves to the writer can be indicated by comparing the composition of a victim-of-society novel with that of a tragedy. If, as George Steiner suggests, tragedy began to die when Rousseau and others led people to believe that "the quality of being could be radically altered and improved by changes in education and in the social and material circumstances of existence,"[11] then the victim-of-society novel is the major successor to tragedy. If not, it is a major competitor.

We can begin by observing that some novels are largely devoted to presenting human suffering. In doing so, they concern themselves with the literary motivation of it, and with its possible causes. Although these are numberless, the basic types of causes are not. Freud limits them to three: "the superior power of nature, the feebleness of our own bodies and the inadequacy of the regulations which adjust the mutual relationships of human beings in the family, the state and society."[12] A similar classification can be obtained by noting common responses to suffering. One is to blame the victim, the Katzenjammer response of "you brought it on yourself, Rollo." A second is to assess no human responsibility and blame some metaphysical agent, seeing the suffering as due to what lawyers call an "act of God." A third is to blame "them"—other people, the powers that be, the establishment.

In particular instances the causes of suffering, however classified, usually operate together, so that attributing it to one or two causes can seldom be achieved except by screen-

ing out or de-emphasizing the remainder. Aristotelian tragedy emphasizes metaphysical causation by minimizing the
role of the victim and screening out the social, which gets
assimilated to the realm of necessity as human nature, fate,
or whatever.[13] According to Aristotle tragic heroes are victims of injustice because of the gap between what they do to
bring on their suffering and the suffering itself, but this gap
is filled with the mystery or mystification of Inevitability.
Tragedy therefore affirms the important truth that some suffering must simply be borne, even if unjust.

For writers of victim-of-society novels, however, such
tragedy won't do, not because they have an impure, nonliterary purpose—admittedly the case—but because Aristotelian tragedy has a different impure, nonliterary purpose. It
seeks to console, to get its audience to accept unavoidable
injustice. The writers considered here seek to prevent such
consolation, that their readers may reject avoidable injustice.
In Aristotelian terms, they need to socialize hamartia and
deny catharsis. To do so, they place the major flaw motivating the protagonist's suffering in an antagonist who can exert
the power of human institutions. Insofar as they succeed,
they will go far toward solving the problems of clarity and
hope. To be sure, this is no easy task, but it should be no
more difficult to show social causation than to screen it out.

The clarity problem centers largely around the antagonist, or victimizer. The target of criticism may be the state,
society, culture, or a ruling class such as the aristocracy, bourgeoisie, or bureaucracy. It may even be a nonruling group,
an adversary organization of radicals or revolutionaries, or a
counter culture. Even when the victimizer in the real world
might be thought one person, a Hitler or a Stalin, and such
a person is presented, as in the rare case of Solzhenitsyn's
First Circle, the target can most accurately be described as
some human institution.

Because they are the logical source of motivation for unjust suffering, antagonists may be realized as major characters, such as Falkland in *Caleb Williams*. I can think of no other
antagonist of comparable stature, perhaps because, as Hazlitt

11

claimed, he is the first, rather than the second, person in the novel.[14] I prefer seeing him as a limit case for the antagonist, the maximum exposure possible without becoming the protagonist. The character used to motivate the victim's suffering must be carefully motivated in turn. A predominantly personal motive will not do because it would make the protagonist simply a victim of another person and create only a novel of victimage. Godwin's solution was to motivate Falkland by a diseased sense of honor. Because this hamartia originates socially and leads Falkland to use the social power of the government against his enemy, Caleb Williams is a victim of society. When Falkland himself later starts to suffer from guilt and fear, it becomes obvious that he too is a victim of society. As the presentation of antagonists becomes fuller, they almost inevitably turn into victims themselves and start to command sympathy.

The other limit case for presenting victimizers is to avoid presenting them. In his preface to *Days of Wrath*, a novel treating Nazi persecution of Communists, Malraux explained, "If I had had to give Nazis the importance I give Kassner, I should obviously have done so in terms of their basic emotional drive—nationalism."[15] In 1935 Malraux was not prepared to give nationalism the minimum sympathy he had extended to capitalism in his rather full portrait of Ferral in *Man's Fate*. For the same reason, some victim-of-society novels merely mention victimizers and others give them even less attention, making them presences felt by their effects on their victims.

Between these two limits, the nearly absent antagonist and one almost as important as the hero, we find the presentation of unjust institutions. The antagonist function is often split among many characters in order to suggest more clearly that the target is social. Sometimes it is assigned to protagonists as false consciousness at odds with what is best in them.

Representing antagonists is not entirely a literary problem. Most of us, like Huck Finn's father, often cuss the government, but like him we usually experience it as a shadowy

12

presence. Society is even more difficult to grasp—not because it is abstract, but because in one sense it is all around us and in another it is nowhere. T. W. Adorno has dwelt at some length on attempts to define it.

> The idea of society confirms Nietzsche's insight that concepts "which are basically shorthand for process" elude verbal definition. For society is essentially process; its laws of movement tell more about it than whatever invariables might be deduced. Attempts to fix its limits end up with the same result. If one for instance defines society simply as mankind, including all the subgroups into which it breaks down, out of which it is constructed, or if one, more simply still, calls it the totality of all human beings living in a given period, one misses thereby all the subtler implications of the concept. Such a formal definition presupposes that society is already a society of human beings, that society is itself already human, is immediately one with its subjects; as though the specifically social did not consist precisely in the imbalance of institutions over men, the latter coming little by little to be the incapacitated products of the former.[16]

The difficulty of representing society or social institutions, then, affects everyone. For this reason I shall speak of victimizers in many ways, depending at times on how clearly the novels indicate who or what is responsible for the injustice they present.

Unlike the clarity problem, the hope problem centers largely around the protagonists. They must be subjected to injustice and suffer more than they deserve, more than the portion falling to all human beings. In presenting this suffering and subjection, however, the writer operates under another nonliterary constraint, which G. K. Chesterton called the "paradox of reform."

> If we are to save the oppressed, we must have two apparently antagonistic emotions in us at the same time. We must think the oppressed man intensely miserable, and at the same time intensely attractive and important. We must insist with violence on his degradation; we must insist with the same violence upon his dignity. For if we relax by one inch the one assertion, men will say he does not need saving. And if we relax by one inch

13

the other assertion, men will say he is not worth saving. The optimists will say that reform is needless. The pessimists will say that reform is hopeless.[17]

By its nature, suffering tends to be proportional to the power of its cause. Consequently, as our sense of unjust suffering increases, so too, all other things being equal, will our sense of the power of injustice. Only if we see in the victim some of its effects do we see any injustice at all, any reason for social remedies. Only if we see something which injustice has not created or some capacity to struggle against it are we likely to see a limit to its power and thus a reason to hope for effective action.

Because of this paradox, which affects nonpolitical action as well, we may find both sentimental optimism and claustrophobic pessimism in novels. Like other novelists, writers of victim-of-society novels deserve our indulgence in their attempts to navigate between these twin hazards, but they can counter with a major resource—restraint. They exercise it when they refuse to dwell too long or graphically on the details of suffering and when they refuse to exploit it merely for emotional effect. Restraint is commonly considered a literary value, but it helps achieve a worthwhile political purpose by keeping the human being visible in the suffering and thus marking a limit to the power of injustice. Here we have, rather than the incompatibility so commonly found, a harmony of literary and political values. Nevertheless, coping with Chesterton's paradox of reform, avoiding excessive optimism or pessimism, requires more elaborate and involved balancing acts.

Having formulated the problems caused by the purpose of the victim-of-society novel, we can now better address the dangers of the term itself. In looking at the antagonist, we saw that "society" is problematic. Indeed a major difficulty for sociologists is to specify exactly what they take their discipline to be studying and how it is represented. Even if the term were clear, "society" is often not the best way to characterize what the antagonists in these novels represent, what the victims are victims of. "Human institutions" is better be-

14

cause more widely applicable, but it is no easier to define and to refer throughout this study to the "victim-of-human-institutions novel" would mean exchanging a cumbersome term for one still more cumbersome. In looking at the protagonist, we also had difficulty with the term "victim" because, as we have seen, the protagonist needs to be more than just a victim. If we think of either fictional or real people as nothing but victims, we deny or ignore most of what makes them human. We then contribute to injustice by dehumanizing those who suffer from it—a group which, after all, includes everybody at one time or another.

The questions at issue presuppose that novels are written by authors, that authors have purposes, and that these purposes can be frustrated to varying degrees by the resistance of the medium. They are questions of poetics and rhetoric, fields which have been intertwined throughout their history because literature has been defined both as fine art which uses language and as discourse which is fine art. I have chosen to omit the word rhetoric from the title of this book primarily because of fear that it would mislead. Unlike poetics, it is associated mainly with nonliterary discourse.[18] Furthermore, it is so often identified with elocution that many associate it only with matters of diction and not with composition. Nevertheless, I shall be concerned both with poetics in Todorov's sense, as a discipline which "aims at a knowledge of the general laws that preside over the birth of each work," and with the rhetoric of fiction in Wayne Booth's sense, as a study of "the author's means of controlling his reader."[19]

This approach requires some surrender of the reader's perspective which literary criticism usually takes, and adoption of the writer's view of a novel as a project or process—seeing it in what R. S. Crane calls its "constructional aspect."[20] Because either perspective requires that critics of fiction have some fictions of their own about the role of purpose in literary works, I want to take a brief look at these critical fictions here. Those who dislike discussions of methodology should go on to the next section of this chapter.

15

From the reader's perspective we may dispense with notions like "purpose" and "author" and make "discourse" into an agentive noun. This fiction—a hot potato caught by many critics and held only at the expense of some pain by a few—we must drop also because it makes meaningless the questions at issue, which are real enough. E. D. Hirsch has arrived at a reader's fiction more fruitful for our purposes in the opposite manner, positing the author's meaning or intention as the object readers seek in reading or interpreting a text and eliminating from it much of the agency it normally implies, so that we're often unable to say who or what is doing the intending.[21] We read on the assumption that making texts requires writers to make choices. In choosing one word for a certain slot in a sentence, writers reject the alternatives they might have used. In choosing one sentence to follow another, they also choose for it not to precede. In attributing to characters certain qualities and actions, they implicitly reject others. Using the pattern of such choices, we read by intuiting intention or purpose. On the basis of whatever part of the text we have read, we form expectations, guesses, hypotheses, or hunches about the rest, and further reading confirms, disconfirms, or forces us to revise them. We make considerable allowances for cross purposes, however, either in the writers themselves or between them and their public medium. If a text is literary, it carries the weight not only of previous language but of previous literature, the residue of intentions and accidents which are not the writer's, as well as other influences not easy to specify. We value literature in large part because it seems to have purposes of its own which allow writers to speak better than they mean, enabling us to trust the tale rather than the teller. Ignorant about exactly what agencies are operating at what time, but taking the author to be a major one, it is natural to resort to some such abstract notion of intention as Hirsch enjoins.

Hirsch provides a model of the reading act because his object is interpretation, but to see matters of poetics or rhetoric, we need a model of the writing act, one moving *from* purpose or intention rather than *to* it. Fortunately, Kenneth

Burke has spent much of his life providing one and using it to rewrite, reinvent, or regenerate literary works, which he calls "prophesying after the event."[22] Burke has long been fascinated by Poe's claim, similar to the one Godwin made for *Caleb Williams*, that he composed "The Raven" through a deductive process, starting with certain assumed principles: "even if we hypothetically assume that Poe's account of the *poet's* procedure was an absolute lie, I submit that his essay came quite close to the ideal procedure for *critics* to follow, in relating a poem to the principles of its composition" (p. 35). This critical procedure is possible because in art as in nature "a thing's 'purpose' is technically one with its *esse*."[23] Just as we can examine a speech act or an ethical act and render explicit the grammatical or moral principles on which the agent acted, we can examine a literary work and make explicit the principles of composition implied by the authorial decisions. And just as the conscious thoughts of other agents may not extend to the principles implied by what they do, neither may those of writers encompass the principles of composition informing their works.

> Regardless of what an author may or may not have personally intended, the Formalist critic fulfills his "proper" task by imputing to the work whatever design, or intention, he thinks is best able to account for the nature of the work.

> Thus, the question of an "intentional fallacy" becomes quite irrelevant. The *test* of the design is pragmatic. The critic proceeds to substantiate his thesis casuistically, by showing in detail how much the imputed design might account for.[24]

Of course we can know the purpose, design, intention, or principles of composition only by reading the work, but they have nonetheless a *logical* priority which we can use in regenerating or rewriting the work.

The critical fiction in Burke's model of writing consists of treating this logical priority as *temporal* priority in generating the work anew. Such a method deliberately ignores the fact that real writers work in a back and forth manner amid a tangle of conflicting purposes and interacting imperatives. It sees the act of writing not only as teleological but as unidirectionally moving toward accomplishing a purpose. It sees one purpose because it ranks multiple purposes by relative priority. It sees writers as knowing fully what they are doing all along; both writer and purpose are fictions because they are not conceived biographically. The value of this critical fiction must rest on its results, and Burke himself has got impressive results. Like any other methodology, however, it simplifies and therefore carries with it the danger of oversimplifying. As John Reichert points out, "There is something to be learned by operating with the fiction that a work is constructed with a single and clearly conceived aim in view, provided one knows when to drop the fiction before making the work seem simpler than it is."[25]

The main value of Burke's method lies in what it tells us about poetics and rhetoric through its application to more than one work. It can have this application because his model of writing can be reversed to provide its own model of reading. Whereas in writing purpose creates structure and attitude creates organization, we read by seeing that structure reveals purpose and organization reveals attitude. Thus when we read works of similar structure or organization, we look for similar purposes and attitudes. Burke goes beyond Wellek and Warren's principle that a genre has both a common structure and a common purpose to make the stronger claim that it has a common structure *because* it has a common purpose. Using his method, he says, "Art forms like 'tragedy' or 'comedy' or 'satire' would be treated as *equipments for living*, that size up situations in various ways and in keeping with correspondingly various attitudes. The typical ingredients of such forms would be sought. Their relation to typical situations would be stressed. Their comparative values would be considered, with the intention of formulating a 'strategy of strategies,' the 'over-all' strategy obtained by inspection of the lot."[26] Here Burke speaks of studying genre inductively, but we can also do it deductively according to his model of writing. We can generate types or groups of works just as we do individual works by starting with assumptions or hypotheses about their common purpose and principles of compo-

18

sition. This is the main method to be used in this book—generating hypothetical structures deductively, then seeing how they are realized in actual works.

Despite the weight Burke gives to purpose, his use of it has disappointed some. Richard Ohmann believes that Burke treats literary purposes as merely personal, and Fredric Jameson has found Burke's notion of purpose unsatisfactory because it announces his eagerness to relate literature to the real social world, but enables him to retreat into merely literary, and often psychological, preoccupations.[27] Although sharing this disappointment that Burke's criticism is not more social, I want to sound a different caution about purpose, not in his theory or method, but in his practical criticism. When Burke does proceed inductively and move as Hirsch does *to* purpose rather than *from* it, he takes the stance of the exegete. Insofar as he takes purpose itself as the problem, he surrenders his deductive study of rhetoric and poetics for the methods appropriate to interpretation. He does so, I think, not only because he wrote much of his criticism at a time when exegesis was much in demand, but also because he is extremely scrupulous to avoid attributing to any literary work an overly simple purpose. As a result, however, he obscures at times his own critical method. For this reason, S. I. Hayakawa has undertaken to popularize the method by using as his examples literary works which have very obvious purposes.[28]

I shall be doing the same and trying to pick up the other end of the stick, as Burke recommends and as he himself often does—for example, in his fine essay on *Coriolanus*. I see no way to study rhetoric or poetics without beginning with the supposition, however attained, that we already have a good notion of the purpose of the work or type of work we are studying. We can, of course, shift rapidly from the reader's perspective of interpretation to the writer's perspective of composition, just as linguists shift from the synchronic to the diachronic, but we can attend to the one only by not attending to the other. Fortunately, victim-of-society novels, with their relatively manifest purpose, can justify better than most other literary works the suppositions about purpose which allow us to get on with the study of rhetoric and poetics.

In conducting and organizing this book I have adopted from Aristotle yet another critical fiction. In the thirteenth chapter of the *Poetics*, he places himself and his reader in the position of one who has adopted the purpose of composing a play to arouse and allay pity and fear in the audience. He then surveys compositional alternatives, first assuming the critical fiction that dramatists begin to implement their purposes by choosing the character and fate of their protagonists. He then shows the thematic consequences of each possible choice—how well it serves the purpose he has posited. I shall proceed as he does, dividing these alternatives into categories which look moral, but which really have more to do with motivation. Because the writers I treat have a different purpose, composing novels designed to show that the suffering of the protagonist is socially unjust and remediable, the alternatives will be reexplored and partly reformulated in the following chapters. In doing so, we discover that each type of protagonist leads to a different structure or privileged literary form and to a presentation of the antagonist which gives rise to a privileged subject or theme because it conceives differently the operation of institutions. Each therefore discloses a subgroup or subgenre closely united by its own common structure and purpose. Insofar as the alternatives cover the possibilities for protagonists within the overall purpose of victim-of-society novels, the group as a whole should become better defined whether it is a genre or not.

The first alternative, not considered by Aristotle, is the innocent victim, one whose suffering is not appreciably motivated by any character trait. Usually this person lacks the heroic proportions, social elevation, or Aristotelian nobility that screen out ordinary social exploitation as a cause of suffering in the tragic hero. Few novels use this protagonist, but their privileged subject seems to be oppression and their privileged literary form comic romance.

The second alternative is the virtuous victim. Aristotle rejected this type for the tragic hero because he thought the fall of the good disgusting. If such a person suffers not only in spite of goodness, but precisely because of it, disgust should grow into shock. The suffering of the innocent victim can result from the mere ineptitude of institutions. The suffering of those who could more appropriately be rewarded suggests not merely an indifference to the claims of justice, but an active opposition. Injustice comes to appear more systematic. The privileged subject of virtuous-victim novels is political repression and their privileged form tragic romance.

For the innocent and virtuous victims, hamartia rests in the antagonist. Victim-of-society novels, however, also use flawed victims. They differ from Aristotle's tragic heroes in being more gravely flawed, but the purpose is not to criticize them for merely personal characteristics. Almost always the flaw is a product of society, acquired through social experience and indicating victimage even before any downfall or suffering which it motivates within the plot. From the wide range of those possible, two opposed flaws are basic. The protagonist may undervalue individualism and become a conformist victim or overvalue it and become a rebel victim. Each of these victims has not only a character flaw which must derive from social experience, but also a misconception about society, so that the proper conception becomes thematized. Once more the writer is trying to discomfort rather than console the reader, who is being shown that people may be both corrupted and punished by institutions and that their punishment may therefore masquerade as justice. The privileged subject of the flawed-victim novel is the false consciousness which a culture strongly influenced by unjust institutions can promote. The privileged literary form is realism.

Innocent, virtuous, and flawed victims undergo the pathos characteristic of the tragic hero, but another alternative is to forego, background, parody, or delay pathos. The result is the pseudo victim. The privileged subject of the pseudo-victim novel is power. The privileged form is comedy.

In each of the following four chapters, I shall begin deductively by sketching a hypothetical structure from the nature of the victim and the broad purpose of the victim-of-society novel, examine several novels manifesting some or all parts of it, and end by considering problems of political expression, chiefly those of clarity and hope, in relation to the privileged literary form for presenting the victim. Thus the political implications of comic romance, tragic romance, realism, and comedy will be considered, at least as far as the victim-of-society novel assumes these forms.

After exploring the four basic types of victim, I shall consider various permutations and combinations of them. Thus the organization of this book resembles that of a grammar: the basic units, their morphology or the transformation of one into another, and the syntax of putting units together by multiplying victims.

In this way I should provide a fairly comprehensive account of the poetics and rhetoric of the victim-of-society novel. Through exploring its main compositional possibilities and problems, I can assess its capabilities and limitations and thus make a new approach to the question of compatibility between literary form and political expression.

2

The Innocent Victim

Nothing is so rare as to see misfortune fairly portrayed; the tendency is either to treat the unfortunate person as though catastrophe were his natural vocation, or to ignore the effects of misfortune on the soul, to assume, that is, that the soul can suffer and remain unmarked by it, can fail, in fact, to be recast in misfortune's image.

—Simone Weil

I N *Mary Barton*, Elizabeth Gaskell has her heroine visit a sick man, Ben Davenport.

He lay on straw, so damp and mouldy, no dog would have chosen it in preference to flags: over it was a piece of sacking, coming next to his worn skeleton of a body; above him was mustered every article of clothing that could be spared by mother or children this bitter weather; and in addition to his own, these might have given as much warmth as one blanket, could they have been kept on him; but as he restlessly tossed to and fro, they fell off and left him shivering in spite of the burning heat of his skin.[1]

He has no food for himself, his wife, or his children. He has no fuel to combat the Manchester winter. He lives in a dark cellar which oozes with moisture from sewage running in the street outside. In these conditions, he has contracted typhoid fever. He will die soon. This is an innocent victim.

Innocent victims need not be innocent people, for, like

23

innocent bystanders, their innocence is not absolute but relative to the injuries they sustain. Except for supplying their bodies, they do little or nothing to bring about their suffering. To describe them is to describe injustice itself: in literary terms, character does not motivate or determine fate; in nonliterary terms, they suffer what they do not deserve. When we think of victims of society, they are the first ones to come to mind. For some of us, they are the only ones.[2]

Fiction contains many innocent victims. Edgar Johnson has referred to the "countless host of helpless victims of society who throng in Dickens' books," including children such as Oliver Twist, Smike, poor Jo, and Amy Dorrit.[3] One innocent victim in Harriet Beecher Stowe's *Uncle Tom's Cabin* is Lucy, the mulatto woman too exhausted to work quickly. One of Simon Legree's drivers punishes her by driving a pin into her flesh. Another innocent victim is Lalie in Zola's *L'Assommoir*. After her drunken father, frustrated by his own victimage, has kicked her mother to death, she bravely takes over running the household and, like her mother, is beaten every day. More recently, in *One Flew over the Cuckoo's Nest*, Ken Kesey has presented Ellis, a mental patient whose brain has been destroyed by electric shock.

As these examples suggest, most innocent victims in fiction are minor characters. Some are extremely important, such as the ones suffering unjust prosecution in Tolstoy's *Resurrection*, Faulkner's *Sanctuary*, and Harper Lee's *To Kill a Mockingbird*, but we might well wonder why the protagonists are those trying to save the victims, rather than the victims themselves. These novels elevate the usually minor character that folklorists call the "helper" to the status of protagonist, at the same time reducing the usually major function of victim. In short stories and collections of short stories such as Richard Wright's *Uncle Tom's Children* and Harvey Swados' *On the Line*, many innocent victims serve as protagonists. In novels I have not found many: Dickens' *Oliver Twist*, Solzhenitsyn's *One Day in the Life of Ivan Denisovich*, and Arnow's *Dollmaker*—all of which I shall examine in this chapter—and a

24

few other novels such as Diderot's *Nun*, Tillie Olsen's unfinished *Yonnondio*, and perhaps Edward Dahlberg's *Bottom Dogs* or *From Flushing to Calvary*.

Apparently, innocent victims do not readily lend themselves to the demands placed on protagonists in victim-of-society novels. This is not an entirely new problem and H. D. F. Kitto has already illuminated it considerably in treating those plays of Euripides which he calls social tragedies. "The tragic theme is, if we may so generalize it, the social suffering which follows social wrong-doing—the dramatic antithesis of Sophocles' method, an individual fault which leads to individual suffering. Accordingly we have on the one hand the wrongdoers, on the other the wronged, and as the tragic point lies in the suffering rather than the oppression, the drama concentrates on the victims." The first difficulty we can notice here is that an emphasis on oppression seems to require concentrating on the oppressor rather than the oppressed, the antagonist rather than the protagonist. Thus innocent victims may get lost in what is ostensibly their own story because the motives for their suffering lie in their victimizers. Other difficulties result from the lack of motives in the victims. Although Kitto observes with refreshing common sense that "there is no dramatic canon which demands that victims have faults," he shows well the difficulty of presenting protagonists without hamartia because he sees its closely related functions with respect to plot, character, thought, and style. Hamartia contributes to plot logic by motivating the protagonists' suffering—as an element within the beginning from which the end develops. It proportions fate to character—the suffering which befalls them to what they have done. And it indicates the target of intellectual criticism—a habit or principle shown to be wrong, incomplete, or overgeneral by the suffering it brings. Thus to take an innocent victim as protagonist would seem to require at least a different logic in the plot, some incongruity between character and fate, and more explicit means of targeting intellectual criticism. Accordingly, Kitto finds that Euripides was committed to "intellectualism in dialogue and speech from the start, just as he was to his restricted characterization and nonorganic use of plot."[4]

We should now be better able to see the innocent-victim novel from the viewpoint of a writer struggling with such compositional problems. Given the basic purpose of protesting against social injustice by means of a protagonist whose character does not bring about his or her suffering, what hypothetical structure will follow? If the action consists of the protagonist's developing into an innocent victim, the end toward which the plot moves is a fall, the worsening of fortune; and the middle consists of a struggle against the antagonist forces to avoid such a fall. The logical place to begin is thus with a potential for falling, for becoming a victim. In other words, the beginning should establish the protagonist's vulnerability to the antagonist.

Such a plot raises difficulties. If the beginning shows the protagonist becoming vulnerable to the antagonist, that in itself is a fall into innocent victimage; if not, the vulnerability implies such an initial fall. During the middle the protagonist continues to be less active than the antagonist, but any struggle at all requires some inner resources. This resilience marking the limits of subjection to injustice must be considerable if the novel is to have much extent. Indeed, it would seem to require being directly proportional with the magnitude of the novel. The end or the fall proper requires that the protagonist's resilience disappear or diminish sharply for some reason.

But why should such protagonists fall at the end? They are already in some sense victims of society from the beginning, because they are vulnerable to the antagonist, and they show enough resilience to ward off further subjection throughout the middle. Because their resilience comes after their subjection and endures for some time, would not a fortunate ending be more probable? To be sure, they do not have enough resources of their own to bring about a fortunate ending, or they wouldn't likely have had to struggle much in the first place; but, by the same token, the antagonist must not have had enough resources to bring about an unfortunate ending. Although the fortunate ending may be more logical, therefore, any ending will likely require some clanky machinery, some agent of the catastrophe.

The project of writing the innocent victim's story as something akin to tragedy seems to carry by its own momentum to comedy. Trying to write the protagonist's development from not being a victim to being one seems to lead to starting with victimage and ending with release from victimage. If we look about for the literary form to which the adopted purposes lead naturally, we find a variety of what Northrop Frye calls comic romance. Comic romances begin with the heroes' falling from a desired to an undesired world, continue with their struggle to remember their origin and safeguard their real identity against the undesired world's assaults on it, and end with their escape back to the desired world.

> Reality for romance is an order of existence most readily associated with the word identity. Identity means a good many things, but all its meanings in romance have some connection with a state of existence in which there is nothing to write about. It is existence before "once upon a time," and subsequent to "and they lived happily ever after." What happens in between are adventures, or collisions with external circumstances, and the return to identity is a release from the tyranny of these circumstances. Illusion for romance, then, is an order of existence that is best called alienation. Most romances end happily, with a return to the state of identity, and begin with a departure from it.[5]

In the character of the romance protagonist Frye finds expressed "that there is something at the core of one's infinitely fragile being which is not only immortal but has discovered the secret of invulnerability that eludes the tragic hero" (p. 86). Because of this invulnerability the natural end of romance is comic. In the hero's return to the desired world "romance's last vision seems to be that of fraternity" (p. 173)— a suggestion of utopia which causes Frye to see "an inherently revolutionary quality in romance" (p. 139).

Stephen Crane's *Maggie: A Girl of the Streets* is only a borderline case of the innocent victim's story, but it is close enough and familiar enough to illustrate many of the features and difficulties just described. It opens in a slum, so that Maggie is already a victim in an undesired world. Although Crane's purpose was "to show that environment is a tremendous thing in the world and frequently shapes lives regardless"[6] more than environment has shaped her.

> The girl, Maggie, blossomed in a mud puddle. She grew to be a most rare and wonderful production of a tenement district, a pretty girl.
> None of the dirt of Rum Alley seemed to be in her veins. The philosophers upstairs, downstairs and on the same floor, puzzled over it.
> When a child, playing and fighting with gamins in the street, dirt disguised her. Attired in tatters and grime, she went unseen (p. 16).

Maggie's real home seems in a world elsewhere, like that of the romance heroine. This flower-in-a-dump motif, so common in naturalistic writing, establishes here the resilience which allows Maggie to struggle and survive for a time in unfavorable conditions. It is one reason that Charles Child Walcutt can claim for the best naturalism that it "underestimates neither man nor the forces against which he contends."[7]

As the story proceeds, however, we see less of both resilience and Maggie. Her death at the end is not presented at all. In the nineteen chapters of the book, she appears briefly in seven and not at all in eight. She is the main character only in the chapter in which we see her walking the streets on the way to the river. All the other characters but one are antagonists, of whom we see much more. Her brother appears almost as much as Maggie does, and his character is more firmly set before us. Her seducer and his circle receive a great deal of attention and better writing. Her mother's life alternates between alcoholic energy and alcoholic stupor, and Crane renders well the chaos of what mind she retains. If combined into one, these antagonists would deprive the heroine of her centrality altogether. As is, the shift of focus makes Maggie only a borderline case—evidence of a related but different purpose—but in its emphasis on the victimizers Crane illustrates nevertheless what would likely result from an attempt to present the innocent victim in an organic plot that attended fully to the required motives.

We might well expect, then, what in fact we find among innocent-victim novels. Not all present the whole story—the initial fall, the resilient struggle, and the triumph—though they have similar structures. Accordingly, the novels about to be examined display a number of alternatives to the organic plot. Dickens' *Oliver Twist*, which presents the story most fully, will be treated primarily for its ending, accomplished through a *deus ex machina*. Solzhenitsyn's *One Day in the Life of Ivan Denisovich* will illustrate a static plot devoted to the middle of the innocent victim's story. Harriette Arnow's *Dollmaker* ends by resolving side issues rather than its major conflict, but presents in great detail the fall from the desired world which makes up the beginning. After looking at these, we can explore the possibilities comic romance presents for social protest by considering how well the innocent-victim novel handles the problems of clarity and hope.

The *deus ex machina* saving the victim by loosening the plot, the victim looking schematic and a bit incredible because so detached from the conditions of his own victimage, and the hortatory rhetoric explicitly connecting plot, character, and thought because the implicit connection is so tenuous—these may sound like a recipe for a Dickens novel. At least they are for *Oliver Twist*, where Dickens set out "to show in little Oliver the principle of Good surviving through every adverse circumstance and triumphing at last."[8]

Humphrey House has declared that Dickens' "belief in the inevitability of . . . consequences is not borne out in the plots of his stories,"[9] but one could say just as well that his plots do not bear out a belief in the inevitability of consequences. Chesterton found in Dickens "the creaking of the machinery that is to give out the god from the machine,"[10] and Orwell identified the god: "in the typical Dickens novel, the *deus ex machina* enters with a bag of gold in the last chapter and the hero is absolved from further struggle."[11]

The god coming from a machine to end *Oliver Twist* is immanent throughout the novel. In *The Sense of an Ending* Frank Kermode has shown that just as theologians took the Apocalyptic End from outside history and distributed it within history, literary fictions have done likewise: "the End itself, in modern literary plotting loses its downbeat, tonic-and-dominant finality, and we think of it, as the theologians think of Apocalypse, as immanent rather than imminent."[12] The end is immanent in *Oliver Twist* as the resilience that Oliver shows throughout it. In Frye's terms the romance hero is invulnerable and he ultimately escapes from the undesired world. But what is the escape except the invulnerability seen as final, in the perspective of the end? And what is invulnerability except perpetual escape? In Dickens' terms the fact that the principle of Good survives every adverse circumstance implies that it triumphs at last. Thus the two great improbabilities many have found in the novel—Oliver's living uncorrupted through the most corrupting circumstances and his removal from them—have the same basis. Before looking at the imminent end, therefore, it is important to see its immanence in Oliver's resilience.

We first hear this immanent god named in the second chapter, after Oliver has been starved for nine years by Mrs. Mann. It is "nature or inheritance" which has "implanted a good sturdy spirit in Oliver's breast," and "perhaps to this circumstance may be attributed his having any ninth birthday at all" (p. 29). J. Hillis Miller glosses this as "nature *and* inheritance, both the self that Oliver has inherited from his unknown parents, and his 'natural goodness',"[13] but Dickens' meaning is less precise. Though often used in the Rousseauistic sense Miller ascribes, nature is also Wordsworthian. When Oliver is recuperating in the country with the Maylies, "Nature's face" consists of rural scenes which restore people by reminding them either of what they have never experienced or of what they experienced just before or not very long after birth. In chapter 24 Nature's faces are the faces of the young, covered as they grow older with "troubled clouds," which pass off as they near death and "leave Heaven's surface clear" (p. 216). If Nature is one name for the immanent god, then we should not be surprised at finding it a very supernatural nature.

Whatever its name, something enables Oliver to resist the power of circumstances and gives him the potential to develop a character different from what circumstances would make. When Noah Claypole goads Oliver, we can see clearly the contrast between his natural self and the self that social circumstances promote.

> A minute ago the boy had looked the quiet, mild, dejected creature that harsh treatment had made him. But his spirit was roused at last; the cruel insult to his dead mother had set his blood on fire. His breast heaved; his attitude was erect, his eyes bright and vivid; his whole person changed, as he stood glaring over the cowardly tormentor who now lay crouching at his feet, and defied him with an energy he had never known before (p. 70).

On the last page of the novel, this resilience to circumstance having come to fruition in both Oliver and Rose Maylie, its existence, as we might expect, is ascribed "to Him who had protected and preserved them" (p. 480).

An agent of the continuous presence sustaining Oliver is Rose, who takes him in and provides a setting in which the healing powers of nature and education can work. Her own attitudes toward the power of circumstance display the paradox which Patrick Brantlinger has shown the novel to maintain throughout,[14] a paradox congruent with Chesterton's paradox of reform. On the one hand, she simply cannot believe that Oliver, the apparent thief lying unconscious before her, has been corrupted by his association with criminals. On the other hand, she wants desperately to keep him from further association with them and thereby prevent his corruption. She is another of Dickens' angels, like Esther Summerson, and embodies the same Carlylean solution Esther gives to social problems: "I thought it best to be as useful as I could, and to render what kind services I could, to those immediately about me; and try to let that circle of duty gradually and naturally expand itself."[15] Rose is an orphan saved from harsh circumstances by Mrs. Maylie. Seeing Oliver in a similar danger, she wants to help him as she was helped— to expand the circle of duty.

It is Rose who reconciles Oliver to Mr. Brownlow, the *deus ex machina* who brings about the imminent end in the discovery of Oliver's true identity, the restoration of his inheritance, and his return to the desired world. In the scene showing their first meeting, Dickens writes,

> Oliver looked very worn and shadowy from sickness, and made an ineffectual attempt to stand up, out of respect to his benefactor, which terminated in his sinking back into the chair again; and the fact is, if the truth must be told, that Mr. Brownlow's heart, being large enough for any six ordinary old gentlemen of humane disposition, forced a supply of tears into his eyes, by some hydraulic process which we are not sufficiently philosophical to be in a condition to explain (p. 115).

The philosophy alluded to here is utilitarianism, seeing benevolence and other operations of the heart as illusions to be explained by matter and self-interest. Like Rose, Brownlow is dissociated from the view that circumstance governs everything. The imminent god and the immanent one embody the same value, freedom. In the benefactor it makes benevolence possible; in the victim it provides the ground for benevolence to be effective. How effective it can be is debatable. In the failure of Brownlow and Rose's attempt to help Nancy, Dickens shows its limits. But before rejecting it as a solution to the problems presented by the novel, it would be well to look at these problems more closely, for just as the immanent and imminent gods are well matched to each other, both are well matched to their adversary.

In *Oliver Twist* Dickens mentions philosophers only to deride them, and their ideas are invariably utilitarian. Their principal representatives are the governing board of the workhouse and Fagin. In the second chapter, the board, "very sage, deep, philosophical men," has instituted a policy of reduced rations in order to stimulate the poor not to live at parish expense, but in fact it has presented them with the alternatives "of being starved by a gradual process in the house, or by a quicker one out of it" (p. 34). Aside from the philosophic compatibility of this passage with Bentham's *Principles of Morals and Legislation*, it directly refers, according to House, to the New Poor Law of 1834, which was a Utilitarian reform.[16] Furthermore, in chapter 43 Fagin converts Noah Claypole, in a very funny philosophic dialogue, from the vulgar selfishness of looking out for number one to a parody of Bentham's artificial identification of interests. Fagin holds the threat of blackmail over all members of the gang. As a result, he says, "we are so mixed up together, and identified in our interests [that] the more you value your number one, the more careful you must be of mine; so we come at last to what I told you at first—that a regard for number one holds us all together" (pp. 385–86). Both the governing board and Fagin try to motivate people to work through that manipulation which is now called brainwashing, behavior modification, or personnel management. Fagin tries to get Oliver to become a thief by first isolating him from everyone: "Having prepared his mind, by solitude and gloom, to prefer any society to the companionship of his own sad thoughts in such a dreary place, he was now slowly instilling into his soul the poison which he hoped would blacken it and change its hue forever" (pp. 174–75).

Dickens could hardly have wanted it to appear that circumstances are always transcended, because then there would have been no social problem. Though he does not dramatize the point at any length, he does remark that Oliver "was in a fair way of being reduced, for life, to a state of brutal stupidity and sullenness by the ill-usage he had received" (p. 51). Moreover, he shows a great number of victims who do not transcend their circumstances, in whom the doctrine of consequences operates as relentlessly as anyone could wish. For Dickens then, social problems were caused, not solved, by engineering circumstances and encouraging people to act in accord with them.

Utilitarianism affected Dickens' structure too. We need

not go so far as Northrop Frye, who finds "a strongly con-servative element at the core of realism."[17] We can say, how-ever, that Dickens' purposes were not consistent with ob-serving the laws of probability and necessity and that in his time utilitarianism greatly influenced how these laws were conceived by providing the dominant norms for what was to be considered rational. Since his motivation of characters was doomed to irrationality with its framework, he did well to call attention to his own motivational and explanatory gaps, not only sacrificing realism, but indulging in its opposite through such mysticism as we have seen and through invok-ing the magic and spells of romance. Beyond mysticism he appealed to the facts of experience itself, in the teeth of his audience's refusal to believe that a girl like Nancy would en-danger her own life by returning to Sikes: "It is useless to discuss whether the conduct and character of the girl seems natural or unnatural, probable or improbable, right or wrong. IT IS TRUE. . . . It is a contradiction, an anomaly, an appar-ent impossibility; but it is a truth."[18]

From the point of view of either social theme or literary structure, then, Dickens found utilitarianism too confining. As both *Oliver Twist* and *Hard Times* show, it is too "mechan-ical"—to adopt the term he found in Carlyle's well-known attacks on it.[19] We shall see other novelists also pondering the issues it raises, but for now we may notice that in push-ing mechanical explanations so hard, it placed what mecha-nism could not explain entirely outside any explanation. As a result, the mystery it sought to banish abounded every-where. Perhaps any explanatory system takes a similar risk. Kenneth Burke has argued that all have concepts which are designed to explain but not themselves explained, and that we may seek them "in the direction of whatever [is] still un-accounted for." He calls these "god-terms."[20] Such a thought may well suggest that Dickens' *deus* owed much to the *ma-china* of utilitarianism.

The open ending, in which there is no resolution, is an-other alternative to organic plot. The classic case against endings was made by E. M. Forster, who found them unimportant, feebly executed, and untrue. He longed for a new convention permitting the novelist to stop when he got bored,[21] and certainly the value we place upon unfinished novels such as *Tristram Shandy* or *The Man without Qualities* would support his position. More recently, René Girard has urged the importance of endings, seeing the resolution of the plot as the solution to the frustrated desire of the protagonist. "Truth is active throughout the great novel, but its primary location is in the conclusion," because "great novels always spring from an obsession that has been transcended."[22] In the innocent-victim novel, however, where the protagonist's desire is quite legitimate, the open ending is itself a way to transcend obsession, that of the antagonist. It is another way to cope with the paradox of reform, inhibiting both optimism and pessimism by avoiding outright triumph or defeat.

In *The Nun*, Denis Diderot uses an open ending for the story of Suzanne Simonin, a young woman early forced into a religious vocation. She suffers a life she would never have chosen, loses a civil case to have her vows annulled, is punished severely, then is transferred to a different convent, subjected to the homosexual enticement of her mother superior, and helped to escape by a priest only so that he can seduce or rape her. The novel attacks monasticism, particularly the special protections afforded it by French law. Diderot motivates the open ending well by having the novel narrated by the nun herself, writing to a marquis of benevolent repute for his help in securing a modest job to sustain her. If he does not help her and she is forced to return to the convent, she is sure that she will eventually commit suicide. Thus Diderot poses but does not choose between the alternatives avoided by the open ending: victory or defeat, a little man with a bag of gold or a lapse of invulnerability. Judging from the heroine as we know her, such a lapse seems unlikely, but a modern film version ended by adopting it nevertheless.

Open endedness may also be achieved not by stopping short of a resolution, but by attenuating so much our sense of narrative development that we do not even expect one.

This is the case in Aleksandr Solzhenitsyn's *One Day in the Life of Ivan Denisovich* which is devoted entirely to the middle of the innocent victim's story. It shows very fully Shukov's resilience under oppression. Again and again we see his refusal to submit to the harsh pressures of a Siberian prison camp. "Even after eight years of hard labor he was still no scavenger and the more time went on, the more he stuck to his guns."[23] "And he couldn't help it even after eight years of camps. He still worried about every little thing and about all kinds of work. He couldn't stand seeing things wasted" (pp. 124–25). "He'd never given or taken a bribe from anyone, and he hadn't learned that trick in the camp either" (p. 48).

Even though he need not do good work, his pride leads him to. He enjoys it: "Not being let out to work—that was real punishment" (p. 7). He operates as much by his own code as by prison regulations. He eats slowly, never with his cap on, careful to spit fish bones out onto the table instead of the floor, and to eat fish eyes only when they are in place, not when they are floating in his bowl. When he cadges cigarettes or food, he doesn't beg or argue his right to what others have, but simply makes himself useful to them.

Were such characteristics his alone, they would not show so well the limited power of the unjust system; but many other prisoners are shown to resemble Ivan in this respect. In fact, presentations of them emphasize the extent and manner of their resilience. Ivan's gang boss, Tyurin, protects his men, threatening to kill a foreman who wants to report the gang's use of roofing-felt as a temporary window to keep out the cold. When he tells the story of his persecution as the son of a kulak, he does so "without pity, like it wasn't about himself" (p. 100). Alyoshka the Baptist reads his contraband Gospels and rejoices to be in prison. Y-81, an old man who has spent untold years in prisons and camps, sits erect in the mess hall and "you could see his mind was set on one thing— never to give in" (p. 172). These and many more like them contrast with Fetyukov, the pitiful scavenger and scrounge, whom the system has succeeded in degrading.

As noted earlier, innocent victims are usually minor characters, apparently more effective because requiring little in the way of plot motivation. Ivan is simply an extended presentation of such a character. Though certainly major, he too requires little motivation because neither he nor his situation undergoes narrative development. At the end, he has exactly the same character as at the beginning, and he is neither worse nor better off. Though using the diurnal framework, from reveille to lights out, the development is essentially expository rather than narrative. When Ivan and his situation have been fully explained, it is complete.

Despite this static quality *Ivan Denisovich* does not refute Kermode's contention that "no novel can avoid being in some sense what Aristotle calls 'a complete action'."[24] It does have a beginning, middle, and end. The beginning, as in other novels, contains most of the story elements which the plot does not present scenically—those details from the past necessary to understand the present. It also shows us most of the harshness of the camp setting: the bitter cold, inadequate clothing, meager diet, and rigorous discipline. As the novel progresses, however, we get more concentration on the resilience of the prisoners under these conditions. For example, the previously mentioned characterization of Y-81 is given during the evening meal. The observation that prisoners had "a hell of a lot of freedom" to criticize Stalin or the government is made during a scene in the barracks afterwards (p. 177). Alyoshka's rejoicing to be in prison and Ivan's wondering whether he still wants out of the camp are in the final pages. All or any of these could have been placed earlier, but Solzhenitsyn's plot is an expository development from an emphasis on subjection to one on freedom from it.

Our impression of Ivan's resilience depends partly on Solzhenitsyn's considerable restraint in presenting suffering. He does not dwell on it as a passive experience. Instead he lets us see it, as it were, out of the corners of our eyes, while establishing Ivan's very active means for coping with it. He understates it by concentrating on a relatively good day, so that he can tell rather than show the more difficult times in the lives of Ivan and the other prisoners. For Solzhenitsyn this restraint in presenting suffering is much more than a rhetorical tactic. During an interview in August 1973 he said,

> One psychological tendency of man is always astonishing. When happy and carefree he fears even the slightest shadow of trouble on the edges of his existence; he tries to ignore the sufferings of others (as well as those lying in store for him); he gives way in many matters, including those that are truly important and morally essential—all in order to prolong his happiness. Yet suddenly, when he finds himself in great extremity, miserable, naked, stripped of everything that enhances life, he summons up the firmness to carry on to the final step, giving up his life but not his principles.[25]

Freud too cautions about forgetting the resources of body and mind for coping with suffering and thereby attributing to sufferers more than they feel,[26] but Solzhenitsyn sees beyond the numbness that suffering may bring, to heroism.

Nevertheless, Ivan bears the marks of injustice and suffering and not just on his body. He is an innocent victim in that his character does not motivate his suffering, and he is admirable because of his resilience. But, as Francis Barker has suggested, he is a parody of the positive hero demanded by socialist realism rather than the positive hero himself.[27] The indirect free style of the narration, using language appropriate to his mind and point of view, often makes the judgments expressed his judgments. The leniency, for example in his refusal to condemn Gopchik's not sharing his packages from home, helps to make him more attractive. Occasionally, however, these judgments are not at all lenient. Ivan is incensed at the Moldavian who is late for the afterwork muster. Then we see that he is very human, not a paragon of virtue.

His behavior is also mixed. In the mess halls he is, as we might expect, at his least appealing. Getting a tray which had been promised to another, he says, "Let the bastard wait. He should have been sharper" (p. 166). There, he observes, "it was every man for himself" (p. 83). This commitment to the "law of the jungle" may remind us of Fagin's exposition of utilitarianism, but it forms only a part of Ivan's character—a necessary defense, as *The Gulag Archipelago* makes plain, in such harsh and unjust circumstances. He wishes things were different. "Who is the prisoner's worst enemy? The guy next to him. If they didn't fight each other, it'd be a different story" (p. 146). Or, "Alyoshka would never say no. He always did whatever you asked. If only everybody in the world was like that, Shukov would be that way too. If someone asked you, why not help him out? They were right, these people" (p. 120).

Ivan Denisovich is a static character with the same mixed ingredients that we are accustomed to see built into characters intended for later development. Thus we have neither the plot of character in R. S. Crane's sense—"a completed process of change in the moral character of the protagonists"[28]—nor the novel of character in Edwin Muir's: "All it need do is to bring out their various attributes, which were there at the beginning; for these characters are almost always static."[29] Instead, we see the potential for character development without the development itself. It exists, as potential must according to Edward Albee's Martha and other philosophers, as something actual. It exists as a source of incoherence in what is otherwise coherent. In characters which develop, we can see their potential for it long before the development proper. In Ivan we can see the potential for development in the main character of a novel which at the same time attenuates our expectation of narrative development. It is a striking way to present the experience of imprisonment.

Georg Lukács has captured well Solzhenitsyn's intrusion of dynamism into a basically static plot. He sees as prefigured an end which could not actually be presented: "The austere abstinence from any perspective itself contains a concealed perspective. Without it being stated, every proving of oneself, and every failure to prove oneself point to the future normal mode of human relations; they are—implicitly—preludes to a real future life among men."[30] I find this argument

ent in Ivan and his group. Frye has spoken of the utopian fraternity at the end of romance. Orwell has spoken of Dickens' novels ending, after the hero gets money, in a little community consisting of other good characters, and Oliver Twist's group, Dickens tells us, is "a little society whose condition approached as nearly to one of perfect happiness as can ever be known in this changing world" (p. 478). This ending, both immanent and imminent in *Oliver Twist*, is immanent, but not imminent, in *Ivan Denisovich*.

A slightly less upbeat innocent-victim novel is Harriette Arnow's somewhat naturalistic *Dollmaker*, first published in 1954 and rediscovered in a 1971 essay by Joyce Carol Oates.[31] It is the story of Gertie Nevels and her family, who migrate from the Kentucky hills to Detroit because Gertie's husband, Clovis, wants to work in a war plant. The novel takes note of exploitative industrial conditions, but examines also the spiritual debasement of men, women, and children in a culture of poverty within an impoverished culture. That Gertie Nevels, without becoming debased, observes the debasement of those she loves keeps her an innocent victim and testifies to her resilience. Unlike the static *Ivan Denisovich*, the novel develops both the plot and the protagonist and provides a strong sense of an ending. Nevertheless, the conflict between Gertie Nevels and the undesired world of Detroit could be resolved only by her defeat or escape, neither of which occurs. The real end, as in *Ivan Denisovich*, is immanent in the protagonist's preservation of identity and humanity.

Though *Ivan Denisovich* and *Oliver Twist* devote little space to the protagonists' lives before becoming victims, the first quarter of *The Dollmaker* presents very fully the beginning of the innocent victim's story. Gertie and her family live contentedly, though not prosperously, in a desired world, Kentucky. The opening scene establishes at once her heroic stature—uneducated but strong, resourceful, independent, and entirely fearless. She stops an army car to insist that a soldier and a general help her take her choking little boy to a doctor.

40

When the child's condition becomes desperate, she compels the men by the force of her character to hold the boy while she uses her pocketknife to make an incision in his throat so that he can get air. The reader can hardly help but respond as the soldier and the general do, with faintness and near nausea but also with admiration.

Gertie's only two goals are to stop sharecropping by getting a small farmstead and to find just the right face to carve in a fine block of cherry she has. She is well on her way to getting a farmstead, and her life is already something of an idyll. She seems to have little to lose, but when she leaves Kentucky and we, like she, measure her losses against this Eden, they turn out to be considerable. Yet Gertie herself remains strong, resourceful, independent, and fearless throughout.

As in many other victim-of-society novels, the wife suffers to some extent because of her husband, who mediates to her the unjust economic system from which he suffers by venting his job frustrations on her. By concentrating on the wife, Arnow spotlights the resilience of the woman rather than the debasement of the man. Even when Clovis wants to be generous and buys a refrigerator, a washing machine, or an extravagant Christmas, Gertie sees him as afflicted with a consumerism which frustrates her desire for freedom. She also suffers more serious losses. Her youngest daughter is killed by a train on an unprotected track near the housing project where they live. Her oldest son resents her having left Kentucky and returns there. Two of her children take to Detroit all too well, quickly assimilating the values purveyed at school and on the radio, so that she feels she is losing them also. Her woodcarving turns from a fulfilling hobby to a largely wearisome labor for money. Clovis, by urging her to use mass-production methods, would transform their home into a dismal imitation of his own unsatisfying workplace.

According to Frye the romance hero has a firm identity in the desired upper world and never really loses contact with it, even though it is obscured and assaulted in the lower world. By showing the continual demand that Gertie adjust,

41

The Dollmaker develops this theme fully, and one of the novel's achievements is to help readers not only to feel the pressures exerted by modern urban culture but also to know that many are grounded in propaganda. From the moment Gertie leaves Kentucky, her children are embarrassed by her ignorance of the trivia they have learned, and in Detroit they seek to instruct her so that she will not merit the dreaded name of "hillbilly." She nevertheless remains committed to her spiritual home and appalled by her surroundings:

> She had never lived with a clock since leaving her mother's house, and even there the cuckoo clock had seemed more ornament than a god measuring time; for in her mother's house, as in her own, time had been shaped by the needs of the land and the animals swinging through the seasons. She would sit, the knife forgotten in her hands, and listen to the seconds ticking by, and the clock would become the voice of the thing that had jerked Henley from the land, put Clovis in Detroit, and now pushed her through days where all her work, her meals, and her sleep were bossed by the ticking voice (p. 210).

Although she sometimes thinks she should adjust, she seems incapable. Like the romance hero, she has no real choice but the alienation she feels. She manifests not only the negative aspect of alienation in her hatred of where she is, but also the often overlooked positive aspect, the longing for an alternate world.

The end of *The Dollmaker* is marked by the end of the war and the death of old man Flint, an often mentioned but never present antagonist who is an automobile magnate strongly recalling Henry Ford. Gertie has developed somewhat. She has come to regret not having defied her mother by staying in Kentucky, and since she has seen in Detroit more of the effects of her mother's stern God, she has become something of a freer thinker. Her financial prospects brighten, but she shows no signs that she can be bought off. She gets a large order for dolls and faces the wearisome work of producing them, for that purpose splitting up her beautiful block of cherry. Although Joyce Carol Oates finds this a defeat, it is not defeat of spirit or surrender of identity. Indeed, it further manifests her constant personal strength. The end is quite open, with her husband on strike and showing signs of homesickness for Kentucky. Considering her character, much is possible except real defeat. She suffers greatly, but her triumph is immanent. It is made all the more credible because Arnow has so firmly and fully grounded her resilience in a Kentucky idyll little affected by technology, mass media, and other traps of the modern world.

In *The Secular Scripture* Northrop Frye speaks of "an element of social protest inherent in romance." That many romances in fact legitimate rather than protest the status quo he thus feels compelled to explain as a "process of what we call 'kidnapping' romance, the absorbing of it into the ideology of an ascendant class."[32] In *Anatomy of Criticism*, on the other hand, Frye's earlier position was that romance has potentials usable by opposed political ideologies.

> The romance is nearest of all literary forms to the wish-fulfilment dream, and for that reason it has socially a curiously paradoxical role. In every age the ruling social or intellectual class tends to project its ideals in some form of romance, where the virtuous heroes and beautiful heroines represent the ideals and the villains the threats to their ascendancy. This is the general character of the chivalric romance in the Middle Ages, aristocratic romance in the Renaissance, bourgeois romance since the eighteenth century, and revolutionary romance in contemporary Russia. Yet there is a genuinely "proletarian" element in romance too which is never satisfied with its various incarnations, and in fact the incarnations themselves indicate that no matter how great a change may take place in society, romance will turn up again, as hungry as ever, looking for new hopes and desires to feed on.[33]

This is better than Frye's later claim for a generic bias in romance because it does not suppose that a bias can be both inherent and subvertible.

The novels we have seen show that comic romance can be of use for social criticism, but if Frye's later position is right, there should be many more innocent-victim novels. If they are rather rare, this is eloquent, authoritative testimony that they leave something to be desired. In order to explore what this lack might be, let us look at how well they solve the problems of clarity and hope which confront all writers of victim-of-society novels.

The presentation of antagonists, which largely determines clarity, follows two lines in innocent-victim novels because they envisage two different falls. The fall from the desired world, through which the protagonists become innocent victims initially, requires at least one antagonist. The struggle against a further fall within the undesired world itself also requires at least one. These may or may not be the same character. In *Oliver Twist* we learn that Oliver's initial fall was engineered largely by Monks, his half brother, in order to cheat him of his inheritance. Monks is also behind Fagin's attempt to bring him even lower. By choosing this selfish, unbrotherly act as the ultimate motive, Dickens makes a basically moral criticism much in keeping with his attack on utilitarianism and defense of benevolence. One can object to such a choice of target, with the remedy it implies, as Raymond Williams once did in charging Dickens and other Victorian social novelists with diverting their attention both from politics and from the social situations needing remedy, or one can defend Dickens' benevolence as genuinely political, as Raymond Williams has more recently done.[34] The first of these viewpoints, as applied to *Oliver Twist*, would have more to recommend it if the novel unfolded in chronological or story order. But long before we learn why Oliver falls initially, we see more specifically social and political criticism in the antagonists who actually come later to threaten a further fall: the parish board, Fagin, and Fang. For this reason Dickens' criticism is somewhat broad, but since he characterizes all antagonists with the same oppressive self-interestedness, it is coherent and not merely moral.

Dickens' use of a personal motive as the ultimate one for Oliver's initial fall does not result from the nature of his medium. This point is clear from Solzhenitsyn's use of a decidedly political motive at a similar juncture in *Ivan Denisovich*.

44

Ivan is in the prison camp, readers are eventually told, because the Russian government, fearing disloyalty, imprisoned those of its soldiers whom the Germans had made prisoners in World War II. The antagonists we see Ivan vulnerable to, however, are prison officials and guards. The novel could easily have become an attack on the administration of prison camps, but Solzhenitsyn screens out much of this potential by keeping the officials largely out of view and having Ivan say of the guards on one occasion, "It was no fun for them either" (p. 43). By preventing his target from becoming diffuse, Solzhenitsyn got the novel published as the attack on Stalinism which it is. Like Monks, Stalin is behind both the initial fall and the threat of a further one. Unlike Monks, Stalin does not appear in the novel. He is merely mentioned in conversations.

The Dollmaker is more broad in its criticism than *Ivan Denisovich* and less coherent in its broadness than *Oliver Twist*. Gertie Nevels leaves the desired world of Kentucky because of pressure from her mother and husband. That she decides to leave does give her some responsibility for the ensuing suffering, but the pressures are so great that I have not hesitated to treat her as an innocent victim. Since her mother has part of the antagonist function, the novel attacks her and the Christianity which impels her. Since Gertie's husband has another part, it attacks male dominance. In the undesired world of Detroit Gertie continues to be her husband's victim at the same time that he is becoming more and more a victim himself. But the antagonist function is still broader. The school system, the mass media, the exploitative conditions in her husband's job show oppression with only a glance at oppressors. The fact that Gertie suffers from assaults on her woodcarving craft makes industrialism an important target, and this impession is strengthened when the end of the novel is marked by the death of Flint, the presence which is never really presented. Because we have little guide to the relative importance or mutual relations of these targets, the novel's attack is diffuse.

Both diffuseness and indistinctness are risks to clarity

which the innocent-victim novel must run because of its problems in presenting antagonists. As we saw in *Maggie*, they will eclipse the protagonist and create a different kind of novel if given space commensurate with their importance in motivating the plot. To prevent this, the writer may distance them to the point of indistinctness, and we get shadowy or offstage antagonists such as Monks, Stalin, and Flint. In any case, the need for more than one antagonist may cause some diffuseness. Nevertheless the risks to clarity are not fatal, as the novels we have seen demonstrate. The privileged subject of the innocent-victim novel is clearly oppression,— even if a somewhat generalized oppression.

The problem of hope in the innocent-victim novel centers around the protagonists and three questions: what is the desired world from which they initially fall, what is the source of their resilience, and what, if any, is the desired world to which they escape? *Oliver Twist* ends with a middle-class utopia of benevolence and prosperity much like that from which the hero was originally expelled, and his resilience comes from vague sources, including the influence of his original world. Here again, the novel is very much of a piece. To such a source of hope one can make two different objections, that it is utopian or that the utopia is badly chosen. One can object to utopianism that it provides the grounds for despair, not hope. Because neither benevolence nor prosperity is likely to become widespread enough to solve the social problems Dickens presents, the novel may encourage readers to overlook other solutions and therefore to do nothing. On the other hand, one can defend utopia,[35] perhaps on the ground that any ideal worth serving ought to be impossible to realize, and still object to Dickens' utopia. Prosperity is by no means without problems of its own. Benevolence may be less fraternal than paternalistic. Nevertheless, we can give Dickens credit for avoiding the excesses of optimism and pessimism. He shows that his solution sometimes does not work, his innocent victim is not altogether invulnerable, and his other victims are extremely vulnerable.

Like Oliver, Gertie gets considerable resilience from the

46

desired world she originates in, but that world is very different from his. Since we see more of it, utopia seems too strong a word for it. Unlike the tragic hero, who often begins in the company of gods and royalty only to end by envying the lot of beggars, the innocent victim makes a short drop in falling from the desired world. For this reason, it is only relatively better than the undesired world. Certainly Gertie's Kentucky Eden has some snakes: it has plenty of poverty, it is not exempt from the perils of war, its religion is often inhuman and demeaning, and its innocence rests largely on ignorance. Nevertheless, it sustains Gertie. Its desirability may be only relative, but it becomes clearer and clearer the more we see of Detroit. Furthermore, the very fact that the novel ends with no resolution of Gertie's problems allows it to suggest a desired world not identical with Kentucky. Her alienation from industrialism, media claptrap, consumerism, conformist education, and so on, together with her ability to resist each, holds out some possibility which the novel does not make explicit. It lacks the detail of Dickens' little utopia, but it may be all the more attractive for that reason.

Solzhenitsyn's desired world is the most implicit of all. What little we know of Ivan's life before prison discloses neither utopia nor idyll. Even if relatively desired because the prison is so undesired, it contrasts with Oliver's and Gertie's because we are not invited to take it as a source of the hero's resilience. Nor, despite his wanting to be released, does any desired world await Ivan outside the prison camp. His letters from home show it as a shallow place in which socialist or communal ideals are crumbling, along with the collective farms to which they gave rise. Instead, Solzhenitsyn invites us to take hope from a resilience based on experience within the undesired world, much as the prisoners snatch it from oppression itself, using resources available to all human beings, not just the bourgeois or the rural. In the prisoners we see a shape for the future in a better society than any mentioned in the novel. It consists of the best that is in all of them, brought out by the harshness of their conditions.

For Frye, the undesired world of romance is aligned with

the reader's real world, and the desired world from which the protagonists fall is the same as that to which they return. If both were always the case, romance would indeed be generically biased toward social criticism, and it could not be kidnapped. As we have just seen, however, the desired worlds invoked at the beginning and at the end of romance need not be the same. Furthermore, the one from which the innocent victims initially fall has problems of its own which help to make possible falling from it. Thus it is only relatively desirable. The desired world invoked at the end, on the other hand, needs no such flaws. It is more than relatively desirable. Instead of Frye's circularity, therefore, we have seen something more like Blake's pattern of innocence, experience, then organized innocence, and if we look beyond social protest novels to a comic romance such as *Gawain and the Green Knight*, we see Blake's pattern again rather than circularity.

The pattern of comic romance can be used for conservative purposes simply by aligning the reader's world with either of these desired worlds. The reader's world is aligned with the desired world from which the protagonist falls in many anti-utopian novels, such as *1984* or *Brave New World*. An important point in such novels is that we already have a better world than the undesired worlds that are trying to be utopias. To be sure, such novels are not entirely conservative or devoid of social criticism. The desired world is only relatively better because it has considerable potential for developing into the undesired one. That too is an important point.

The reader's world can also be aligned with the desired world at the end of comic romance, to generate even less social criticism. Since many historical novels and films adopt this strategy, it probably derives from the *Waverley* novels, in which Scott often used it. At the end of *Old Mortality*, for instance, the violence of the undesired world gives way to the settlement produced by the Glorious Revolution of 1688, a settlement at the heart of Scott's conservatism and one that he was defending against nineteenth-century British radicalism. To be sure, the conservatism in *Old Mortality* is not undiluted, but when William Hazlitt thought Scott's novels might be misfiring because the past did not look much like the good old days, he should have recognized that it was not always designed to.[36]

If comic romance is not inherently biased one way or the other, and if the novels we have seen manage clarity and hope fairly well despite some difficulties with these problems, the question remains: why do there seem to be so few innocent-victim novels? A partial answer at least is that these novels cannot be written without inorganic plot, and many novelists of the past hundred or so years have felt obliged to try to produce organic plots. A better answer, I think, can come into view only by looking beyond the innocent-victim novel itself to the other options available. Like it, they run certain risks. More than it does, however, they derive many strengths from the very task of managing these risks. As a result, the virtuous-victim novel, for one, can do anything as well as the innocent-victim novel can, and it does some things much better. Let us turn to the virtuous-victim novel, then, as many novelists have done.

3

The Virtuous Victim

Justice is the only virtue which is regarded as benefiting
someone else than its possessor. For it does what is to
the advantage of another, whether he is in authority or
just a partner. As it is the extreme of wickedness to prac-
tise villainy towards one's friends, as well as to debauch
oneself, so the highest virtue is shown not by the man
who practises it in his own case but by the man who
performs the difficult task of practising it towards another. Thus righteousness or justice, so understood, is
not a part but the whole of virtue, while injustice, its
opposite, is not a part but the whole of vice.

—Aristotle

INNOCENT victims are innocent because they do little or
nothing to motivate the fate which befalls them. Their suffering is caused by antagonists. Virtuous victims, although
also brought to suffer by antagonists, make substantial con-
tributions of their own. In large part their character does
determine their fate, not through some flaw, such as the hamartia of Aristotle's tragic hero, but through some excel-
lence.

As we have seen, innocent victims are not simply victims
who happen to have moral innocence. In fact, they may have
little or none. Similarly, virtuous victims may or may not be
conspicuously virtuous people. Although they must have some

51

virtue to motivate their suffering, they may be quite flawed. Ernest Everhard, in Jack London's *Iron Heel*, is a moral exemplar, and Robert Jordan, in Hemingway's *For Whom the Bell Tolls*, is only slightly less so. But Winston Smith, in Orwell's *1984*, has the flaws of a very ordinary man, and Pietro Spina, in Silone's *Bread and Wine* and *Seed beneath the Snow*, has plenty of faults, despite his inclusion, along with some other virtuous victims, in Theodore Ziolkowski's *Fictional Transformations of Jesus* and R. W. B. Lewis's *Picaresque Saint*.[1]

Virtuous-victim novels solve the main formal problem of innocent-victim novels by showing strong narrative development and organic plot. Indeed the desire for organic plot— as much as any desire to uplift readers with positive heroes who can preach the right values—goes far to explain why so many novelists have chosen virtuous victims as protagonists. A virtue works quite as well as any flaw or mistake to motivate a fall in fortune, to proportion fate to character and to direct intellectual criticism naturally to where it belongs—to the antagonist.

Nevertheless, Aristotle has objected with great fervor to the possibility of showing the good suffering despite their virtue. His objection would apply still more strongly to any who suffered because of it: "Neither should virtuous men be shown shifting from good fortune to bad, for this is not fearful, and not pitiable either, but morally shocking." To be sure, he deals here with the proper form of tragedy, but his objection goes well beyond any failure to inspire pity and fear. "Morally shocking" is *miaron*, which Gerald Else renders also as "'filthy,' i.e., morally revolting, disgusting."[2]

Obviously the objection is not basically literary. In *The Nicomachean Ethics* Aristotle puts forward a moral optimism by conceiving the good as that which tends to bring happiness. Thus he can account for the fact that good men suffer only by supposing in such cases "atrocious luck or ill-treatment."[3] Accordingly, O. B. Hardison has argued that he rejects the downfall of good people not only because it should not occur, but also because presenting them as victims of luck would violate the laws of probability and necessity.[4] Gerald

Else, on the contrary, has suggested that presenting them would show not atrocious luck, but ill-treatment.

Whatever the precise grounds, Aristotle's proscription of the virtuous victim indicates once more in his literary theory a bias against the presentation of social injustice. The writers studied in this chapter can hardly be expected to share this bias. Some do not believe happiness to be the true aim of human beings, but they are by no means moral pessimists. On the contrary, they believe strongly that virtue should not and need not cause suffering. They believe it so strongly as to incite their audiences to the outrage that Aristotle prohibits.

In arguing for social protest in the theater, Augusto Boal has described a character much like the virtuous victim by turning Aristotle upside down and speaking of "negative harmartia." He illustrates it in Dumas' *Camille.*

> The universe of the work is one, and our universe, or at least our momentary position during the spectacle, is another. Alexander Dumas (Dumas fils) says in effect: here you see what this society is like, and it is bad, but we are not like that, or we are not like that in our innermost being. Thus, Marguerite has all the virtues that society believes to be virtues; a prostitute must practice her profession of prostitute with dignity and efficiency. But Marguerite has a flaw which prevents her from practicing her profession well—she falls in love. How can a woman in love with *one* man serve with equal fidelity *all* men (all those who can pay)? Impossible. Therefore, falling in love, for a prostitute, is not a virtue but a vice.
>
> But we, the spectators, who do not belong to the universe of the work, can say the exact opposite: a society which allows and encourages prostitution is a society which must be changed. Thus the triangle is established: to love, for us is a virtue, but in the universe of the work, it is a vice. And Marguerite Gauthier is destroyed precisely because of that vice (virtue).[5]

Similarly, in the virtuous-victim novel, the reader and the antagonist must perceive the protagonist's character very differently.

The need for a protagonist who can be viewed in such

opposite ways underlies the basic dynamic of the virtuous-victim novel, strongly affecting its content and form. For this reason, the best place to start deriving its hypothetical structure is with the need for an antagonist who will view a virtue as a vice.

There is little danger that antagonists will overshadow protagonists, because virtuous victims furnish important motives for their own suffering, but antagonists also motivate it and therefore assume considerable importance of their own. Because they can be given space fully commensurate with their importance, we can expect the institutions attacked by virtuous-victim novels to be clear. These institutions give antagonists the power to inflict suffering without falling afoul of the law themselves and furnish the standards for judging the protagonists' virtue as vice. In short, antagonists should be a part of a legal *system*, or the *legal* system itself, and their inflictions upon protagonists represent the operation of that system. Since readers are to question their judgments of protagonists, the legal system grounding such judgments should be brought into question also. Thus virtuous-victim novels should set up a conflict between legality and morality.

There are two reasons for a legal system to oppose anyone: that the person is a threat to the common good or that the person is a threat to the system itself. Antagonists may well believe the first to be their motive, but if they are to attack anything which readers will take to be a virtue, it cannot be. Readers must see them as merely defending the system. They must see the antagonists as the real opponents of the common good and, therefore, question the very legitimacy of the legal system.

If antagonists are really defending the legal system, how should protagonists be presented? What virtue can readily be mistaken for vice because it is a threat to the system? I submit that a legal system can be threatened by one thing and one thing only: rival power. To pose such a threat, protagonists must be perceived by antagonists as either having such power or as having some potential for generating it.

54

Therefore protagonists must have some virtue which tends to develop a power that threatens the legal system. Since we are talking about political power, there can be only one source for it, some *polis*. Protagonists must have, or at least be viewed as possibly getting, a constituency or community which opposes the legal system. A bare minimum for their virtue then is that it tend to engender community. What makes community possible? Social theorists from Plato through Hobbes to the present have agreed that it is the surrender by individuals of merely individual rights and powers. This self-abnegation or selflessness has often been thought not only a virtue, but the basis for all virtues. Well it might be. It gives rise to community, and community naturally enough designates the antisocial as the chief vice.

If some such dynamic seems called for by the very project of writing a virtuous-victim novel, its privileged subject will be repression, suffering inflicted in order to protect an unjust system. In treating repression, the virtuous-victim novel brings into question the very legitimacy or sovereignty of the system, its right to exercise power. It shows that system opposing the common good and attacking the ties among human beings which bring society into being. In short, it shows the system to be antisocial.

In treating this privileged subject, the virtuous-victim novel figures to have a structure somewhat as follows. The beginning, whatever else it may do, should establish the protagonist's virtue and indicate its origin. The middle should show the protagonist's struggle against the antagonist, perhaps alongside the community which the virtue engenders. The end should show a decided downturn in the protagonist's fortunes, and its effect on the community.

The privileged literary form of the virtuous-victim novel we may take to be tragic romance, which Northrop Frye treats as "an incomplete form of the total picture."[6] For Frye, tragic romance is truncated romance, with the hero's defeat blocking reentry into the desired world. The virtuous-victim novel is somewhat different. The protagonists begin in an undesired world, finding within it a desired world or community where they are not alienated from their authentic identity. In their struggle against the antagonists, they are heroic because they fight from a position of some strength, but the strength is not theirs alone. In the end the desired world is usually intact, still within the undesired world itself. Its continuing invulnerability is suggested all the stronger when that of the protagonist ends. Thus virtuous victims begin with a rise and end with a fall, reversing the innocent victim's development from fall to rise. In doing so, they make clearer than the innocent victim does the communal source of all power, including that which makes heroes heroic.

Because Maxim Gorki's well-known *Mother* incorporates all these components, it can illustrate the whole story, but we should bear in mind that the virtuous victim's community is usually less organized than Pelagueya Vlasov's. At the outset of the novel, she is an innocent victim. In drunken rages her husband has repeatedly beaten her, thereby working out the pain of his own oppression. Because of these beatings she has become degraded—fearful, melancholy, ignorant, submissive, and alienated. In her poverty of body and soul she shows full subjection to the tyranny of her condition. Her conversion to community begins when her son Pavel, who has got out of the round of exhaustion, drunkenness, and brutality, confesses to her that he reads illegal books. It is completed by the socialist revolutionaries in Pavel's group, who meet in her home. Although they read together and heatedly discuss social issues, Gorki has chosen a heroine who cannot be converted by abstract arguments because she cannot understand them. Instead, she is slowly converted by admiring and sharing the group's community and its work and by seeing the repression against it. She becomes free of her fears and passes from death to life, darkness to light, and brute to human.

The middle of the novel focuses on the group, which Vlasova joins, and their struggle against tsarism. The scenes devoted to the socialist revolutionaries show a community of human people prefiguring the society which ought to emerge if they triumph. In them readers can see an idyll, a glimpse of something like utopia. Along with their idealism, the socialists have considerable earthiness. They resemble the earlier narodniks as well as today's dissidents, who still struggle for greater freedom in Russia. Gorki presents their antagonists much less fully than he might have. They appear as soldiers and policemen interfering with the spread of socialism and as bored judges presiding over the trials of Pavel and others. The novel ends as Vlasova is trying to disseminate leaflets containing one of Pavel's speeches. Police beat her, but she defies them, shouting to the crowd around her to give up their fear as she has done. She sees and feels the crowd's sympathy with her and her cause and knows that the repression against her will create many more like her.

To explore the virtuous-victim novel in greater detail, the rest of this chapter treats Victor Hugo's *Les Misérables* largely for the beginning of the story, Herman Melville's *Billy Budd* for the presentation of antagonists in the middle, Graham Greene's *Power and the Glory* for the hero's community in the middle, and Harriet Beecher Stowe's *Uncle Tom's Cabin* for the end. This done, I take up some aspects of romance disregarded previously and assess the capabilities and limitations of tragic romance by seeing how well the virtuous-victim novel deals with the problems of clarity and hope.

Before looking at the conversion with which Victor Hugo establishes his hero's virtue and begins *Les Misérables*, we should consider conversion itself and its structure, because the conversion with which the whole story of the virtuous victim begins has a beginning, a middle, and end all its own.

Many readers feel put off by literary conversions. For the sake of following the adventures or wit of an unregenerate life, they may tolerate or even welcome a conversion at the end, but especially if it is more than perfunctory, they know that the writer's rhetoric is trying to hook them—that the protagonist's fictional conversion is given as a pattern for their own real one. By and large, they are right. Lovelace's conversion attempts to convert them to Christianity; Stephen Daedalus's, to the religion of art. Those in eighteen proletarian novels cited by Walter B. Rideout urge them to socialism or communism.[7] Nevertheless, conversion has its supporters. Jerome Hamilton Buckley has shown that the *Bildungsroman* usually ends with the hero's reappraisal of values through some epiphany,[8] or muted conversion, and René Girard not only defends fictional conversions but chides his fellow critics for minimizing their importance.[9]

In a thoughtful treatment of nonreligious conversions, Kenneth Burke argues that they obey a "lex continui," so that they "are generally managed by the search for a 'graded series' whereby we move step by step from some kind of event, in which the presence of a certain factor is sanctioned in the language of common sense, to other events in which this factor had not previously been noted."[10] Seeing the intermediate stages, rather than merely the starting and ending points, does make conversion more intelligible, just as it does any other complex development—just as Saussure showed it to do for linguistic change. It does not, however, dissipate the mystery. Although we see more continuity as we look closer, we also become more aware of discontinuity. No momentous issues need be involved to reveal the discontinuous nature of conversions, but we can get an illustration from Thomas S. Kuhn's account of scientific revolution, which for the scientists involved he calls "a conversion experience that cannot be forced" or "resolved by proofs." First the old way of thinking, or paradigm, must be in considerable trouble, failing to solve important problems. Next, a new one must be available. Ideally it should hold some promise of solving problems better, but since any such claim could be proved only by adopting it, some intuition of fruitfulness by a number of people together must serve in place of proof. Therefore esthetic standards such as beauty, elegance, or economy become as important as logical standards, and Kuhn can describe conversion proper as a leap of faith.[11] Although not irrational, this process is not logical either. Indeed, it much resembles the hermeneutic circle. In both cases, one might say "credo ut intelligam."

Kuhn's account of conversion finds in it three moments—dissatisfaction with a current outlook, an alternative outlook, and a leap from the first to the second. These mark fictional conversion too. The source of dissatisfaction in protagonists designed to become virtuous victims is almost inevitably that they are already victims of society, like Vlasova. Thus a previous fall is implied, similar to those we saw early in the innocent-victim novel, but we seldom get a glimpse of it. In general, the protagonist begins very much in an undesired world, and we do not see the desired world until a conversion occurs.

Because the conversion of virtuous victims occurs in the beginning rather than the end, it cannot be motivated by the whole weight of accumulated experience already presented to the reader. Partly for this reason and partly to show that the conversion which will make the hero community-engendering is itself community engendered, writers usually rely on "helper" characters. The helper embodies the alternative outlook required for the second moment of conversion, its middle. Because this alternative is some form of selflessness, the helper not only embodies it but acts selflessly toward the protagonists, doing something to their advantage without worrying about whether they deserve it. This gratuitous act of generosity disorients the protagonists because the outlook with which they are dissatisfied has not led them to expect it. They therefore compare outlooks. They already know the consequences of their present one, but can only imagine those that would attend their adoption of the alternative. Because our minds can know little or nothing of the future, they have a problem which cannot be altogether logically solved.

The leap with which conversion ends is its most mysterious component, but we must remember what good reasons the protagonists have for repudiating their old outlooks, whatever the alternatives may entail. At any rate, the leap is a gratuitous act of their own, called out by the helper and testifying to the lessening power of unjust conditions over them. They become, like the helper, capable of such acts toward other people. With the helper, they make up a community all the more obvious if, as in *Mother*, the helper function is split among many characters.

Because real conversions are discontinuous, we can expect to find the fictional conversions of virtuous victims incompletely motivated. Like real conversions too, they are illogical without being irrational or unreasonable. Nevertheless, since selflessness has its own illogicality, particularly for those who think no human act adequately explained until shown to be grounded in self-interest, the motivational or explanatory gap may widen to a chasm. In *Resurrection*, Tolstoy anticipated such a response to Nekhlyudov by placing it in his bailiff: "the thought that every one is concerned only for his own profit, to the harm of others, was so deeply rooted in the bailiff's conceptions that he imagined he did not understand something."[12]

The conversion of Jean Valjean in *Les Misérables* is one of the best known in fiction. Originally sent to prison galleys for stealing a loaf of bread to feed his sister's famished children, he has already passed from an innocent to a flawed victim when the novel opens. He has just been released from prison, with an ex-convict's yellow passport describing him as a very dangerous man. Like a millet seed under a millstone, he feels the weight of human society on his head. Like a man fallen overboard at sea, he feels dreadfully alone. He finds the external world almost unreal and his internal world is a tangle of hatreds.

> At times he did not even know exactly what were his feelings. Jean Valjean was in the dark; he suffered in the dark; he hated in the dark; we might say that he hated in his own sight. He lived constantly in the darkness, groping blindly and as in a dream. Only, at intervals, there broke over him suddenly, from within or from without, a shock of anger, an overflow of suffering, a quick pallid flash which lit up his whole soul, and showed all around him, before and behind, in the glare of a hideous

light, the fearful precipices and the sombre perspectives of his fate.[13]

Hugo raises the question of what potential he has for reversing the damage which the law has done to his character, whether there is "in the particular soul of Jean Valjean, a primitive spark, a divine element, incorruptible in this world, immortal in the next, which can be developed by good" (p. 77). From a materialist perspective capable of seeing the awful effects of injustice on him, such a possibility, Hugo says, would be denied: "a physiologist would have seen in Jean Valjean an irremediable misery" (p. 77).

The helper is Bishop Myriel. We should look at him closely to see not only the motivation but also the alternative outlook that Jean Valjean will convert to. We first see him as a good man and a good bishop. From the Gospels he has acquired what others find "a strange and peculiar way of judging things" (p. 13). Although a Royalist, he is haunted by the idea of justice. In the long scenes devoted to his past, we find that he has undergone something of a conversion himself. In the tenth chapter we are shown his visit, long ago, to a dying old conventionist. The bishop treats him with some severity, but the conventionist, still proud of his part in the Revolution, defends his republicanism ably and with dignity. Warming to him, the bishop asks the old man to make peace with God before he dies, only to discover that the conventionist is already at peace.

"I was sixty years old when my country called me, and ordered me to take part in her affairs. I obeyed. There were abuses, I fought them; there were tyrannies, I destroyed them; there were rights and principles, I proclaimed and confessed them. The soil was invaded, I defended it; France was threatened, I offered her my breast. I was not rich; I am poor. . . . I have done my duty according to my strength, and the good that I could. After which I was hunted, hounded, pursued, persecuted, slandered, railed at, spit upon, cursed, proscribed. For many years now, with my white hairs, I have perceived that many people believed they had a right to despise me; to the poor, ignorant crowd I have the face of the damned, and I accept, hating no man myself, the isolation of hatred. Now I am eighty-six years old; I am about to die. What have you come to ask of me?"

"Your benediction," said the bishop. And he fell upon his knees (p. 39).

After this experience, the bishop "redoubled his tenderness and brotherly love for the weak and suffering." His opinions changed little, but abstract thought had never been important to him. Even in religion "he had no systems; but many deeds" (p. 48). His Christianity is so basic as to contrast sharply with both the church and the society he serves. He represents values admired as well by many varieties of humanism, including the nineteenth-century romantic humanism which developed by secularizing Christianity. Thus we do not expect any converts he makes to become theologians or to practice cloistered virtues. Jean Valjean fully confirms such expectations.

Myriel takes in and feeds Jean Valjean after many others in the town have refused to sell food or shelter to the traveling ex-convict. He does not preach to his guest. He does not worry about being robbed. He simply trusts and helps. The first step toward conversion comes when Jean Valjean hesitates for a moment before he steals the bishop's silver. When the police bring him back with the silver, the bishop claims to have given it to him. Jean Valjean is released, and the bishop enjoins him to use the silver to become an honest man. He leaves and begins to wander, dazed and disoriented. "He saw, with disquietude, shaken within him that species of frightful calm which the injustice of his fate had given him. He asked himself what should replace it" (p. 90). The scent of flowers brings back memories of his childhood. He loses himself in reverie all day, not eating. Near nightfall, a small boy comes by, happily throwing coins into the air and catching them. When one falls and rolls to him, Jean Valjean abstractedly puts his foot on it. The boy cannot penetrate his reverie enough to get him to remove his foot, and walks away frightened. Some time later Jean Valjean moves his foot, sees the coin, and knows what has happened. He feels wretched; he is already a changed man.

At this point Hugo creates a flashback to a few hours before. As we see Jean Valjean leaving the bishop's house once more, we get a question: "Did a voice whisper in his ear that he had just passed through the decisive hour of his destiny, that there was no longer a middle course for him, that if, thereafter, he should not be the best of men, he would be the worst, that he must now, so to speak, mount higher than the bishop, or fall lower than the galley slave; that, if he would become good, he must become an angel; that, if he would remain wicked, he must become a monster?" (p. 94) Though not unequivocally imputing this knowledge to Jean Valjean's conscious mind, Hugo does point out the shape of the issues involved. Jean Valjean faces extremely sharp alternatives. Neither will permit him to remain the same as before meeting Myriel. In other words, immediately after leaving the bishop Jean Valjean undergoes a conversion which we never see, a conversion to becoming either much worse or much better. Already we have a discontinuous event operating at some inaccessible level of consciousness.

Depriving the boy of his coin, however unconscious, gives shape to the alternative of becoming even worse, and Jean Valjean's wretchedness contains his rejection of it. In a hallucination, he sees figures representing his alternatives. One is a phantom of himself which he does not immediately recognize. When he does so, he recoils in horror. The other, a light which assumes the figure of the bishop, grows and brightens. The Jean Valjean figure becomes a shadow and disappears. He weeps as he rejects the horror which the contrast with the bishop has made plain. He has participated in a choice that we cannot say he has consciously made.

In one sense Jean Valjean's conversion is complete at this point, but as Georges Piroué has observed, he works at the task of conversion all his life.[14] His crises of conscience show marked resemblances, particularly when we compare two of the most extended, the initial conversion and the decision to confess in order to save Champmathieu. Jean Valjean is each time secure enough to exclude his acting under the pressure of adverse circumstances. Each time he passes into and out of a trance or reverie, unable to control the ebb and flow of mental events. He notices irrelevancies in his surroundings, entertains childhood memories of doubtful application, and observes natural phenomena portentous with pathetic fallacy. Some fundamental chaos is evoked, which clarifies to a contrast between light and dark, and the interior chaos resolves into a hallucination embodying one image of himself as a wretched man and another image representing an alternative. Then Hugo takes a stance outside his mind altogether and suddenly presents an act indicating a resolution of the conflict by self-sacrifice. The will has been not so much exercised as suspended. The closer we get to the conversion, the closer we get to an explanatory gap. We cannot really identify a proximate cause. If we try to get rid of the indeterminacy we feel, we can only label our ignorance or accept Hugo's labels.

Hugo's labels are Providence and progress, the latter of which is the announced subject and "true title" of *Les Misérables* (p. 1024). He makes explicit the connection between his hero's crises of conscience and the political crises underlying progress when, during the revolutionary uprising of June 1832, Jean Valjean is wrestling with the question of giving up Cosette. "What are the convulsions of a city compared with the émeutes of the soul? Man is a still deeper depth than the people. Jean Valjean, at that very moment, was a prey to a frightful uprising. All the gulfs were reopened within him. He also, like Paris, was shuddering on the threshold of a formidable and obscure revolution. A few hours had sufficed. His destiny and his conscience were suddenly covered with shadow. Of him also, as of Paris, we might say: the two principles are face to face" (p. 965). But, an uprising becomes a revolution only if the people concur. "Repression has as many regiments as the barricade has men, and as many arsenals as the barricade has cartridge-boxes. Thus they are struggles of one against a hundred, which always end in the destruction of the barricade; unless revolution, abruptly appearing, casts into the balance its flaming archangel's sword. That happens. Then everything rises, the pavements begin to ferment, the redoubts of the people swarm, Paris thrills sovereignly, the *quid divinum* is set free" (p. 1016). In 1832 the people did not concur. According to Hugo, interests prevailed over principles. Conversion is thus used, as André Brochu has argued, as an analogue of revolution.[15] The mystery of individual progress helps to elucidate the mystery of collective progress, which occurs when collective conversion manifests itself. Political revolution resembles individual conversions and the collective conversions of scientific revolution. According to Crane Brinton, who strongly influenced Kuhn, it requires a dissatisfaction with the old in the presence of an alternative and a shift of commitment which cannot be logically explained, or even accurately described in its onset.[16] It attests in a sudden and dramatic form to what Hugo thought not simply an ideal, but a fact—that real sovereignty rests with the people.

Such a conviction, whatever the logical difficulties of maintaining it, underlies the attack on the legitimacy of legal systems which all virtuous-victim novels make.

Herman Melville's *Billy Budd*, left unfinished in 1891 and published first in 1924, not only omits any conversion of the hero to virtue, but denies that one took place. Melville speaks of Billy as an unfallen Adam and conceives of his story as the tragedy of Rousseau's naturally good man. For this reason the novel provides a good introduction to the middle of the virtuous victim's story, especially to its presentation of antagonists.

One shortcoming of Aristotle's criticism is that it can easily lead us to underestimate the middle of a literary work in favor of the end. If not careful, we may think of the middle simply as a contrivance for getting to the end from the beginning. Actually, the purpose of a novel should be, as we have seen among innocent-victim novels, fairly manifest in the middle, since that is where the conflict or center of interest is most evident. The middle of the innocent-victim novel shows the hero, with some degree of resilience, struggling against an injustice which would inflict further injury by destroying the self. The middle of the virtuous-victim novel also presents a struggle, but the virtue of the protagonists makes it different. Since they are perceived as threats, they are stronger than innocent victims, so that we may more accurately speak of resistance rather than resilience. This strength not only motivates the representatives of the legal system to oppose them, but also makes those representatives intrude more into the action than do the antagonists of the innocent victim. Indeed, getting antagonists who are more visible and official is another good reason to choose a virtuous victim in the first place. Injustice cannot be seen as an accident or as the result of personal corruption. It looks more systematic because we see more of the system.

Les Misérables presents two major antagonists: Javert, the policeman and pillar of rectitude, and the Thenardiers, rapacious, unscrupulous, and petit-bourgeois. These antagonists enable Hugo to show the opposition to Jean Valjean at its best and its worst and as embodied both in the state and in the economic system. Such an arrangement has proven very durable in virtuous-victim novels, and in *Billy Budd* Melville uses a similar pair. The dishonorable antagonist is John Claggart, the master-at-arms. He soon notices that Billy's cheerful innocence makes him popular with the crew. Having a "natural depravity" as unmotivated as Billy's goodness, he senses his opposite and starts to persecute him. Melville spends three chapters on Claggart's motive, and it all comes down to envy, a "cynic disdain, disdain of innocence."[17] Like Iago, to whom he is often compared, Claggart is a moralist of cynicism, outraged at selflessness and eager to destroy it because he so desperately needs to believe it impossible. He has, like some devils and demons in Spenser and Milton, what might be called the problem of good: how, in a world ruled by omnipotent evil, can so much good exist?

After this malice has led to Billy's unintentionally striking Claggart dead, Captain Vere, though knowing Billy innocent, condemns him to hang. Through this honorable antagonist, Melville allows the case for an unjust punishment to be made with the strongest possible arguments: the wartime conditions, the possible epidemic of mutiny, the need for military discipline and social order, and the likelihood of the crew to interpret any leniency as weakness. Vere has so many different arguments as to have led some readers to see him as hiding a more important ulterior motive. He has such good ones as to have led some to think him right. He is so attractive as to have led some to believe him the hero of the novel.

Much criticism of *Billy Budd* has centered on whether Captain Vere is justified, supposing that insofar as he is wrong we have a novel about social injustice, and insofar as he is not we have one about cosmic injustice or the frailty of innocence.[18] Interpretation, however, may not really be at issue. Melville's well-known ambiguity is here a sign, as it often is both for him and other writers, that the issue in question simply isn't important. Just as Melville leaves open the question of whether Vere is temporarily insane because any inference the reader makes is beside the point, he leaves open the question of whether Vere is intellectually or morally justified in executing Billy. For that reason, let us assume that Vere is both sane and guiltless. Despite his being an instrument of the English government during one of the most repressive decades in its history, let us accept Vere's argument at face value, ignoring all the doubts about it raised by the narrator and other characters. We will still find that Billy is a victim of earthly and institutionalized injustice.

Captain Vere bases his argument on necessity, but Melville has him base that necessity itself on a political reality he fully manifests to the court-martial as contrary to nature. Vere says:

"How can we adjudge to summary and shameful death a fellow creature innocent before God, and whom we feel to be so?— Does that state it aright? You sign sad assent. Well, I too feel that, the full force of that. It is Nature. But do these buttons that we wear attest that our allegiance is to Nature? No, to the King. Though the ocean, which is inviolate Nature primeval, though this be the element where we move and have our being as sailors, yet as the King's officers lies our duty in a sphere correspondingly natural? So little is that true, that in receiving our commissions we in the most important regards ceased to be natural free agents. When war is declared are we the commissioned fighters previously consulted? We fight at command. If our judgments approve the war, that is but coincidence. So in other particulars. So now. For suppose condemnation to follow these present proceedings. Would it be so much we ourselves that would condemn as it would be martial law operating through us? For that law and the rigor of it, we are not responsible. Our vowed responsibility is in this: That however pitilessly that law may operate in any instances, we nevertheless adhere to it and administer it" (pp. 110–11).

We can fully accept this argument, forgetting Vere's failure to persuade his own audience and the failure of similar arguments to persuade real courts. Our doing so, however, simply brings into stronger relief the injustice of the political necessities to which Vere bows.

The immediate necessity he feels is the Articles of War, which mandated capital punishment on conviction for striking a superior acting in the line of duty—making irrelevant both the effect of Billy's blow and the intention or lack of intention behind it. Clearly, this law is unjust because it makes innocence no protection from summary execution. By removing all grounds for judicial discretion, it causes rather than cures injustice.

But Melville did not write *Billy Budd* simply to attack one badly conceived and superseded law. He is concerned with the arbitrariness—the contrariness to nature—represented by that law and other laws, particularly those endured by sailors. He was indeed, particularly late in life, a conservative exponent of law and order, but we must not miss the radical criticism such conservatives make. Melville opposes lawlessness even when used as an arm of the state. In *White-Jacket* he repeatedly notes illegal acts committed by the very commanders sworn to defend the law and the Constitution. Even when acting legally in accord with the lights of the Navy, moreover, they observe "arbitrary laws" punishing "things not essentially criminal."[19]

Melville didn't lose interest in arbitrary laws during the years separating *White-Jacket* from *Billy Budd*. Once more we may simply take Vere at face value. He admits that extenuating circumstances would really extenuate "before a court less arbitrary and more merciful than a martial one" (p. 111). Not only is martial law arbitrary, so is naval discipline. Vere uses this point to argue that the crew would not understand clemency even if the court were permitted to use it. "Even could you explain to them—which our official position forbids— they, long molded by arbitrary discipline, have not that kind of intelligent responsiveness that might qualify them to comprehend and discriminate" (p. 112). Arbitrary discipline, according to Vere, has created a body of men who do not understand real justice. In *White-Jacket* Melville makes a similar argument in commenting on the riotous effects of letting the crew go on liberty ashore: "Such are the lamentable effects of suddenly and completely releasing *the people* of a man-of-war from arbitrary discipline. It shows that, to such, 'liberty,' at first, must be administered in small and moderate quantities, increasing it with the patient's capacity to make good use of it" (pp. 226–37). If arbitrary discipline has such effects the solution, for Melville, is to attack arbitrariness, not to forfeit justice or liberty.

The virtuous-victim novel, particularly if the virtue is given at the outset rather than developed through a presented conversion, tends to focus on political repression rather than on social oppression. In *Billy Budd* the police and judicial power of the state is much in evidence. Social issues such as *White-Jacket* raises—the hunger caused by bad scheduling of meal hours, the sickness brought on by holy-stoning and other fetishes of tidiness, the grogginess of not being allowed sufficient sleep at sea, or the ennui resulting from having nothing to do in port—play no part at all. Instead, the political issues raised by *White-Jacket*—the narrowness of utilitarianism, the legitimacy and extent of power, and the failure of ships to use a separation of powers even when sailing under the flags of countries observing the basic principle— show up once more in *Billy Budd*.

One of the political issues common to both books is secrecy, the refusal to keep the governed informed. Vere's consistent refusal to let the crew even hear the word "mutiny," for fear that it might give rise to the thing itself, causes him to summon Billy to hear a charge that he is entirely unprepared for. When Billy involuntarily strikes out at Claggart, Vere has brought about the very insubordination he tried to avoid. Because he fears what the crew would do if told the truth, his penchant for secrecy continues—an eloquent testimony to his own vulnerability. He may well ponder "the mystery of iniquity," for he himself produces mystifications. He may well think Billy Budd a victim of fate, for he, together with Claggart, is a large part of that fate.

The antagonists of virtuous-victim novels give readers a good look at the legal system and its commitment to law and order. By attacking the protagonists, however, the system finally promotes lawlessness and disorder, because they are the sort of people around whom community forms. After M. Madeleine confesses himself to be Jean Valjean and Javert arrests him, the town he has brought to prosperity disintegrates: "He fallen, every man strove for himself; the spirit of strife succeeded to the principle of organization, bitterness to cordiality, hatred of each against each instead of the good will of the founder towards all, the threads knitted by M. Madeleine became tangled and were broken" (p. 306). Similarly, after Billy Budd is hanged, a murmur arises from the crew. Captain Vere sees it as yet another threat and disperses them by piping the watch. At Billy's burial Vere sees in the crew a threatening movement and acts promptly again to disperse them. Like Jean Valjean, Billy Budd is a peacemaker bringing order and harmony to those around him. When he suffers, the community suffers. In Melville's presentation of Rousseau's naturally good man, we find something of Rousseau's attitude toward the civil institutions in which people live: "the real welfare of the public and true justice are always sacrificed to an apparent order, which is in reality subversive of all order."[20]

Graham Greene's *The Power and the Glory* pays special attention to the virtuous victim's community and to the legal system's attack on it. Just as *Billy Budd* can be compared to the more factual *White-Jacket*, so Greene's novel covers ground he had earlier dealt with in nonfiction. *The Lawless Roads* suggests through its title the attack on law and order that a government ostensibly devoted to those values can make. It reports Greene's 1939 trip to Mexico to investigate the persecution of religion and his simultaneous concern with the rise of fascist totalitarianism in Europe. There one can read of the Mexican government's attempt to dismantle colonialism and build socialism, but the novel devotes little space to these topics. Greene wanted to study the totalitarian state at war with community, principally in the form of a persecuted church.

Greene's protagonist, an unnamed whiskey priest running from persecution and wishing for capture, has none of Billy Budd's innocence or Jean Valjean's grandeur. He is afraid, he drinks too much, he has violated his vow of chastity, and when not persecuted, he is arrogant and ambitious. Nevertheless, he is a virtuous victim. He suffers persecution, sickness, hunger, fatigue, and eventually death because he serves his people. Whether he is right or wrong in thinking himself different from martyrs and saints, right or wrong in thinking, as did his historical prototype,[21] that he is doing the people no good; whether he is motivated also by pride, inertia, and confusion—he suffers death because of what is good in him. When he chooses to leave his refuge and walk into a trap to hear the confession of a dying man, he chooses also to prevent himself from becoming once more an aloof and bureaucratized cleric.

The honorable antagonist in *The Power and the Glory* is the police lieutenant, a good man even in the priest's estimation. Looking at an old, first-communion party picture of the priest, whom he hopes to track down, "he had the dignity of an idea, standing in the little whitewashed room with his polished boots and his venom. There was something disinterested in his ambition: a kind of virtue in his desire to catch the sleek respected guest at the first communion party."[22] In his hopes that the children he sees and loves will not grow up in the misery he knew as a child, he would make his country a desert if necessary, or wall it in with steel if that were possible. He is a disciplined, ascetic, puritanical, manichaean, and paranoid absolutist who undertakes a reign of terror—like the Robespierre of most historians. The chief dishonorable antagonist in the novel is the mestizo who eventually betrays the priest for a reward of several hundred pesos. On first meeting him, the priest recognizes him as a Judas and treats him with the same ironic detachment he has seen Lenten ritual use to keep the enemy of God from looking heroic. The mestizo, however, although he believes his poverty makes him unable to afford goodness, claims to be a good Catholic. Certainly he shows the pietism and superstition which Greene attacks throughout the novel. Even after betraying the priest, he asks for a blessing.

In those who do not betray the priest we see community, in contrast to the solitary mestizo despised even by the solitary lieutenant who uses him. Not a "shallow kinship with all the world" (p. 31), community has a local habitation and a name. It is in the jail the priest is put into when mistaken for a liquor smuggler. He tells his fellow prisoners that he is a priest and that a reward has been offered for him.

> "Nobody here," a voice said, "wants their blood money."
> Again he was touched by an extraordinary affection. He was just one criminal among a herd of criminals. . . . He had a sense of companionship which he had never experienced in the old days when pious people came kissing his black cotton glove (p. 128).

Community is in the village where we see the priest celebrating mass, but there it is pressured by the lieutenant's tactic of taking a hostage from each village and killing him if the villagers shelter the priest. They do not really want the priest and urge him to go, but no one betrays him when the lieutenant calls everyone together and takes a hostage.

Community is also in the persecuted church. The state is seen in its most absolute and the church in its least organized form. Each, simplified in opposite ways, is sharply defined against the other. The contrast is developed most fully during the long discussion after the lieutenant has arrested the priest and is taking him to the capital to be tried in absentia and executed.

"I was never any good at books," the priest said. "I haven't any memory. But there was one thing always puzzled me about men like yourself. You hate the rich and love the poor. Isn't that right?"

"Yes."

"Well, if I hated you, I wouldn't want to bring up my child to be like you. It's not sense."

"That's just twisting. . . ."

"Perhaps it is. I've never got your ideas straight. We've always said the poor are blessed and the rich are going to find it hard to get into heaven. Why should we make it hard for the poor man too? Oh, I know we are told to give to the poor, to see they are not hungry—hunger can make a man do evil just as much as money can. But why should we give the poor power? It's better to let him die in the dirt and wake in heaven—so long as we don't push his face in the dirt."

"I hate your reasons," the lieutenant said. "I don't want reasons. If you see somebody in pain, people like you reason and reason. You say—pain's a good thing, perhaps he'll be better for it one day. I want to let my heart speak."

"At the end of a gun."

"'Yes. At the end of a gun' (pp. 198–99)."

Here is the fundamental issue. The state is directly concerned with power, and when we see it simplified to the absolute of totalitarianism, power is compulsion. The church, on the other hand, is directly concerned with glory, and when we see it simplified as the primitive, persecuted church, power is merely an alien temptation. What Captain Fellows thinks about the limits of parental power applies equally well to such a church: "You cannot control what you love" (p. 36).

One doesn't have to contrast church and state in this way, of course, and Greene reverses his simplifications to provide new ones. The church, seen in its absolute form in the priest's memory of the days before persecution, is merely a pietistic bureaucracy, and parish life an endless series of vacuous meetings, rote masses, and perfunctory confessions. The state is presented in its least absolute form in a scene between the lieutenant and some children. One of them has been resisting his mother's attempts to instill piety in him, but is attracted by the lieutenant's pistol. "The tip of the boy's tongue appeared: he swallowed. Saliva came from the glands as if he smelt food. They all stood close in now. A daring child put out his hand and touched the holster" (p. 58). For the children, the lieutenant represents the state in its most elemental form, security.

Yet the church that we see in the novel, elemental under persecution and purged of almost everything, is a threat to the state: "You're a danger. That's why we kill you" (p. 193). Why a danger? Because it is a community not designed to serve the state. The state can view it only as a parody of the social contract—a community not founded on any human bargain—or as a group of hypocrites really banded together for self-defense. This threatened feeling is well founded, because even a group brought into being by the renunciation of power has plenty of power. Its source is trust, which creates the social bond and therefore the constraints within which any state must operate. By using hostages and informers, the lieutenant seeks to subvert trust. He himself trusts no one. Neither does the state he serves. The governor and the chief of police do not trust each other enough to put an agreement in writing, although they claim that their trust for each other makes it unnecessary to do so. Distrust has spread everywhere, corrupting not only the government but also personal life. The assault on trust and the consequent undermining of the social bonds creating community is what makes totalitarianism totalitarian. Its ideal citizen is the solitary informer. However legal its actions may be technically, it is illegitimate.

The ending of *The Power and the Glory* begins with the priest's temptation to abandon the virtues he has developed under persecution. He is safe in a Mexican state not actively persecuting priests. He sees his former clerical self beginning to take possession of him. In deciding to leave his sanctuary, he rejects that self and thus reenacts the initial conversion that Greene omitted by starting his novel *in media res*. As a result of this reaffirmation of his virtue, the priest is martyred, but his community goes on. The novel closes with the arrival of a new priest to take his place.

The ending of *Les Misérables* has been treated very well in a special issue of *Nineteenth-Century Fiction* devoted to narrative endings. There, Alexander Welsh credits Walter Scott with originating the pattern: "What used to be called Scott's dualism is most importantly reflected in the double fable of most of his novels, wherein the correct hero refrains from acting and survives history but certain active heroes who endorse violence or have the bad luck to stand in the way of the 'whither?' of the action pointedly end their lives with the end of the novel. *Les Misérables* boasts two such contrasting heroes in Marius Pontmercy and Jean Valjean." Welsh goes on to note that "as the nineteenth century progressed, writers began to interpret this fable as marking a division between the claims of the species and the claims of the individual."[23] I think this is true even for Scott. Certainly it is for the virtuous-victim novel, in which what almost always survives is the hero's community.

Harriet Beecher Stowe's *Uncle Tom's Cabin* can illustrate this ending, together with some of its implications. As its title ought to suggest, it is largely the story of a community. According to Stowe's 1878 essay "The Story of *Uncle Tom's Cabin*," the novel's animus was the Fugitive Slave Law of 1850, which required even the citizens of the Free North to consider slaves merely as property by turning them in if they escaped from their masters. Its germ was a story about a young slave woman who escaped with her child by leaping from one ice floe to another on the Ohio River, and the story of another slave who would not escape because he would not violate the trust his master had bestowed on him.[24] It is the story, then, of escape and the refusal to escape, of the Harris family and of Uncle Tom, two different virtuous victims.

Eliza Harris shuns the very idea of escape until threatened with the sale of her son Harry to a trader who has admired the boy's intelligence. Her husband, George, has already decided to escape because his master's envy of his learning and inventiveness has led to a systematic attempt to degrade him. He decides to be free, and from the moment of his decision he is because he is willing to fight to death for his freedom. The successful escape and reunion of his family dominate the first quarter of the novel. Even afterwards, it occasionally counterpoints the sufferings of Tom.

Tom is sold away from his family because he is more valuable than the other slaves. He permits himself to be sold, instead of escaping as he encourages others to do, not because he is the abject and passive Christian darky that James Baldwin and others have seen in him,[25] but because his alternative is to see many of his fellow slaves sold down the river to pay his master's debt. In this respect Stowe varied the story from her original germ. She showed him refusing to escape not out of loyalty to his master, but out of loyalty to his own community. Undoubtedly, she confronted him with such drastic alternatives because it is difficult to write a novel about life under slavery without some characters who do not escape from it.

The stories of Uncle Tom and the Harrises permit Stowe to present an extremely wide array of antagonists throughout the middle of the novel. Tom Loker is a brutal slave-catcher and Marks a canting one who pretends to be humane in order to keep from decreasing the value of those he pursues. Slave masters likewise range from negative to positive antagonists, with a higher proportion of the latter so that Stowe can show slavery at its best and still show it wrong as a system. By showing its terrible effects on masters as well as slaves, she raises the grim possibility that this enormous legalized injustice served no one's real interests. It is this great range and complexity that led Edmund Wilson to count himself with Henry James among the novel's admirers: "The farther one reads in *Uncle Tom*, the more one becomes aware that a critical mind is at work, which has the complex situation in a very firm grip and which, no matter how vehement the characters become, is controlling and coordinating their interrelations."[26] The novel achieves whatever literary value one might assign it largely because of the propagandistic purpose and political passion of its writer, casting great doubt on the presumption that literary and political values must always conflict. And if the story is true that Abraham Lincoln saluted Stowe as the one who brought on the Civil War, then—even allowing for presidential hyperbole—the novel casts doubt too on the presumption that social protest novels have no liberating effects on politics.

The ending of *Uncle Tom's Cabin* was written first, and everything leads to it. In it, as in the end of *The Power and the Glory*, we can see the shape of the beginning of the virtuous victim's story, the initial conversion reported but not presented. Tom is sold from the estate to St. Claire, the most positive of the novel's antagonists, to Simon Legree, the most negative. Like Claggart, Legree has a "native antipathy of bad to good" (p. 352). He too operates by trying to subvert social bonds.

> Legree, like some potentates we read of in history, governed his plantation by a sort of resolution of forces. Sambo and Quimbo cordially hated each other; the plantation hands, one and all, cordially hated them; and, by playing off one against another, he was pretty sure, through one or the other of the three parties, to get informed of whatever was on foot in the place (p. 346).

He is a northerner who has given up his puritanical religion and channeled its intensity into moneymaking. He is a test case for the anti-abolitionist view that masters would take care of their slaves out of their own self-interest. His own is a slender reed bending to an irrationality which ruins not only others but also himself.

Legree buys Tom to use him as a driver, an instrument for oppressing his fellows. When Tom insists on helping a weak mulatto woman, Legree orders him to flog her instead. When Tom refuses, he himself is beaten. He is befriended by Cassy, who urges him to give in.

> "It's no use, my poor fellow!" she broke out at last, "it's of no use, this you've been trying to do. You were a brave fellow,— you had the right on your side; but it's all in vain, and out of the question, for you to struggle. You are in the devil's hands;—he is the strongest, and you must give up!" . . .
>
> "There's no law here, of God or man, that can do you, or any one of us, the least good; and, this man! there's no earthly thing that he's too good to do. I could make any one's hair rise, and their teeth chatter, if I should only tell what I've seen and been knowing to, here,—and it's no use resisting" (pp. 360–61).

Tom continues to resist Legree, but becomes despondent and enters a dark night of the soul.

Legree comes to pressure him anew. He is desperate because of Tom's resistance. He wants to crush it and substitute himself for the church that sustains it, but he shows Tom all too clearly the alternatives.

> When a heavy weight presses the soul to the lowest level at which endurance is possible, there is an instant and desperate effort of every physical and moral nerve to throw off the weight; and hence the heaviest anguish often precedes a return tide of joy and courage. So was it now with Tom. The atheistic taunts of his cruel master sunk his dejected soul to the lowest ebb; and, though the hand of faith still held to the eternal rock, it was with a numb, despairing grasp. Tom sat, like one stunned, at the fire. Suddenly everything around him seemed to fade, and a vision rose before him of one crowned with thorns, buffeted and bleeding. Tom gazed, in awe and wonder, at the majestic patience of the face; the deep, pathetic eyes thrilled him to his inmost heart; his soul woke, as, with floods of emotion, he stretched out his hands and fell upon his knees,—when, gradually, the vision changed: the sharp thorns became rays of glory (p. 393).

This reaffirmation of an earlier conversion makes clear the values of resistance and community which motivate Tom throughout the novel. Legree's power starts to break, and

Tom becomes a center holding the slaves together. He can encourage others to escape and help them, but he cannot leave his beleaguered community. For helping others, he is killed by Legree, and the novel shifts to the survivors, including the Harrises. Once more, a double ending serves to contrast not passivity and activity but the death of an individual and the survival of his community. The community survival in the end is immanent in the invulnerability it lends the hero; the death of the individual in the end is immanent throughout in his selflessness. It is a fall, but not entirely a defeat.

One support for Northrop Frye's claim that romance is naturally comic is that "comic romance" seems a redundant expression for something which can be treated simply as romance. The term "tragic romance," on the other hand, seems not one thing, but two. It could be replaced here by "romantic tragedy" except for the accidents of historical usage, or "romance-tragedy" except for the warning figure of Polonius. For this reason I have not hesitated to take from Frye the term but not entirely the meaning he assigns to it. He has in mind *Clarissa*, *Romeo and Juliet*, and *The Bride of Lammermoor*, but I think it arguable that even Romeo finds his desired world in an undesired one and rises to it at the beginning through something like conversion. Frye traces his hero back to the heroes and gods of myth. I suggest for a prototype of the tragic romance hero represented in the virtuous-victim novel someone like Moses, who also found a desired world only in the undesired one, struggled against an unjust but legal system together with his community, and led it toward a promised land he could not personally enter. At any rate, the previous chapter could treat comic romance as essentially romance and defer most discussion of comedy. Now, treating the capabilities and limitations of the virtuous-victim novel for political expression requires bearing in mind that tragic romance, its privileged form, is somewhat like romance and somewhat like tragedy. Even so, it is sufficiently different to make irrelevant most claims about the ideological bias of either.

79

The problems of clarity and hope in the virtuous-victim novel consist of its risking too much of each. It may be so clear as to oversimplify social reality, because it relies on the melodrama common among romances. It may be so hopeful as to dissolve the very social problems it treats into nonproblems, because its heroes have the romance hero's invulnerability. When this does give way in the end, they achieve something like tragic transcendence, which compensates them considerably for their suffering.

In presenting a combat between a strong hero of some virtue and a strong antagonist seeking to punish it, the virtuous-victim novel figures to be melodramatic, and this strongly affects its clarity or targeting. Like other literary forms, melodrama has the weakness of its strengths. The strengths were hardly evident some years ago, however, when Richard Chase helped make melodrama respectable by showing that important achievements of American novelists stemmed from their ability "to take advantage of the abstractness of melodrama and its capacity to evoke ultimates and absolutes, in order to dramatize theological, moral, and less frequently political ideology."[27] As for its weakness, Eric Bentley and others have defended melodrama from the charge that it exaggerates for the sake of effect by pointing out that such an objection applies to all art and that even writers who scorn melodrama have bootlegged it into their work so often as to have made it a major modern form.[28]

Because the main expressive advantage of melodrama is the moral clarity achieved through its sharp contrasts, the main justification of it as rhetoric lies in its ability to counter muddle and nihilism. In real people and situations, good and evil mingle so much as to tempt us to mingle them conceptually as well—to take them as merely one more set of reconcilable opposites, to despair of accomplishing any good, and perhaps even to traffic with evil. Melodrama, on the other hand, asserts the absoluteness and irreconcilability of good and evil. This strength leads to the major risk of using it. According to Frye, "The popularity of romance, it is obvious, has much to do with its simplifying of moral facts. It relieves us from the strain of trying to be fair-minded, as we see particularly in melodrama, where we not only have outright heroism and villainy but are expected to take sides, applauding one and hissing the other." Similarly, Bentley finds that "melodramatic vision is paranoid," and Peter Brooks calls it manichaeistic.[29]

Applied to politics, which is particularly open to manichaeism and paranoia, such a vision may encourage unjustifiable polarization and a siege mentality. However, these dangers need not lead us to see any generic political bias in melodrama, since simplification can serve any ideology, including that of moderation. As is the case with other literary forms, claims of generic bias tend to cancel one another out. When we find James L. Rosenberg asserting that melodrama offends the bourgeois sensibility and Wylie Sypher arguing in the same collection of articles that it is "a notoriously bourgeois aesthetic," it is easy to agree with Brooks that "its social implications may be variously revolutionary or conservative," and with Chase that it is "as good a vehicle for radical opinions as it proves for conservative ones."[30]

To guard against the manichaeism of melodrama, the writer can dilute it. If George Worth is correct, seeing vice and virtue as social products is itself a move away from simplification and melodrama: "In the *Sketches by Boz*, vice—to the extent that it is to be found at all—is not embodied in greedy, larcenous, lecherous, or murderous men, as it is in melodrama. Rather, it stems from the corrosive effects of poverty and other forms of deprivation, whereas virtue consists in the ability to surmount such pressures and kindred temptations. Since vice is depersonalized in this way, there can hardly be palpable, audible encounters between it and virtue."[31] Essentially, melodrama is diluted by assigning limitations to the hero's goodness and/or the antagonist's evil. Bootlegged melodrama often disguises the hero in whatever vices are currently thought amiable, and Greene's priest has several of these. The virtuous-victim novel can also suggest complexity in the protagonist through psychodrama, despite the fact that its psychodrama almost invariably and inevitably ends by reaffirming conversion and banishing once more the hero's old self. It also gets some complexity in the antagonist, as we have seen, by often having a positively presented one to go with a negative one. The dynamics of the innocent-victim novel give rise naturally to more than one antagonist, but since the virtuous-victim novel has no such pressure from plot, the presence of two or more antagonists seems designed to increase complexity. In this way what could have been a source of weakness is transformed into a source of great strength, for in multiplying antagonists in this way and drawing multiple distinctions between and among them, writers such as Stowe and Hugo make their novels extremely convincing, both artistically and politically.

Because diluting melodrama obviously risks forfeiting its benefits as well as its drawbacks, the writers we have examined also seek to avoid excessive simplification or clarity by thematizing the hazards not only of muddle but also of clarity itself. Claggart, the Thenardiers, and St. Clare's brother have plenty of clarity and simplicity. It accounts in part for the evil they do. Javert, a positive antagonist, needs clarity so much that he can accommodate no moral ambiguity at all. He is capable only of rectitude, and when ambiguity invades him, bringing about his one really good act, he can no longer live. In these and others, writers have taken the manichaeism which threatens the virtuous-victim novel and located it in the mental habits of antagonists. Instead of diluting melodrama, they have, as it were, increased it and turned it on itself.

Alan Swingewood has objected to Gorki's *Mother* as melodramatic propaganda unfaithful to the complexity of social life: "The revolutionaries are portrayed as wholly good, the representatives of the Russian autocracy as degenerate and evil."[32] In fact, one or two blemishes can be found among the revolutionaries, and Gorki mentions several times that the Tsarist officials are the same sort of people as their victims, more to be pitied than hated. Instead of, or in addition to, diluting the melodrama, however, Gorki might well have increased it. He does not show the antagonists enough to justify much of any attitude toward them, and when he does, he is so intent on minimizing their power—which he has already achieved—that he makes them ineffectual, muddled, and comic. He celebrates political manichaeism by concentrating clarity, not virtue, in the revolutionaries. By denying his heroine worthy opponents, furthermore, he diminishes her own stature.

Although melodrama has become fairly respectable, sentimentality, one of its most frequent features, has not. Yet sentimentality also comes naturally to the virtuous-victim novel. The suffering and death of such a positively conceived character, so readily loved by admirable children who suffer or die themselves, appeals openly to the softer emotions of readers. Even Graham Greene, who caters to the taste of his time by toning down such appeals more than do Stowe or Hugo, is writing a sort of hagiography. If sentimentality is bad, the virtuous-victim novel has a serious limitation. But is it? Brian Wilkie has examined carefully the handbook notion of sentimentality as the arousing of tender feeling in excess of what a situation warrants and found it not only unworkable, but also biased socially and philosophically. "My point, then, is not that a work can survive or compensate for sentimental blemishes; sentimentality may in some cases sentimental blemishes; sentimentality may in some cases be an organic part of a large vision of life that is valid both morally and as art. Granted that such instances of 'formally necessary' sentimentality are unusual, they are still part of the whole of literature, and one must not theorize about sentimentality in such a way as to exclude or prejudice them."[33] We might ask, then, what necessity, formal or not, might justify the sentimentality of the virtuous-victim novel.

This question should be addressed from the perspective of a writer such as Harriet Beecher Stowe. She knew that slavery could be accepted only through a widespread atrophy of feeling, which allowed human beings to be treated as things. She saw the bonds of society disintegrating as slavery divided the families of both slaves and masters. She thought slavery could be opposed only by stimulating the creation of the bonds it was undermining. Social bonds, however, are in large part affective bonds depending upon positive emotions. They must be in excess of what a situation warrants, if the situation is analyzed logically. Clearly, Stowe's purpose must lead to sentimentality. But just as clearly, the insistence—moralistic in its own way—that sentimentality is an evil which no purpose can justify merely masquerades a political censorship as a neutral literary principle.

Virtuous-victim novels also risk excessive hope or optimism because of their affinities with both romance and tragedy. The protagonists have even more of the romance hero's invulnerability than do innocent victims because they stay more closely tied to their own community, getting from it and giving to it the power to resist. That source also underlies what seems to be their transcendence of their final suffering, a characteristic often associated with tragic heroes. Many have described tragic heroes as looking back after their suffering and experiencing an epiphany or access to wisdom. Kitto calls this "the doctrine of *pathos mathos* (learn by suffering)."[34] This moment may be the point for which the resources of tragedy have been marshaled, the answer to the old question of what pleasure the spectator can get from witnessing pain. Of course, not everyone agrees that tragic heroes do, or at least should, transcend their suffering. George Steiner cautions that compensation for suffering may trivialize it,[35] and virtuous-victim novels seem to invite a similar objection—that a *quid pro quo* transaction takes place which costs a bit of suffering but buys a lot of satisfaction. If so, the optimism this transaction suggests may be so great as to swallow up the very social problems treated, because seeing these depends on our taking the suffering seriously.

There are two ways of meeting such an objection, at least as far as it applies to virtuous-victim novels. First, I think the ending may be misconceived if seen as transcendence. In the last chapter we saw Frye's observation that the hero of comic romance looks weak but proves invulnerable, whereas the tragic hero looks invulnerable but proves weak. Accordingly, I suggested that the triumph or partial triumph of the innocent victim helped to satisfy the paradox of reform by insisting on some freedom from the tyranny of circumstances to go along with the subjection to them. In the case of virtuous victims a very similar balance exists for the same reason. Their death or defeat balances the aura of invulnerability which has come to attend them. Thus the defeat is a correction factor. As to the victorious element in the ending, it corrects this correction. It insures that defeat will not eclipse the victory seen throughout the novel. It performs the same function as the death or defeat of the antagonist, which also tends to mark the ending, for the antagonist's defeat also corrects the impression of defeat in the victim's end.

Perhaps instead of seeing the virtuous-victim novel as using something other than transcendence, we should conceive transcendence itself differently, even in tragedy. Kenneth Burke has done so, using the musical terms chord and arpeggio to distinguish the simultaneous from the serial.

> In the arpeggio of biological, or temporal, growth, good *does* come of evil (as we improve ourselves by revising our excesses, the excesses thus being a necessary agent in the drama, or dialectic, of improvement: they are the "villain" who "competitively cooperates" as "criminal Christ" in the process of redemption). But when you condense the arpeggio of development by the nontemporal, nonhistorical forms of logic, you get simultaneous "polarity," which adds up to good and evil as consubstantial. Now if one introduces into a chord a note alien to the perfect harmony, the result is a discord. But if you stretch out this same chord into an arpeggio having the same components, the discordant ingredient you have introduced may become but a "passing note." "Transcendence" is the solving of the logical problem by stretching it out into a narrative arpeggio, whereby a conflicting element can be introduced as a "passing note," hence not felt as "discord."[36]

Here Burke conceives transcendence not (or not simply) as a triumph of good over evil but as a serializing of their simultaneity. Thus in the virtuous victim we can see at one given moment both suffering and resistance. They are inversely proportional, so that a limit to suffering is a limit to the power of the antagonist and an indication of the victim's resistance. When one is emphasized the other is de-emphasized, so that

85

we get a series of highs and lows. Transcendence is such a serialization, or at least the effect of it, so that we see the highs in the light of the lows and vice versa. Each is a correction factor to the other. Which one comes last may not matter except to the rigid Aristotelian. We see defeat in the light of triumph and triumph in the light of defeat, so that either one, in its pure form, is negated. Thus we find once more that optimism can be kept from excess by the avoidance of outright triumph.

Regardless of how we conceive the typical ending of the virtuous-victim novel, we should bear in mind that the triumph, like the invulnerability which it reaffirms, is basically the community's. It has a better claim to immortality than the protagonist. If the protagonist feels a triumph that compensates somewhat for suffering, it is their triumph—the triumph of the crew, church, party, or cabin. And just as the protagonist triumphs through them, because a part of them, they suffer through the protagonist's suffering. Suffering is not trivialized—we will see really trivialized suffering later—but it does lose its finality.

When all is said and done, however, defeat is de-emphasized somewhat by juxtaposition to triumph. The risk of excessive optimism in the virtuous-victim novel, though it should not be exaggerated because it is not unmanageable, will not simply go away. Nor will the risk of excessive clarity, despite all the resources writers bring to cope with it. However, any writer or reader unwilling to accept the risks of the virtuous-victim novel can turn to a different type of novel—and to different risks.

4

The Flawed Victim

Free will does not mean one will, but many wills conflicting in one man.

—Flannery O'Connor

A LTHOUGH using innocent and virtuous victims as protagonists, the novels so far considered present other
victims of society who suffer partly because of flaws in character. Solzhenitsyn's Fetukov has lost his self-respect through
parasitism, and Stowe's Prue has lost herself in alcohol trying
to forget a child taken from her. Unlike innocent victims,
flawed victims contribute substantially to motivating their
own fate. Unlike both innocent and virtuous victims, their
characters provide a major target of social criticism. Nevertheless, they need not be entirely flawed. Just as innocent
victims need not be innocent people or virtuous victims extremely virtuous ones, flawed victims are not victims who
happen to be flawed. They are simply characters with some
defect which helps to bring about their suffering. They may
be quite admirable otherwise.

Such characters, at least when used as protagonists in
flawed-victim novels, incorporate much of the antagonist
function also. This dynamic underlies the poetics of these
novels and thus makes possible hypothesizing about their
structure. The beginning, like that of the virtuous-victim novel,
should establish the internal characteristic which is to motivate the hero's suffering. Because this is a flaw, we can look

for a negative conversion, one which locates an antagonist within the protagonist. The middle should present a struggle between the two, inside the hero, as well as a test of the flaw outside the hero through another struggle with some external antagonist. By the end, the flaw should fail the test. To the extent that the hero makes sense of the experience, he or she should drive away the inner antagonist and undergo a positive conversion, coming finally to resemble a virtuous victim.

As is the case with the previous types we have seen, only the middle need be presented to have a flawed-victim novel, but we see the whole in Dickens' *Great Expectations*. Pip first undergoes a negative conversion, conforming to the code of the gentleman-snob. He then struggles because his former self limits his adherence to it and because it is inadequate in the face of experience. After it fails him entirely, he ends with a positive conversion, helping the criminal who befriended him, giving up his snobbery, and withdrawing from his life of idleness. Such a story, or at least the middle of it, may be seen in Defoe's *Moll Flanders*, von Kleist's *Michael Kohlhaas*, Flaubert's *Madame Bovary*, Dostoevsky's *Notes from Underground*, London's *Martin Eden*, Conrad's *Under Western Eyes*, Fitzgerald's *The Great Gatsby*, Hemingway's *To Have and Have Not*, Faulkner's *Light in August*, Mann's *Dr. Faustus*, Bellow's *Seize the Day*, and many other, less illustrious, works.

Flawed-victim novels can use almost any flaw to motivate the suffering. In *Of Mice and Men*, for example, Steinbeck's hero is mentally retarded. Most novelists, however, do not use natural flaws, but choose one which is socially induced. They conceive character dynamically, forcing us to make some such distinction as Richard Bjornson makes between "character as nature" and "character as process."

In the European picaresque, the self is frequently depicted in the traditional manner as an inherent "nature" which is tested and revealed for what it is during the course of the hero's fictional adventures.

What the anonymous author of *Lazarillo* portrayed was something quite different. Faced with the common human problem of providing himself with both physical sustenance and a psychologically satisfying self-image, his picaresque hero internalizes the dehumanizing behavior patterns of the dominant society and thus acquires a character which he did not have by nature.[1]

Those whose character has thus been deformed need not even be brought to suffer at the hands of social institutions. They have been misfit for living fully, and almost any of their failures will make a social criticism.

Unfortunately, we sometimes cannot readily distinguish between character as nature and character as a social product. Godwin motivates Caleb Williams by an "insatiable curiosity" which leads him to pry into Falkland's affairs, for which he suffers unjust punishment. We may see this flaw as socially caused, a natural result of the excessive secrecy and distrust brought about in England by fear of sedition in the aftermath of the French Revolution. A similar point may be made about the heroine of Mary Wollstonecraft's *Maria*, who has so much romantic imagination that she marries without due consideration for the faults of her husband. When these grow intolerable, she is punished by the laws which prevailed before the Married Woman's Property Act. Such romanticism may be considered a part of the social subjugation of women, a natural outcome of the ignorance in which they were kept and the triviality of the little they were taught, as Wollstonecraft makes clear in *A Vindication of the Rights of Woman*.

Even without historical considerations, however, we know that curiosity and romanticism, unlike the mental retardation of Steinbeck's hero, cannot be congenital, and we should see some social criticism in any flaw which can originate only in social experience. Still, most writers of flawed-victim novels require of us no such interpretative arts. They give their heroes the flaw of having difficulty relating to other people. As a result they insure that we recognize a social origin for the flaw and highlight their social theme. Such a flaw makes the hero exactly opposite to the virtuous victim. The selflessness of the latter, as we have seen, is community-engendering.

Flawed victims, whether selfish or not, have some character-istic that is community-inhibiting. The virtuous victim har-monizes the claims of the individual and the group, as does any society to the extent that it is just. Flawed victims do not. They may display excessive individualism and an inability or refusal to associate, so that we may call them rebels, so long as we distinguish their solitary rebellion from the resistance of the virtuous victim. Or they may show too little individ-ualism by adopting the values of the dominant society, in which case we may call them conformists. Although oppo-sites, rebellion and conformism are quite similar. Both re-quire the hero to endure solitude, even if in a crowd. More-over, both may be realized in the same character, since both derive from the same underlying flaw and people are not always consistent. Thus we need not always worry about discriminating them. We should simply expect most flawed victims to have some difficulty associating with other people. Their flaw, we may say, is that they are not like virtuous victims. Their story implies the same social ideal.

In the virtuous-victim novel antagonists play a large part, usually as agents of the state, and the privileged subject is the contest between resistance and repression. In the flawed-victim novel, on the other hand, we find few Javerts and Simon Legrees, because the antagonist function is largely given to the protagonists themselves, who interiorize the master or slave values around them. Their struggle is largely internal, fighting the inauthenticity which has invaded them. Consequently, the privileged subject of the flawed-victim novel is false consciousness and the ideological oppression bring-ing it about. We can expect little of the sort of attack Dickens made on the Poor Laws, Solzhenitsyn on the Soviet regime, Stowe on the Fugitive Slave Law, Greene on the persecution of Christians, or Melville on naval discipline. The flawed-victim novel tends rather to attack a culture—the source of the false values the heroes adopt.

Flawed victims are the most subjugated of all victims of society, because injustice damages their character as well as body. They may even lack enough privileged inner space or self to resent the injustice against them or to attribute their suffering to the right causes. The deformation of their character indicates both the pressure and the nature of the environment or milieu in which they live. Thus the privileged literary form for presenting the flawed victim, despite some gothicism in *Caleb Williams*, is realism—more accurately, the tragic realism which John Orr has found in the social criticism of so many novels.[2]

This chapter examines Theodore Dreiser's *American Tragedy* for the beginning of the flawed victim's story, Emile Zola's *L'Assommoir* and Richard Wright's *Native Son* for the largely internal conflicts common in its middle, and Stendhal's *The Red and the Black* for its ending. Finally, a discussion of how well the flawed-victim novel copes with the problems of clarity and hope throws light on realism as a means of political expression.

By showing Clyde Griffiths eventually convicted and executed for an accidental death, Theodore Dreiser used *An American Tragedy* to protest the punishment of an innocent man: the legal system was overly sensitive to public opinion and private manipulation, its jurors subject to economic reprisals for following their consciences, and its lawyers less dedicated to justice than to their own careers. As the nature of these charges suggests, however, changing one or two laws, or even installing a new political regime, could not begin to remedy the injustice. That would require cultural change, a widespread shift in social attitudes extending beyond the sort of people who victimize Clyde Griffiths to the antagonist within him and those like him—a large number, judging from the fact that so many readers wrote to Dreiser saying that Clyde's story could have been their own. Thus, although he is a legally innocent man, Clyde Griffiths is no innocent victim, no harbinger of a better society. He is part of the problem and the worship of success which brings him to the bar of justice subjects him to the judgments of those flawed in the same way as he. Like most flawed victims, he resembles his adversaries. Unfortunately, such resemblances

91

have led at times to the libel that all victims are similar in character to their victimizers.

Although Dreiser gives Clyde a "bump of position and distinction," suggesting through phrenology that his desire for success is innate, he actually shows this desire developing from an underlying conformism which is widespread, for Clyde has "that old mass yearning for likeness in all things."[3] This conjunction of conformism and devotion to success lies at the root of Clyde's tragedy and gives to it its specifically American features, making him, as F. O. Matthiessen some time ago remarked, "a victim of the contemporary American dream."[4] Clyde wants to be like other people, and like other people he wants social distinction, which can consist only of being unlike other people. This contradiction at the heart of American culture gives rise to many absurdities, as we sense in Dreiser's mockery of a plush hotel purveying "exclusiveness to the masses" (p. 45). More importantly, it gives rise to a war of each against all. As an innocent victim Clyde is opposed by the establishment and its functionaries; as a flawed victim he is opposed by almost everyone, including members of his own social class. Conformism then, although it seems a social orientation, leads to attitudes and consequences as antisocial as those of rebellion.

Although bringing him to prize success, conformism incapacitates Clyde for achieving it. He does not lament, as Dreiser does, that his education has been very impractical, "for true to the standard of American youth, or the general American attitude toward life, he felt himself above the type of labor which was purely manual" (p. 80). As a result he is a dreamer or romantic, lacking "that mental clarity and inner directing application that in so many permits them to sort out from the facts and avenues of life the particular thing or things that make for their direct advancement" (p. 188). He sees puritan self-discipline in some of the wealthy and resolves to adopt it, but with a "disposition which did not tend to load itself with more than the most immediate cares" (pp. 328–29) he cannot handle the calculation of consequences. A lawyer later sent to help him prepare his defense concludes that "as a plotter of crime Clyde was probably the most arresting example of feeble and blundering incapacity he had feeble and blundering incapacity he had ever met" (p. 627).

With such ineptness, Clyde's method for succeeding can consist only of waiting for a "break." To him success is a mystery: "Who were these people with money, and what had they done that they should enjoy so much luxury, where others as good seemingly as themselves had nothing?" (p. 62) He is the perfect protege, looking for patrons who will lift him to "position." Like many other flawed victims, he abandons himself to chance, and for a while it serves him well. But continuing to rely on it threatens to get him married to the poverty of Roberta. Only then does he try to become someone who makes things happen. Since he is entirely unfit for the role, chance betrays him. Dreiser, the champion of self-reliance, sees to that.

So much for Clyde's flaw and the disaster it brings him to. Now let us take a closer look at its origins. *An American Tragedy*, like *Les Misérables*, begins with a conversion which establishes the personal characteristics which will lead eventually to the victim's suffering. It thus shows fully an important compositional option which many other flawed-victim novels, to varying degrees, dispense with.

As we saw in the case of Jean Valjean, the process of conversion has three moments—a beginning, middle, and end—which together make up the beginning of the whole story. The protagonists must have some potential for changing or some dissatisfaction with their current outlook. They must have an alternative, because they cannot leap without having something to leap to. Then there is the leap itself, which is nonetheless a leap into the unknown, because the full import of the alternative cannot be clear until well afterward.

For protagonists who will become flawed victims the source of initial dissatisfaction, like that of those slated to undergo conversions and become virtuous victims, is that they are already innocent victims of society. Occasionally the process of becoming an innocent victim, falling out of a desired world, will be presented.[5] *An American Tragedy*, how-ever, begins with innocent victimage, and it is twofold: Clyde's entire family is poor and thus outside the dominant society, and he is the innocent victim of his family. His parents are street-corner evangelists who expect him to go with them to sing hymns, an experience he hates more than he does his poverty, which he blames on them. He "looked upon himself as a thing apart—never quite wholly and indissolubly merged with the family of which he was a member" (p. 30). This sense of double alienation—from both the dominant society and the more immediate society of family, race, or social class—often marks the flawed victim.

Double alienation was even more evident before Dreiser revised *An American Tragedy*. In one of eight canceled early chapters he presented in some detail his hero's early encoun-ter with people outside his family. Clyde makes a friend at school, visiting his home in a better part of the city. He con-ceals his own home life because he is ashamed of the store-front mission where he lives, but his friend finds out, and other boys, not at all friendly to Clyde, discover that he sings at his parents' street-corner meetings. They involve him in a fight, despite his vigorous and false denials of their taunts. His friend tries to help him, but is repelled by his lies. Thus in this version of the novel Clyde's first attempt at substantial association outside the home is rebuffed. Dreiser ends the chapter claiming that this fact considerably strengthened his desire to associate.

A deep psychic wound had been delivered which was destined to fester and ramify in strange ways later on. It convinced him of the material—even the spiritual—insignificance of that which his parents did. They seemed, if anything, more hopeless and incompetent than ever. It sickened him of this school—and this type of school work as well as of this type of prosperous youth. But by some psychic process of inversion, it gave him a greater awe of wealth and comfort—or at least a keener perception of the protective qualities of a high social position in life. Other boys were not like him. Other boys did not need to do, had never been made to do, the things which he and his sisters had been made to do. Oh, to have good clothes, a nice home, free of such things as this mission work—money to spend, pleasure to indulge in—such as theatres and the like—not to have to slip around in this way. If only he could have been or could be from now on, like other boys—happy, independent, respected, removed by comfort from any possibility of such indignity as this! Oh![6]

Getting rejected provides a plausible motive for a more intense desire to join those in a higher social position, but it can also motivate the protagonists' rejection of the society which rejects them, as Dreiser recognizes in supposing a "psychic process of inversion." For this reason frustration of the fundamental desire to associate is a common event in the early lives of both conformists and rebels in flawed-victim novels.

The alternative making Clyde Griffiths' conversion possible, its second moment, is seeing the attractiveness of the larger social world outside his family, the dominant society represented in his consciousness by the great resonance of the words *others* and *normal*.

> To-night, walking up the great street with his sisters and brother, he wished that they need not do this any more, or at least that he need not be a part of it. Other boys did not do such things, and besides, somehow it seemed shabby and even degrading. On more than one occasion, before he had been taken on the street in this fashion, other boys had called to him and made fun of his father, because he was always publicly emphasizing his religious beliefs or convictions. . . .
>
> On this night in this great street with its cars and crowds and tall buildings, he felt ashamed, dragged out of normal life, to be made a show and jest of. The handsome automobiles that sped by, the loitering pedestrians moving off to what interests and comforts he could only surmise; the gay pairs of young people, laughing and jesting and the "kids" staring, all troubled him with a sense of something different, better, more beautiful than his, or rather their life (p. 22).

Seeing the world of comparative wealth from outside and contrasting it with his own, Clyde cannot see any tawdriness in it or any dissatisfactions among its inhabitants. Because he lacks experience, he adopts as his desired world what the previous novels we have seen present as the undesired world. It comes within reach when he gets a job as a bellhop in an imposing hotel, which he invests with all the romantic aura of an Arabian Nights tale. As Ellen Moers has said, "Nothing in Clyde's story is more tragic or more American than his too early, too swift, and too magical transport to the cave of wonders."[7]

To make the leap to the alternative, the flawed victim, like the virtuous victim, usually needs a helper or helpers, although this term is much less appropriate for negative conversions, in which the function has sometimes been realized by characters with a strong aroma of brimstone. Clyde's fellow bellhops are the helpers. They embody the alternative world of drink, partying, sex, money, and glamor as fully as the hotel itself. The very different world of Clyde's parents provides little resistance to his conversion.

> What would they think of him if he didn't drink something? For ever since he had been among them, he had been trying to appear as much of a man of the world as they were. And yet back of him, as he could plainly feel, lay all of the years in which he had been drilled in the "horrors" of drink and evil companionship. And even though in his heart this long while he had secretly rebelled against nearly all the texts and maxims to which his parents were always alluding, deeply resenting really as worthless and pointless the ragamuffin crew of wasters and failures whom they were always seeking to save, still, now he was inclined to think and hesitate. Should he or should he not drink?
>
> For the fraction of an instant only, while all these things in him now spoke, he hesitated, then added: "Why, I, oh—I think I'll take Rhine wine and seltzer, too" (pp. 74–75).

From repressive puritanism he moves quickly to values and beliefs which Donald Pizer has well summarized: "that hypocrisy, dishonesty, role-playing, and sexual deceit and cruelty are the ways in which one gains what one desires."[8]

Like Jean Valjean, Clyde Griffiths undergoes other conversions which parallel, develop, and reaffirm this one. He has other schools of manners. He raptly observes the behavior of others, especially when he himself is unobserved. He observes himself, sometimes in mirrors, to measure his ability to act as expected. Being a conformist and wanting to act like "others" may appear to simplify one's choices, but he finds, as do many, that the norm in the normal can be terribly difficult to determine. He follows the lives of the fashionable in the society pages, but when he at last gains admission to Sondra Finchley's exclusive set, he still must learn how to adjust his face, wardrobe, deportment, and personal history. His struggles with his conscience mark still other developments or reaffirmations of his conversion. Yet, like other flawed victims, he can never accommodate himself fully to the dominant society, and the beginning of his story shows him taking only a first step into it. In this respect flawed victims resemble the picaresque hero from whom they may derive, the hero whom Claudio Guillén has well called a "half outsider."[9]

Most flawed-victim novels do not show the protagonists acquiring their flaw, relegating anything pertinent about it to brief exposition. Many omit such information. A few, such as *Of Mice and Men*, make it as natural as Melville tried to make Billy Budd's virtue. In planning the character of Gervaise in *L'Assommoir*, Emile Zola apparently wanted to show the strong influence of heredity in her prehistory.

> Gervaise must be a sympathetic figure. Formerly at Plassans, her mother made her drink anisette, and she became pregnant by Lantier at fourteen. Explain these beginnings. She is by temperament yielding and passionate; that will do as a fault. As for drunkenness, she drank because her mother used to drink. But at bottom she is a sodden beast, devoted like her mother. She is an exact reproduction of "Fine" (her mother) at the moment of conception (later, even, I have her grow fat like her mother). . . . By heredity, she is much like her mother, a beast of toil, devoted; some natural weaknesses; she is like a thing thrown into the air, to fall by chance head or tail. *Her environment will determine her lot.*[10]

Whatever the mix of heredity and environment planned here, the novel itself, although presenting no negative conversion, assigns considerable weight to the action of environment in the deformation of Gervaise that has already occurred when it opens. The writer who had studied "temperaments, not characters" in *Thérèse Raquin* became, as Harry Levin has pointed out, "less interested in genetic traits and more interested in conditioning factors. There was less *histoire naturelle* and more *histoire sociale*."[11]

Gervaise's flaw, being "yielding and passionate," is by no means an unmixed one. Indeed, F. W. J. Hemmings seems to deny that it is a flaw: "her best virtue—simple good-heartedness—is the soft spot through which circumstance wounds her mortally, and her modest demands of life are cruelly rejected."[12] Hemmings is certainly right here to see a basic sociability unmarred by any corrupting ambition such as Clyde Griffiths has. It probably explains much of her appeal to readers. Her good-heartedness, however, is a soft-heartedness. Insufficiently corrected by other values, her sociability becomes complaisance or conformity, and Zola was justified in conceiving it as a fault. Moreover, he presents her as conscious of the fact: "Her one weakness, she asserted, was being too soft-hearted, liking everybody, getting passionately fond of people who afterwards caused her heart-aches."[13]

For the origin of Gervaise's basic characteristics we are alerted to the role of her past experience even in the first description of her, with "finely drawn features already beginning to reflect the strain of her hard life" (p. 14). In the exposition devoted to her past we learn that since the age of ten she has worked as a laundress. Unhappy at home largely because her drunken father, Macquart, beat and kicked her without reason, she sought satisfaction outside and became pregnant at fourteen. Her parents would not consent to her marrying her lover, Lantier. Later we are told,

> She was like her mother, a hard worker who died in harness, after serving Pére Macquart like a beast of burden for more than twenty years. She herself was still quite thin, while her mother's

shoulders had been heavy enough to smash through doors, but that didn't keep her from having a soft heart like hers, one that could get madly attracted to people. Even the fact that she limped a little she had from the poor woman, whom Pére Macquart used to beat unmercifully. Hundreds of times her mother had told her about nights when Macquart would come home drunk and make love to her so brutally as to leave her black and blue. Undoubtedly she had been born with her dragging leg as the result of one of those nights (pp. 44–45).

In these few facts we get little reason to assess what follows as a tragedy of temperament. When the innate does make its appearance, her lameness gets attributed to prenatal experience. The other information also requires us to give considerable weight to her experience and environment, whatever we give to heredity. We need give little to it, since a mother who acted compliantly and a father who beat both of them go a long way to account for Gervaise's complaisance. To be sure, any signs of negative conversion we might see in her past would indicate an experience different from Clyde Griffiths', but we can note that she too is marked early by innocent victimage, double alienation, and the sense of an alternative, embodied in a helper.

The middle of *An American Tragedy* consists of a rather one-sided battle between Clyde Griffiths' conformist commitment to success on the one hand, and on the other his ineptitude, his fear, and the *nachschein* of a Christianity which initially glowed but faintly. As Richard Lehan has shown, the divided self of the beginning continues throughout the novel, often subliminally through Dreiser's invocation of second selves of various sorts.[14] In *L'Assommoir*, however, we get a more even struggle in a consciousness divided between complaisant conformism and self-disciplined individualism. The opening chapter presents Gervaise's abandonment by Lantier, but not before she has tried to persuade him that with a little firmness and hard work they can escape their poverty. Later, in resisting the entreaties of Coupeau, who wants to become her lover, she tells him, "my hard luck has been a great lesson to me" (p. 41). She has determined to look at things seriously, to take no other lover, to keep working hard at her job, to raise her children properly, and to look out for her future: "She stated all these things as a woman who had made up her mind, with her plan of life settled, while Coupeau, never forgetting his yearning to possess her, made a jest of it, converting everything into ribaldry" (p. 45). As they grow closer in the ensuing month, Coupeau admires her courage and self-discipline, even though he continues to believe, because he never worries about the future himself, that she takes life too seriously. She hastens to correct his impression: "He was wrong to think of her as especially strong-willed; on the contrary, her will power was very weak. Again and again she had let herself be pushed into things because she didn't dare hurt someone's feelings. Her one hope now was to live among decent people, because if you're among bad people, she said, it's like being conked on the head by a bludgeon" (p. 54). Coupeau continues to admire Gervaise, and eventually her complaisance leads her to consent to marry him: "She was in one of those moments of weakness she so greatly mistrusted, persuaded at last, too stirred emotionally to refuse anything or to hurt anyone's feelings" (p. 58).

Despite some lack of seriousness or concern for the future, Coupeau makes a good husband at first. He too works diligently and avoids hard drinking because his father's life has shown him its dangers. He and Gervaise prosper, and she gets her own laundry shop. Several years after their marriage, however, his self-discipline starts to give way when he is injured falling off a roof he is working on. From this moment on he no longer supports Gervaise's better self, but undermines it. Just as we can see her resolution struggling against her complaisance in the scenes leading up to their marriage, we can see the same struggle and surrender later. Although we have not really seen a negative conversion in the beginning, we get something like reaffirmations of one, just as we noticed in *An American Tragedy*. There are several of these key points in Gervaise's downward progress. In a scene at the end of the eighth chapter she breaks her resolution not to sleep with Lantier, falling into a degrading *mé-*

nage à trois largely because Coupeau has come home drunk and vomited all over the bedroom. Soon she cares as little for the future as he does. In a long scene at the end of the tenth chapter she breaks her resolution to avoid hard liquor, falling into alcoholism when Coupeau urges her to drink. Soon she passes, as he does, from conviviality to solitude. Let us examine an earlier scene, however,—one very well known partly because Zola suggests that it marks the height of prosperity and the beginning of decline. It illustrates well the internal struggle marking the middle of the flawed-victim novel.

On a very hot and busy June afternoon, made even hotter in the laundry shop by the irons and the coke fire needed to heat them, Clemence, one of the women hired to iron, removes her blouse. Mme. Putois, an older employee, notices and rebukes her for indecency because some men outside have stopped to stare. Gervaise agrees and orders her to put it back on. Soon the washerwoman comes unexpectedly early for a batch of clothes to wash, and Gervaise stops her ironing to sort them out, after objecting to having her schedule disrupted. Although she does not mind the strong smell of the dirty clothes, she seems to get drowsy and intoxicated, and Zola remarks, "It may be that the beginnings of her laziness came from that, a kind of asphyxiation caused by dirty clothes poisoning the air about her" (pp. 158–59). During this process Coupeau comes in, tipsier than he has ever been, and everyone begins laughing at him and with him. Amid the piles of laundry she sorts, Gervaise then regains "her air of composure, her calm smile of a careful, attentive proprietor" (p. 161). Coupeau decides that he wants to kiss her. She pushes him away so that he won't mix up the sorted piles, but when the other women claim that she is too hard on him she presents her cheek to him. He grabs her breasts, then her body. As she abandons herself to him, Zola comments, "The long kiss that they exchanged, mouth to mouth, amid all this accumulated filthiness of soiled laundry, was perhaps a first step downward in the gradual corruption of their life together" (p. 162). After the washerwoman leaves, Gervaise hangs a sheet over the front windows to keep out the sun, and Clemence takes off her blouse again, this time unreproved. After the women have resumed ironing for a while Coupeau starts teasing Clemence, admiring her breasts and pinching her bottom. Noticing this, Gervaise stops him and puts him to bed. She goes back to the shop, makes excuses for Coupeau, and rationalizes her indulgence of him.

Since Gervaise undergoes some development in this scene, the division of her consciousness between complaisance and the values which oppose it becomes quite evident. Since she is at the height of her prosperity in the first place because she has been keeping her complaisance fairly well under control—we can see that Zola, like Dreiser, has determined to promote the values often associated with puritans or the bourgeoisie but actually antedating either. Gervaise's yielding, complaisance, conformism, or oversociability clearly constitute the false consciousness, and the better self that struggles against it is relatively individualistic—devoted to hard work, responsibility, thrift, sobriety, personal integrity, seriousness, foresightedness, decency, self-discipline, and so on. We can gauge the strength of her false consciousness by its very triumph in this scene. We can gauge the strength of its opposition not only in her initial resistance to the carnival which develops, but less directly. To motivate its defeat, Zola goes to extraordinary lengths. He uses extreme heat, a girl very sensitive to it, and the unexpected arrival of both a tipsy Coupeau and a washerwoman sympathetic to merely tipsy husbands because her own husband is often sodden drunk. As he often does, Zola attributes to odors or air pollution what we can only call occult qualities. Yet despite all this machinery and the rhetoric asserting its momentous effect on Gervaise, the first step downward is a very small one. Complaisance does not triumph entirely.

The internal division between false consciousness and a better self appears also in other ways. Gervaise often remembers her native Plassans, much to the disadvantage of the polluted and crowded Paris around her. She prefers the most rural parts of the city, looks forward to some day retiring from it, and wishes, in the depths of her degradation, that she had taken a train and left it. Zola helped make such starved pastoralism, which we have seen in previous novels, a staple of the naturalistic novel. A more interesting manifestation of Gervaise's divided consciousness, however, comes from the love plot of *L'Assommoir*.

If we recall the virtuous-victim novels of the preceding chapter, we may notice that they lack much in the way of love plots. In flawed-victim novels, on the other hand, love triangles abound. Like the *Bildungsroman* to which many of them conform, they often expose the protagonist to what Buckley has seen as "at least two love affairs or sexual encounters, one debasing, one exalting." We can explain the relative sexlessness of the virtuous victim, if we wish, by supposing the existence of many readers unable to conceive virtue without it. We can attack it, as Uncle Tom has been attacked, for libeling the virility of the oppressed. Or we can psychologize it, as is done in the further victimization of Billy Budd by some literary critics. But if we can set aside for the moment whatever belief we have about the importance of sexual activity in real life, we can assume that the presence of the love plot in flawed-victim novels calls for explanation as much as does its absence in virtuous-victim novels. Then we should be able to see that the different possible sexual partners represent, among other things, different aspects of the protagonist's divided consciousness. Buckley notes that the love plot of the *Bildungsroman* demands that "the hero reappraise his values."[15] In the flawed-victim novel the values are social, different visions of association and community.

We have seen that Gervaise marries Coupeau in a moment of weakness, afraid to hurt his feelings, and his influence dominates the key points of her decline. His lack of self-discipline exacerbates her own and proves fatal to both of them. In this process Lantier, also a parasite, assists him. Opposed to both of these is Goujet, whom Gervaise comes to love after her marriage. He is a proletarian blacksmith with the frame and aspect of a god. Like Gervaise, he comes from outside Paris and has embraced sobriety and discipline partly because of seeing his drunken father's fate. Unlike her, he is somewhat obstinate. Unlike Coupeau, he does not reject politics: "He was concerned about politics, being a republican by conviction, for the sake of justice and human welfare. Yet he hadn't fired a gun, giving his reasons as follows: the common people were getting weary of fighting battles for the benefit of the middle classes, who usually collected the chestnuts the workers pulled out of the fire, getting their paws singed in the process" (p. 123). When Coupeau's fall uses up the savings Gervaise wanted for establishing her shop, Goujet lends her the necessary money. In one scene in which he and another blacksmith contest to see who can make a bolt faster, she watches him as if he were her knight. When she feels herself drawn into the *ménage à trois* with Coupeau and Lantier, she is more concerned about disloyalty to her chaste relationship with Goujet than about infidelity to Coupeau. In a pastoral setting on a vacant lot they enjoy a brief idyll, during which she refuses his suggestion that they go away together. After she succumbs to Lantier and Goujet finds out, he is terribly hurt and asks her to leave him. She does, "after a final look around the neatly arranged room where she seemed to be leaving some part of her better self" (p. 314).

Coupeau, like the bellboys who assist Clyde Griffiths' negative conversion, is a helper attractive to the weak side of Gervaise. Goujet is a helper appealing to the part of her divided consciousness which opposes her fall. Now perhaps we can see why love plots do not mark the virtuous-victim novel. There, protagonists form part of a community, perhaps together with the helper(s) who assisted their positive conversion. Since their social relations are unproblematic, so is their sex life. A sexual triangle in which they were torn between two or more possible partners might detract from the virtue they represent, not because they must be sexless, but because, regardless of what other faults they may have or what enmity with the antagonist, they do not engender social strife. Despite any psychomachia they may engage in or doubts they may show, they have a basically undivided consciousness. The flawed victim, on the other hand, usually has trouble relating to other people, and this difficulty can be effectively manifested in the love plot as a triangle. If the helpers of virtuous victims are to find a place in the flawed-victim novel, and thus render more explicit the call to community which it makes, they do not have to enter as rivals for the protagonist's love, but if their deep appeal is to be established, that is certainly the readiest way.

As we are about to see, however, the consciousness of the flawed victim may be divided not between authenticity and inauthenticity, but among a mélange of conflicting, mostly inauthentic, selves.

In Richard Wright's *Native Son* the flaw of Bigger Thomas is rebellion. Individualism, which struggles against a dominant conformism in Clyde and Gervaise, provides in Bigger the main source of a false consciousness little relieved by sociability. Like Lermontov's Pechorin, Dostoevsky's Underground Man, and many other rebels, he finds love, friendship, and other human relationships difficult because he can conceive them only as requiring dominion over another person or being dominated. Since oppression dominates him so much, he craves power over others as a testimony to his personal identity. When he occasionally achieves it, he simply passes on the oppression he has felt, alienating his victim as he has been alienated. His rebellion thus shuts him out from the relations with others which lie at the roots of any power capable of resisting social injustice. Wright has said that he wanted to show "how oppression seems to hinder and stifle in the victim those very qualities of character which are so essential for an effective struggle against the oppressor"—a statement of purpose which could serve for almost every flawed-victim novel.[16] The hero lacks the harmony of sociability and individualism seen in the virtuous victim, qualities on which both personal authenticity and political resistance depend.

As to the origin of Bigger's flaw, the novel tells both too much and too little. The many statements such as "he was a long, taut piece of rubber which a thousand white hands had stretched to the snapping point" (p. 214) seem to attribute his character to the way all black people are treated, ignoring that he differs from other blacks and is also alienated from them. On the other hand, we get little information about his prehistory, and what we get, unlike that provided by Dreiser and Zola, is both too little and too late to help us see the hero in terms of a past that is distinctly his own. We can make out a history of innocent victimage and double alienation, and in his relations with his own gang we can see a group of helpers and the alternative life crime provides. In this remnant of negative conversion, however, we cannot really tell what has made him. James Baldwin has argued that information of this sort is essential if we are to accept the premise of *Native Son* that "we are confronting a monster created by the American republic"; yet he charges that Wright tells us "little about the social dynamic which we are to believe created him. Despite the details of slum life we are given, I doubt that anyone who has thought about it, disengaging himself from sentimentality, can accept this most essential premise of the novel for a moment."[17]

Wright met such an objection in an article significantly entitled "How 'Bigger' Was Born," and now serving as a preface to *Native Son*. Although he claimed emphatically that *"what had made him and what he meant* constituted my plot" (p. xxvii), he felt it necessary to address at some length how he supposed Bigger's flaw originated.

> Why did Bigger revolt? No explanation based upon a hard and fast rule of conduct can be given. But there were always two factors psychologically dominant in his personality. First, through some quirk of circumstance, he had become estranged from the religion and the folk culture of his race. Second, he was trying to react to and answer the call of the dominant civilization whose glitter came to him through the newspapers, magazines, radios, movies, and the mere imposing sight and sound of daily American life (p. xiii).

We can gather as much from the novel, but it is hard not to wish Wright had told us more about the "quirk of circumstance" which disengaged Bigger from his own people. Indeed, the wealth of such information about Wright himself in *Black Boy*, his autobiography, has given Ralph Ellison reasonable grounds for preferring it to *Native Son*.[18]

How can we explain the paucity of information about that part of Bigger's past which was most his own and the abundance of assertions that oppression created him? Part of the answer may be suggested by looking again at *An American Tragedy* and *L'Assommoir*. These novels give us exactly what *Native Son* does not—enough of the protagonists' past to account for the false consciousness they present. As a result we see more clearly in Clyde and Gervaise consciousnesses divided by a struggle between inauthenticity and authenticity. Similarly, if Wright had presented some quirk of circumstance separating Bigger from the black community, the middle of the novel would have tended to suggest that he is torn between an inauthenticity associated with white people and an authenticity grounded in the black community. Although Baldwin would have preferred such a novel, it is one Wright chose not to produce. Instead, he wanted to establish that white and black alike are oppressed, that racism divides the opponents of oppression, and that a multiracial resistance on communist lines provides the best avenue Bigger Thomas could have taken for achieving authenticity. At one time he shows this ideal appealing to Bigger, but in his consciousness it collides not only with his rebellion but also with many other temptations, most of them illusory. His consciousness is drawn not in two different directions, but in many. He is a chaos of conflicting values covering most of the options open to oppressed blacks. Out of this chaos, Wright, not Bigger, achieves considerable clarity. A major achievement of *Native Son* consists of showing the confusion which oppression can foster in its victims, a confusion in which the various alternatives for remedy tend to cancel each other out.

Before taking up these inner struggles, we should look briefly at the outer ones. Only against the rat in the opening chapter does Bigger win. In the following scenes he struggles against his family, his friends, and his white supporters. He mistrusts and antagonizes all of them, showing the extent to which rebellion misfits him for ordinary life. The power arrayed against him looks omnipotent to him, and he does not want to display weakness or vulnerability to anyone. Since this makes impossible all ties—of family, friendship, love, race, or whatever—his entire outer life is a struggle. His fear of being caught in a vulnerable position leads him to accidentally kill Mary Dalton, the white girl trying to help him. After disclosing the fact to his black lover, Bessie, in order to impress her with his power, he feels vulnerable again and murders her intentionally. The legal system which catches him is concerned primarily about the death of the white girl, so that in his struggle against it in the last third of the novel he, like Clyde Griffiths, has some technical innocence, and many of the issues of the latter part of *An American Tragedy* surface here also. While in jail he thinks that "he could not fight the battle for his life without first winning the one raging within him" (p. 337), but he loses both inner and outer battles.

Of the many selves struggling inside him, the most basic and least authentic is the fearful Bigger. Book 1 of the novel, "Fear," begins by establishing this and ends with its consequence, when Bigger's fear of being caught in Mary Dalton's bedroom proves stronger than his knowledge that he is innocent of anything other than helping a drunken girl to bed. His fear of being charged with rape if discovered leads him to stifle her noise so forcefully that she dies. This accidental murder suggests that the fear of the oppressor which injustice arouses in its victims does not always serve to protect society. Later, when Bigger's lawyer, Max, tells the court that a mountain of fear in blacks could explode, Wright opens himself to the charge of trying to increase white fears, which could fuel further injustice. But he anticipates such an objection by having Max deny that he wants to raise the "guilt-fear" of white people (p. 360). Fear in each side for the other leads to irrational violence: the killing of Mary Dalton by a black and of Bigger Thomas by whites.

The indifferent Bigger is an inauthentic self which arises when he tries to overcome with cool his shame at feeling fear and helplessness: "He hated his family because he knew that they were suffering and that he was powerless to help them. He knew that the moment he allowed himself to feel to its fullness how they lived, the shame and misery of their lives, he would be swept out of himself with fear and despair" (p. 13). Bigger hates not only others but himself. In this reflexive action the hated self is ridden with fear and shame, the hating self at one remove from it. The indifferent self, still further removed, tries to mask both from consciousness. When Bigger adopts this indifferent self, as he does frequently, Wright speaks of him as going behind a curtain to protect himself from others. This should not be confused with his playing the dumb darky or with any of the other hypocrisies which he recognizes as such. His indifferent self attempts to mask his fear, shame, and self-hatred not only from others but from himself.

Such a tactic cannot wholly succeed, and its failure calls for still another mask, the violent Bigger. "These were the rhythms of his life: indifference and violence; periods of abstract brooding and periods of intense desire" (p. 31). Bigger's violence is first used to try to mask his fear from himself and his own gang. It ministers also to his need for excitement, power, and something like punishment. The suffering which it brings him he can know for sure that he has caused. It indicates to him some control of his own life. It even brings him a sense of freedom after he has committed murder.

The more socially conscious Biggers are the Black Nationalist and the American, or Native Son—suggesting the alternatives of separationism and integrationism. We see the latter when he watches an airplane and wishes he could fly one and in the game of playing white, in which he pretends to be J. P. Morgan, then the President. Yet along with the appeal of America comes knowing that its promise is not for him. When we watch Bigger watching a movie glamorizing rich people, we can understand his failure to see any snake in the American paradise. In this respect he resembles Clyde Griffiths, but whereas Clyde responds to glamor itself, false though it may be, Bigger responds more to images of glamor in the mass media. Exactly which of Bigger's characteristics we attribute to his being a Native Son depends partly on what we think of America. James Baldwin has attributed his rebellion itself to this source: "Bigger has no discernible relationship to himself, to his own life, to his own people, nor to any other people—in this respect, perhaps, he is most American."[19] Whatever we may think of this, it is hard not to see Bigger's worship of success as particularly American. He admires wealthy Americans so much that he fails even to consider that they might have something to do with his own poverty. He attributes the poverty of blacks and the racism against them to poor whites.

Bigger's admiration for rich whites and his hatred of black people ought to make black nationalism impossible for him. They do not because it consists of little more than despair of achieving the American dream. Thinking of it quickly brings more despair: "There were rare moments when a feeling and longing for solidarity with other black people would take hold of him. He would dream of making a stand against that white force, but that dream would fade when he looked at the other black people near him" (p. 109). Bigger goes on to wish for a black leader strong enough to unify black people and later wishes for one he can admire as much as he does Hitler and Mussolini. Bigger's black nationalism does not have to be tainted with fascism to expose his misdiagnosis of his own case. When he believes his problems are racial, he naturally enough is attracted to a racial solution for them. Only occasionally does he suspect that some of them are simply human and that most result from an exploitation inflicted also on many who are not black. In talking to Bigger, Max tries to help him see this wider perspective, but his speeches to the jury at the trial have to emphasize racial rather than economic oppression. As a result, some readers have attributed Bigger's confusion to Wright. Both Baldwin and Ellison have charged him with treating a class problem as if it were a caste problem.[20]

There is also a Christian Bigger of sorts, although he has long ago given up Christianity. Considering the world in which he lives, he thinks, "If only someone had gone before and lived or suffered or died—made it so that it could be understood! It was too stark, not redeemed" (p. 226). On the whole, however, any residual or potential Christianity in Bigger is clearly part of his false consciousness, because he connects it with resignation in the face of social injustice. Unlike that shown in *Les Misérables*, *Uncle Tom's Cabin*, or *The Power and the Glory*, it concerns this world very little.

With such a multitude of selves, each inconsistent with the others, Bigger's false consciousness lacks the unity of those we saw in Clyde and Gervaise. We can hardly wonder that his grip on reality is so tenuous, or that any potential authenticity gets quickly lost. At times he does feel "some obscure need to be at home with people" (p. 255). While he is in jail Max helps bring him to "the verge of action and commitment" (p. 319), and later he wonders: "If he reached out with his hands, and if his hands were electric wires, and if his heart were a battery giving life and fire to those hands, and if he reached out through these stone walls and felt other hands connected with other hearts—if he did that, would there be a reply, a shock?" (p. 335) This thought quickly vanishes. At the end Bigger is more confused than ever, holding on to his murders and trying to find in them some meaning for his life. The dismay with which Max leaves him is hard not to share.

To see a further point to which the flawed victim can develop, we must look to a different novel.

In *Memoirs of an Egotist* Stendhal recalls a day in London on which he heard that eight people were to be hanged. "When a robber or murderer is hanged in England," he comments, "it is the aristocracy sacrificing a victim to its security, for it is the aristocracy that has reduced him to becoming a criminal, etc. This truth, so paradoxical today, will perhaps be a commonplace by the time my chatter is read."[21] This truth has indeed become a commonplace, partly because of Stendhal's own *The Red and the Black*. Other reasons have already been seen in this chapter; Clyde and Bigger, like

Stendhal's Julien Sorel, are eventually executed after a trial *by* the establishment has turned into a trial *of* it. *The Red and the Black* shares with other flawed-victim novels much more than the commonplace that oppression can cause crime. In Julien's prehistory we can make out signs of a negative conversion: he is an innocent victim of poverty, doubly alienated from family and the dominant society, and he has adopted an alternative to it, thanks to a helper who had been a surgeon-major in Napoleon's army. His flaw is ambition, together with the rebellion and hypocrisy which ambition requires of him. His standards of success—like those of Clyde, Gervaise, or Bigger—are largely determined by others, so that he suffers both internally and externally from the culture in which he lives. His false consciousness struggles with a better self, and this internal struggle is mirrored in the two women he loves.

It is mainly the ending that distinguishes *The Red and the Black* from other flawed-victim novels. There, the heroes often fail to learn from their suffering, to experience that quiet moment in which the tragic hero achieves enlightenment. Certainly their suffering ought to make them wonder about its cause, and they may question the values which have contributed to it. But the tenacity of their flaws inhibits or prevents such questioning. Gervaise understands all along that her complaisance brings her heartache, but the very stupefying suffering she endures does not make for clear thought. She never sees her basic character as a product of social experience and treats her weakness as a personal quirk. Bigger, in trying to understand what happened to him, struggles hard for a vision of community only to reject it for a view of life which, despite its lack of clarity to him or us, appears even worse than the false consciousness with which he begins. Clyde's struggle to understand, presented even more fully, shows him no better at self-analysis than he has been all along. The hero of Carlos Fuentes' *Good Conscience* develops at the end from rebellion to a conformism which is even worse. Saul Bellow's flawed victim in *Seize the Day* starts to see the light at the end, but it is little more than a glimmer. In *To Have and Have Not*, Hemingway's hero makes further progress, mumbling incoherently before dying the point that all rebel-victim novels make—that no man is much good alone. In *Under Western Eyes*, Conrad's hero comes to the farthest point to which the flawed victim develops: he rejects the negative conversion with which the novel begins by means of a positive conversion which makes him, in his last suffering, almost a virtuous victim. In *The Red and the Black* Julien Sorel does not develop quite as far, but he does undergo a positive conversion in which he repudiates his flaw.

The ending of *The Red and the Black* consists actually of two endings not easily reconciled. The first is Julien's achievement of success, marked when he says, "the novel of my career is over, and the credit is all mine."[22] At this point he has become a chevalier, a lieutenant in the hussars, a landowner, a wealthy man, and the intended fiancé of the beautiful Mathilde, daughter of his patron, the Marquis de la Mole. This success is not a case of building a tragic character up just before a fall, but part of the fall itself, because it is accompanied by the moral deterioration of the hero. From the start Julien has been apprehensive lest his poverty, ambition, and hypocrisy lead him to participate in the shabby deals he condemns all around him. What he fears comes to pass. He helps make questionable political appointments, telling himself, "There are plenty of other injustices which I will have to commit if I'm to be successful" (p. 225). When he makes no objection, asking instead an appointment for his father, whom he hates, the Marquis is pleased to find him "shaping up." Just before winning Mathilde by more cool calculation than he has shown before, he helps in a political plot directed against everything he believes in. In short, he becomes a part of the very system of oppression from which he has suffered. On a much grander scale than Clyde or Bigger, his sense of injustice against himself leads him to inflict injustice upon the innocent. Like his first patron, he becomes the hammer in order to avoid being the anvil.

After the first ending establishes a rise in fortune accompanied by a fall in character, the second develops Julien's fall in fortune and his rise in character through renunciation of his ambition. Thus the novel shows in complementary forms the lack of connection between character and fate on which our perception of injustice depends. The second ending begins when Julien discovers that the Marquis de la Mole will oppose his marriage to Mathilde more firmly because he has received a letter from Mme. de Rênal exposing her former lover as one who uses seduction to serve his ambition. Julien shoots Mme. de Rênal. In prison and faced with death, he loses his ambition. When he finds out that Mme. de Rênal will recover, his love for her blossoms once more. He refuses all assistance in avoiding the death penalty for his attempted murder and is executed. To many critics of *The Red and the Black* much of this has seemed hurried, irrational or inconsistent, and even those who feel otherwise find several problems. Our thread through the maze is that Stendhal wanted to bring about in Julien something of a positive conversion and designed the actions accordingly. Let us look at them backwards, therefore, in the hope that concentrating on the author's motives will make clearer those he assigns to his hero.

Why does Julien frustrate Mathilde's attempts to get him acquitted? She has influenced the jury strongly in his behalf through astute bribery, but in his speech at his trial Julien claims that his crime merits the death penalty and condemns the jury as an outraged bourgeoisie intent on punishing a peasant for mingling "with what the arrogant rich call good society" (p. 388). He seems to want death, so much so that it is hard not to agree with Mathilde's accomplice and call him suicidal. But before imputing such a motive to him, we should look at the choice that Stendhal contrived to confront him with. Julien does not so much choose death as reject the alternative to it—life with Mathilde, profiting through her influence. In short, he rejects a return to the high fortune and low character he has known at the first ending. He does so because he has undergone a positive conversion which he refuses to reverse.

What brings about this conversion? Stendhal has warned us to tread carefully at this point. He prefaces the chapter preceding the trial with an epigraph from Goethe: "It is because I was foolish then that I am wise today. O philosopher

114

who sees nothing but the fleeting moment, how short is your vision! Your eye was not made to follow the underground working of the passions" (p. 381). Nevertheless, we can make out the conditions needed for conversion. To begin with, Julien finds it impossible to continue with his old outlook. When he first enters prison he thinks Mme. de Rênal dead and his own death impending. As a result, his ambition gives way: "Each of ambition's promises had to be ripped in turn from his heart by this great thought: *I am going to die*" (p. 365). When he discovers that Mme. de Rênal will live, he discovers also his own joy at that fact and looks forward confidently to her forgiveness and love: "He thanked heaven that he had not wounded her mortally. Astonishing thing! he said to himself; I thought that by her letter to M. de la Mole she had destroyed forever my future happiness; now, less than two weeks from the date of that letter, I never give a thought to the things that used to occupy me completely. . . . Two or three thousand florins a year to live peacefully in a little mountain town like Vergy . . . I was happy then. . . . I didn't know how happy I was" (p. 368). This alternative vision, of happiness rather than ambition, he adopts so strongly that he will not surrender it even to escape death. He becomes more honest and much happier than he has ever been.

Why did Julien shoot Mme. de Rênal in the first place? Apparently, Stendhal has him do so in order to provide one motive for his moral regeneration. Just as apparently, he imputes no clear motivation to his hero. Immediately before the event and during it, he rather puzzlingly denies the reader access to Julien's otherwise well-documented consciousness, imputing to him some mental abstraction. Only in bits and pieces, after the fact, do we get his comments on his motives. He claims he wanted revenge, presumably against Mme. de Rênal, but he also speaks of having settled his score with humanity. Later he blames the shooting on his ambition and his love for Mathilde. Since all this does not add up, it has much exercised Stendhal's critics. Many of their suggestions have been considered by Michael Wood, who puts forth a worthwhile idea of his own: "The point of his act for Stendhal is that it is a passionate act, rising from regions within Julien which the errors of his calculating mind could not touch."[23] Such an explanation accounts well for our lack of access to Julien's consciousness at the time. It also does well to see passion as the antithesis of calculation, for one of Stendhal's main criticisms of the culture he depicts is that its excessive prudence makes passion too rare. Nevertheless, I do not know that we should so fully dismiss Julien's own explanations of his act, as Wood does, on the ground that they demean his character. Without attributing much calculation to his decision, we can remember that at the time he makes it his character is at its least admirable.

Julien's motives, both at the time of the shooting and after, may seem irrational because he does what he believes will bring death to him, but to Stendhal they were probably quite rational. One of his favorite philosophers was Helvétius, who had argued prior to Godwin that a nation's vices result from the form of its laws and government—a view Julien endorses when he rejects the idea of any natural law in morality and claims that everything depends upon positive legislation (p. 400). To those who objected that ascribing all human actions to self-interest would not explain heroism, Stendhal liked to reply with Helvétius' answer citing the example of Regulus, who kept his honor to both his country and his adversaries knowing that he faced certain death.

> In almost all the circumstances of life, a generous mind will perceive the possibility of certain actions, the idea of which a commonplace mind is incapable of understanding. The moment that the possibility of accomplishing these actions becomes apparent to a man of generous sentiments, it is immediately in his own interests that he should carry them out. If he fails to, he feels the sting of self-abasement and, as a result, becomes unhappy. This principle, taught by Helvétius, is true, even in the wildest aberrations of passion, even in suicide. In a word, it is contrary to man's nature and even impossible for him not to do what he thinks may lead to his own happiness, the moment the possibility of doing so is presented to him.[24]

Although Julien Sorel is no Regulus, the principle is the same. The idea that acting to preserve self-esteem may answer a deeper need than life itself should seem irrational only in times as prudence-ridden as Stendhal considered his own. He expected more of posterity.

For all its rationalism, however, this utilitarianism is another revisionist variety, leading inevitably to its own negation in the existentialism so many have found in Stendhal. Once we suppose anyone with a stronger desire for self-esteem than for life or pleasure, the foot is in the door for the gratuitous act, designed to win one's own self-esteem by the sacrifice of self-interest itself. If, like Leon Blum,[25] we take Stendhal's revisionism to consist of substituting happiness for Helvétius' self-interest as the ultimate motive of all human action, we can see yet another germ of existentialism. The happiness Julien actually achieves, depending as it does on Mme. de Rênal, cannot be his motive for shooting her. As Michael Wood emphasizes, "Julien did not, then, shoot Mme de Rênal just because he loved her. But his crime does in effect allow him to learn the truth about this love, it restores him, *by another road*, to Mme de Rênal and to himself."[26] In the relationship of means to ends here, we find an indirectness also affecting other possible motives. If ambition is the motive, ambition is subverted; if love for Mathilde, that love evaporates; if the desire to settle a score with humanity, Julien nevertheless finds more of a place within it. Indeed, the ending of *The Red and the Black* illustrates well an observation by another revisionist utilitarian, John Stuart Mill:

> I never, indeed, wavered in the conviction that happiness is the test of all rules of conduct, and the end of life. But I now thought this end was only to be attained by not making it the direct end. Those only are happy (I thought) who have their minds fixed on some object other than their own happiness; on the happiness of others, on the improvement of mankind, even on some art or pursuit, followed not as a means, but as an ideal end. Aiming thus at something else, they find happiness by the way.[27]

This, according to Mill, is the anti-self-consciousness principle of Carlyle, an anti-utilitarian who scoffed at the idea of making even happiness one's main goal.

We can also see the subversion of utilitarianism leading to existentialism in Julien's changing relationship to his own future. We may recall that Zola marks the deterioration of Gervaise by having her adopt Coupeau's unconcern about the future, and Dreiser criticizes Clyde for his inability to appropriate present means to future ends. Partly as a result, they imply a liberal utilitarianism as a solution to the injustices they present. Stendhal, however, uses a loss of concern with the future to motivate Julien's moral rise, not his fall. Since the future is the *sine qua non* of any utilitarian calculation, we seem to have in *The Red and the Black* a transcendence of time and self not easy to reconcile with utilitarianism. The lack of this transcendence, without which the flawed victim cannot reach the end of his story, dooms Bigger and Clyde to failure in their struggle to understand their lives. They remain in moral solitude to the end, for as we saw in the preceding chapter, the transcendence which concerns us requires that the hero have some place in a community.

The transcendence marking the end of Stendhal's novel, like that we have seen in novels focusing on innocent and virtuous victims, is immanent throughout. Julien's shooting of Mme. de Rênal and his refusal to avoid execution are not his first acts defying prudence. From the first we see his consciousness divided between hypocrisy and a need for self-respect which makes his hypocrisy a torture to him. Several times his need to know that he is not a coward makes him place himself in danger. Early and often Stendhal notes that Julien owes his success less to the prudence and calculation designed to bring it about and more to luck and the passion of his better self. Julien makes a very elaborate campaign plan to seduce Mme. de Rênal, but he gains "a victory to which all his clumsy subtleties would never have conducted him" because he "forgot all his empty projects and recovered his natural self" (pp. 68–69).

The ending of *The Red and the Black* is not unanticipated then, for it consists of Julien's once more coming to possess his better self. Even when Stendhal speculates about how Julien would have developed if his life had not been cut short, he says, "Instead of treading the common path from softness to cunning, like most men, advancing years would have given him easy access to a fund of generous feeling; he would have overcome his morbid mistrust" (p. 371).

Writers have produced flawed-victim novels partly out of dissatisfaction with the alternatives. In explaining the composition of *Native Son,* Wright recalls his dissatisfaction with the reception of *Uncle Tom's Children,* a collection of short stories dealing with many innocent victims: "When the reviews of that book began to appear, I realized I had made an awfully naive mistake. I found that I had written a book which even bankers' daughters could read and weep over and feel good about. I swore to myself that if I ever wrote another book, no one would weep over it; that it would be so hard and deep that they would have to face it without the consolation of tears" (p. xxvii). We can see similar apprehension in Zola's first sketch of *L'Assommoir:* "Do not flatter the worker, nor blacken his character. An absolutely exact reality. At the end the moral standing out inevitably. A good worker to play the opposite part, or rather no, don't fall into the *Manual.* A frightful picture which will carry its own moral lesson."[28]

Nevertheless, flawed-victim novels produce some dissatisfactions of their own. After *Native Son,* Wright turned, in *The Outsider,* to a black hero who claims not to be a victim of racism, injustice, or oppression, but to have personal, moral, and metaphysical problems. After seeing readers miss the obvious but implicit moral of *L'Assommoir,* Zola discovered, according to Hemmings, "that it was not enough, then, simply to imply the need for extensive, costly, and in many ways revolutionary social reforms: the need would have to be urged, and urged in the pages of his novels. But this meant a complete break with the aesthetic of impartial statement that Zola had inherited from Flaubert."[29]

The virtuous-victim novel overcomes the disadvantages of the innocent-victim novel—nonorganic plot, sketchy characterization, and loosely integrated theme—by risking some disadvantages of its own. Its moral clarity may suggest a manichaean view of politics, and its optimism, founded on the weakness of the victimizer and the strength of the victim,

119

may suggest to readers that little needs to be done, or that they cannot attain the level of heroism which resistance demands. The flawed-victim novel overcomes all these disadvantages, yet still has the problems of clarity and hope. It shows injustice strong enough to corrupt its victims and thus establishes the complexity of the issues it treats, but its complexity can confuse readers, and its demonstration that something *needs* to be done can undermine their belief that anything *can* be. It threatens the paradox of reform in exactly the opposite way from that of the virtuous-victim novel. Indeed, in the frequent objections to flawed-victim novels as pessimistic or confused we can often see the wish that they were more like virtuous-victim novels. When Baldwin, for example, suggests that Bigger should have been presented in some sort of relationship to black people, he is asking for at least one step toward the integration of victim and community that we have seen in Pelagueya and Uncle Tom.

The advantages and disadvantages of any type of victim are those of the privileged literary form for presenting it. For flawed-victim novels, realism rather than romance predominates. In fact, many descriptions of realism itself stress the penetration of character by milieu that flawed victims so commonly present. Erich Auerbach, for example, says, "the serious realism of modern times cannot represent man otherwise than as embedded in a total reality, political, social, and economic, which is concrete and constantly evolving."[30] René Wellek describes nineteenth-century realism as "the objective representation of contemporary social reality."[31] According to George Levine, "the characteristic subject of realistic fiction is the contest between dream and reality; the characteristic progress, disenchantment. The single character is implicated in a world of the contingent and must make peace with society and nature or be destroyed."[32] Harry Levin has noticed in nineteenth-century French realism a concentration on "the revolt of the individual against society," and in the twentieth century, a frequent conflict "between an active and a passive role, between participation and withdrawal—*solidaire* or *solitaire*, in Hugo's equivocation." He quotes as particularly appropriate to realism Dostoevsky's claim that "the basic idea of the art of the nineteenth century is the rehabilitation of the oppressed social pariah," and he sees in the modern realistic detective novel a defeat for "the anti-social energies of the hero-villain."[33]

Although we can readily see an overlap between the flawed-victim novel and the realistic novel when the latter is positively described, the most satisfying descriptions of realism are not positive. Auerbach, reluctant to define it, describes it here and there as rejecting romance, comedy, the idyll, melodrama, and didacticism. Wellek likewise makes what realism excludes much clearer than what it includes: "It rejects the fantastic, the fairy-tale-like, the allegorical and the symbolic, the highly stylized, the purely abstract and decorative. It means that we want no myth, no *Maerchen*, no world of dreams. It implies also a rejection of the improbable, of pure chance, and of extraordinary events."[34] Among the many who characterize realism negatively, Harry Levin has best grasped the need to do so and its consequences. Realism resembles freedom, he says: "Both are relative terms, referring us back to a definite series of restraints from which we have managed to secure some degree of release. When we call a book realistic, we mean that it is relatively free from bookish artificialities; it convinces us, where more conventional books do not. It offers us *realiora*, if not *realia*, as Eugene Zamyatin succinctly put it: not quite the real things, but things that seem more real than those offered by others."[35] Conceiving realism in this way lends Levin's observations about it a coherence that is quite persuasive. We can better see the underlying reasons when he points out that it has often originated in parody, that it works through the rectifying process of disillusionment, that its protagonists are often outsiders, that its technique is iconoclastic, and that one age's realism provides the standards against which its successor's realism will rebel. Levin's viewpoint also enables him to solve a persistent terminological problem, the lack of an English word meaning "an extended, realistic prose fiction." He suggests "anti-romance."

The political implications of realism have often been discussed, at least since the time of Brecht and Lukács. Roland Barthes, David Caute, Alain Robbe-Grillet, Terry Eagleton, Leo Bersani, and others have questioned it on the ground that it strengthens the establishment and have urged literary modernism instead. Erich Auerbach, John Orr, Gerald Graff, W. J. Harvey, George Levine, and others have defended it, often making the counterclaim that the status quo is well served by modernism.[36] The fact that these critics disagree so much about what bias realism has leaves reasonable doubt that it has any which will align on a political axis. We should hesitate, I think, to surrender the naive but at least firm perception that some realistic works are progressive and others not, and that the same is true of nonrealistic or modernist works.

If realism is a relative term, any discussion of it will actually center on what term it is opposing at the moment. This sometimes makes a bit unreal itself the debate about its political implications. Robbe-Grillet, for example, opposes realism in the name of a newer realism because of the remnants of romance and idealism he finds still in it. His position very much resembles that of the naturalists. If Levin and Levine are right in seeing the history of realism as a series of revolts against previous novelists for not being realistic enough, there is as much reason to call Robbe-Grillet and Zola realists as there is for calling what Flaubert developed from Balzac and Stendhal realism. Lukács, on the other hand, defending realism by opposing it to naturalism, actually advocates the measure of romance which naturalists oppose, so that those who find idealism in his aesthetics seem well justified. Then there is Brecht, who claimed to be a realist on the ground that his works were true to social reality. He is now seen as a nonrealist in his opposition to Lukács, and his theories are much admired by the proponents of modernism. These theories, developed from expressionism and advocating "epic" theater, defend episodic or montage structure, open didacticism, and a disintegration of character brought about by deliberate violations of dramatic illusion which emphasize the artifice of both life and art. Essentially, these proposals advocate comedy, as Terry Eagleton has shown.[37] Since comedy is the dominant literary form of our high culture, it is easy to see how Brecht could provide the basis for at least one variety of modernism.

Although leaving much of the debate about realism to others, I think there is much to be said for examining comedy, romance, and other negations of realism directly, rather than in the mirror provided by realism. Perhaps when their limitations become clearer, those of realism will seem of less moment. The relativity of realism, which reflects the reciprocality already noted between flawed-victim novels and those devoted to other types of victims, has several consequences of immediate concern, however. First, any problems with the flawed-victim novel treated in this chapter as problems of realism could be treated in other chapters concerning forms which realism negates. In fact, the two previous chapters, treating romance, have already dealt with issues which could have been treated here, and the next chapter, in discussing comedy, will do the same. Second, we must be prepared to tolerate, to some extent, the disadvantages of any type of victim-of-society novel for the sake of its advantages—a problem not confined to social protest novels. If we are not careful, a justification of any type and its privileged form may seem an attack on other types and forms. Finally, the very oppositions on which realism is founded exert some pressure within it, so that, as already noted, the basic political ideal implied by the flawed-victim novel is the same as that more explicitly presented by the virtuous-victim novel. In "The Fate of Pleasure," Lionel Trilling made a similar point more broadly—perhaps too broadly, as he himself seems to have later suspected:

Whenever in modern literature we find violence, whether of represented act or of expression, and an insistence upon the sordid and the disgusting, and an insult offered to the prevailing morality or habit of life, we may assume that we are in the presence of the attempt to destroy specious good, that we are being confronted by that spirituality, or the aspiration toward it, which subsists upon violence against the specious good.[38]

With these caveats out of the way, we can turn to the problems of hope and clarity in flawed-victim novels.

If the pessimism often found in these novels comes from the same source as their strength, from their protagonists' being denied the degree of freedom we have in innocent and virtuous victims, it cannot be swept away by any magic wand. Nevertheless, we can try to understand better its rationale and how it can become qualified. To begin, let us look at a couple of well-developed objections to pessimism and the features which give rise to it. In "The Nature of Art under Capitalism," Kenneth Burke argues that "pure" literature, by promoting acquiescence in what is, keeps us healthy by enabling us to tolerate for the moment, as we must, even those conditions which we might oppose as unjust. "Propaganda" literature, on the other hand, promotes rejection of what is by adopting impurity, even though we now read as if they were pure many of its great nineteenth-century monuments. Burke concludes,

> Much of the harsh literature now being turned out in the name of the "proletariat" seems inadequate on either count. It is questionable as propaganda, since it shows so little of the qualities in mankind worth saving. And it is questionable as "pure" art, since by substituting a cult of disaster for a cult of amenities it "promotes our acquiescence" to sheer dismalness. Too often, alas, it serves as a mere device whereby the neuroses of the decaying bourgeois structure are simply transformed to the symbols of workingmen.[39]

As an alternative, Burke recommends, "more of Dickens is needed, even at the risk of excessive tenderness" (p. 278).

In "The Intellectual Physiognomy of Literary Characters," Georg Lukács argues that portraying the commonplace rather than the "awake" consciousness ignores the future progress latent in the present, renounces "the portrayal of social contradictions in their most fully developed and purest

124

form"[40] and thus serves as an apologetic for the status quo. He objects to naturalism in Zola and in Flaubert, who portrays "the crisis of bourgeois ideals . . . as the collapse of all human strivings" (p. 109). He indicts modernism as well, because "both of them start with the solipsistic conception of man hopelessly isolated in inhuman society" (p. 112). Both Burke and Lukács object to the assignment of bourgeois consciousness to the victims of the bourgeoisie on the ground that it confines our vision of human and social reality within an oppressor's ideology, with results not only discouraging but untrue. For a remedy Burke suggests Dickens as a model, and Lukács goes on to recommend Gorki's *Mother* and the positive heroes of socialist realism. Thus both would have writers move away from the flawed victim and toward romance.

For an articulate and certainly authoritative response to arguments such as these, we can turn to Zola's classic essay, "The Experimental Novel." Essentially, he defends himself from the charge of fatalism by accusing his critics of confusing conditions with consequences. Given certain conditions, certain consequences follow necessarily. If we impute the necessity of the consequences to the conditions, fatalism results, because then we can do nothing about either. If we do not, conditions are open to intervention. Zola does not limit his scientism to a respect for observation, but seeks to imitate the activism with which scientists intervene in nature after they have learned its laws. Like scientists, those who would intervene politically can do so to the extent that conditions are not necessary, and as a result of their intervention different consequences follow, necessarily. Such an argument, which any political activism must make, seems to imply in the intervener a freedom to act or not act, or to act in one way rather than another. However that may be, what is important is that the conditions lack the necessity with which they bring about consequences.

If in the real world fatalism comes about as Zola says, we can find a novel fatalistic by imputing necessity to the consequences developed from its conditions or givens and then confusing the two. Unfortunately, readers may do just that. Henry James's often-cited remark that we must accept the *donnée* of a novel, but may quarrel with its treatment, or Coleridge's that *King Lear* is not marred by its opening implausibility because it proceeds logically thereafter may suggest to some that a literary work is not only an axiomatic system, but one in which all the axioms are established early. However, the givens of a literary work, in which it establishes conditions, are by no means confined to its opening pages. Nor is the movement from them to their consequences strongly marked by necessity. As Aristotle pointed out in his praise of Homer, necessity in the literary work is only apparent.

To establish these points and get closer to the problem of pessimism, let us look again at the laundry scene in *L'Assommoir*. The consequence being motivated is Gervaise's taking an important step from the height of her prosperity toward her ultimate degradation, a step signalized by her finally consenting to kiss passionately the tipsy Coupeau. Some of the many conditions are the extreme heat, the need to sort dirty laundry, and Mme. Putois' sympathy with Coupeau. These help bring about the consequence quite nicely. But the fact remains that there is a gap in motivation. We can see it if we suppose that at the crucial moment Gervaise had persisted in her intention not to indulge Coupeau in the kiss: she could have continued in her businesslike mood and put Coupeau to bed at that moment instead of later. Our supposed consequence would follow just as logically as the actual one. It has plenty of motives to support it, in the very grounds for Gervaise's initial resistance. Since two opposed consequences would follow plausibly, neither can be necessary, and a motivational gap must exist. Her internal struggle means that a gap will occur regardless of what Zola has her finally do, and this internal struggle is a manifestation of the divided consciousness we have noted among flawed victims.

What are we to make of this and similar gaps? What are we to make of the gap in motivating Clyde Griffiths' failure to save Roberta or Bigger's suffocation of Mary Dalton? We

126

cannot take them fatalistically, at least in Zola's sense, because there is no logical necessity in the consequence, so that statements such as Hemmings' that Gervaise's plunge to degradation is "inexorable"[41] can be accepted only as relative or exaggerated. Zola would probably have explained Gervaise's act as free, had he not tended to reserve that term for what he thought impossible, being unaffected by any conditions. Certainly his criticism of both Gervaise and Coupeau on one occasion implies her freedom: "Unquestionably, the Coupeaus should have done something about this. No matter how hard up you are, you can always pull out of trouble somehow if you practice order and thrift" (p. 360). Such an authorial statement contrasts strongly with the fatalism Gervaise herself expresses when Zola presents her rationalizing her actions as "the law of nature" (p. 308). To attribute fatalism to the flawed victim, as Wright and Dreiser do also, is one means of undercutting pessimism. Just as writers of virtuous-victim novels undercut the manichaeism toward which their form tends by assigning it to an antagonist, so writers of flawed-victim novels can assign fatalism to the false consciousness of inner antagonists as a sign of the oppression in the protagonists. This way it highlights rather than denies their freedom, and freedom in the victim, as we have already seen, is one ground for hope that greater justice may be achieved.

If we do not take motivational gaps to indicate such freedom, we can think of them simply as what in any case they are, indications that external conditions pull the heroes in opposite directions. We see social reality, environment, or milieu as heterogeneous, as containing contradictions. Even though these may not have the clarity demanded by Lukács for the presentation of social contradictions, they too contain the seed for future social development. Whether we see flawed victims as free or not, then, the motivational gaps to which their divided consciousness (if nothing else) gives rise offer some relief from pessimism. We may not get hope—which writers are not obliged to give us—but we do get the grounds for it, which writers are obliged to give by the project of writing a victim-of-society novel. In this way they do not undermine the paradox of reform. To be sure, we get more grounds for pessimism than for optimism, but that is the price paid for attributing to injustice the considerable power needed to corrupt its victims.

The price paid for avoiding the simplifications of melodrama and showing moral complexity is the lack of clarity so often besetting flawed-victim novels, a lack reflected in the rather vague statements I have had to make about their targets. Of course, many other literary works have proved difficult to interpret. Despite its melodrama, *Billy Budd* has had interpretational problems. But these center around Captain Vere, whereas those of flawed-victim novels center around the protagonist. To devote to Billy Budd an article like the one which Robert M. Adams devotes to the question of whether readers should "like" Julien Sorel[42] ought to be unthinkable, even if it isn't. Interpretational problems often arise when one character serves two functions, and they can become acute when the functions are hero and villain. Readers may find it impossible to tell the better self from the worse, as Hemmings seems to have done when he admired the softheartedness of Gervaise as good-heartedness. If the false consciousness under attack is sufficiently widespread to be a real social problem, moreover, readers may misread, perhaps even knowingly, as Budd Schulberg discovered in reactions to *What Makes Sammy Run?*: "the book I thought I had written as a warning against unsocial behavior is in danger of becoming a business manual, a fictionalized how-to version of a current bestseller, *Looking Out for Number One.*"[43] Just as often, the authors themselves are contaminated by the same false consciousness they attack. Whatever Flaubert's "I am Madame Bovary" might mean, Dreiser certainly had some of Clyde Griffiths' respect for success, Wright Bigger's *ressentiment*, Hemingway Harry Morgan's Tommy-gun individualism, Stendhal Julien Sorel's duplicity, and Dostoevsky his Underground Man's capricious freedom.

The most important interpretational problems stem from the difficulty of controlling reader sympathy for the protagonists. Rebels cause more confusion than conformists, largely because rebellion is closer than conformism to the resistance being promoted, and because readers find it more difficult to tell when individualism becomes excessive. Many literary critics believe there is a bias toward individualism in the novel itself, partly because it is written and read alone, and partly because it emerged at the same time as the bourgeoisie did[44] Even if they are correct—and Michel Butor has persuasively challenged them[45]—the bias is no more inherent than others we have seen, because there are literary means of circumventing it. Since movies also exalt individualism, however, despite their different historical origin and their very communal production and consumption, the source of bias seems more likely to be cultural than artistic, literary, or generic. Wayne Booth devoted the last chapter of *The Rhetoric of Fiction* to the confusion resulting when a reader sympathizes too much with an attractive but immoral character. He urged writers to make their moral norms clear, to insist that characters who punch women in the face or prey sexually upon children are wrong. But readers may be the source of the problem to begin with. The characters he objects to as attractive and immoral are very individualistic, and readers have sympathized with many such characters despite writers' having made their moral norms quite clear. One can resist misinterpretations of Julien Sorel and similar characters, as René Girard does in *Deceit, Desire, and the Novel*, by demanding that the obvious remain obvious, or one can seek in hermeneutics literary laws for restraining interpretation. But many readers will still misinterpret characters like Julien Sorel, just as he, because he was antisocial, misinterpreted *Tartuffe*.

One way that writers attempt to keep their readers from sympathizing too much with rebel victims is to escalate the violence they inflict. Wright has Bigger dismember Mary Dalton's body, and Hemingway has Harry Morgan murder a man as follows: "I got him forward onto his knees and held both thumbs well in behind his talk-box, and I bent the whole thing back, until she cracked. Don't think you can't hear it crack, either."[46] Here Hemingway is not simply indulging a penchant for immediacy, but trying to cause readers enough pain to inhibit somewhat their sympathy for the oppressed hero. Of course such a solution to the problem contains its own risk. Instead of criticizing the excessive individualism because of the cruelty, readers may accept or even admire the cruelty because they do not question the individualism.

A better way to control sympathy for rebel victims is through the temporal dislocations with which the writer can present their story. The beginning, in which they pass from innocent victimage to a negative conversion, places them in a very favorable light. We see them unprotected from harsh conditions, wanting to enjoy the normal human relations for which all strive, and rejected. The negative conversion itself becomes an understandable act of self-preservation. Whatever they do afterwards, no matter how much they oppress in their turn, will be colored by our knowledge of why they became corrupted and antisocial. This is a good reason why writers seldom begin with the beginning of their story. Many omit it altogether. Hemingway, for example, gives us no idea why Harry Morgan became what he did. Many move the details of negative conversion to just before or after the climax of the novel. As a result, we see rebels first in the least flattering light, which continues for most of the narrative. Only after we have had a chance to judge their individualism adversely are we called to sympathy by seeing its causes.

As the title suggests, Budd Schulberg's *What Makes Sammy Run?* keeps us wondering why the rebel hero cannot love or trust anyone and why he seems capable of any treachery. In the ninth of twelve chapters, we find out why. The narrator investigates Sammy's childhood background, in his old neighborhood and school, and gives us the results—a full-scale beginning of his story which takes the narrator and presumably the reader from hatred to compassion. Schulberg would have had even more trouble with misinterpretation if he had ordered his narrative chronologically, in the manner of *Great Expectations*, *An American Tragedy*, or other presentations of conformist victims, for whom reader sympathy needs to be promoted rather than inhibited. In a very good book on temporal dislocations in fiction, Meir Sternberg shows how the timing with which Faulkner releases information about Joe Christmas prepares a trap for the reader of *Light in August*.[47] The most damaging information comes first, and few will sympathize with the withdrawn loner. Then flashbacks start to show us in great detail how the young hero was rejected, beaten, and warped. After the beginning has been fully told, the ending develops the suffering to which his rebellion brings him and some suggestion that he too condemns what he has been.

Dostoevsky's *Notes from Underground* withholds the earliest events in the hero's story until just past the midpoint of the narrative.

> That night I had the most revolting dreams, and no wonder: all evening I was oppressed by recollections about the penal servitude of my school years, and could not rid myself of them. I had been shunted off into that school by distant relatives whose dependent I was and of whom I have never heard since. They left me there, a lonely boy, already crushed by their reproaches, already brooding, silent, looking at everything with savage suspicion. My schoolmates met me with vicious and merciless ridicule because I was unlike any of them. But I could not endure ridicule; and I could not get along with others as easily as they did. I conceived an immediate hatred for them and shut myself away from everyone in timid, wounded, and inordinate pride.[48]

Here we have almost the entire process of negative conversion, placed just before the long sequence of events which will complete it, developing one who already has the underground in his soul to a life of even more severe isolation. Thus the narrative ends with the beginning of the rebel's story, withholding as long as possible the sympathy which goes with it. Dostoevsky actually begins with a set of personal and philosophical reflections, the fruit of the hero's underground life, his attempt to make sense of his experience. Chronologically, this is the ending of the rebel victim's whole story. If placed last, it too would generate more sympathy and even more readily pass for the pure wisdom that it is not.

These temporal dislocations should prevent the very considerable degree of sympathy which chronological order would have promoted. Dostoevsky goes much further, however, to protect his readers from his hero's extreme individualism. Near the end of part one, he has him say, "it's not at all the underground which is best, but something different, something I long for and can never find! To the devil with the underground" (p. 42). In a similarly strategic position near the end of part 2, he has the hero characterize his own narrative as "long tales about how I have shirked away my life through moral degeneration in my corner, through isolation from society, through loss of contact with anything alive, through vanity and malice in my underground" (pp. 151–52). Notwithstanding all these precautions, *Notes from Underground* is often read as advocating the very individualistically conceived freedom which it attacks. Many readers do not see that the need for others implied by the narrator's suffering urges a commitment not only *to* freedom, but *of* it. The hero's freedom, as mechanical as the utilitarianism it rejects, has no content: it consists only of one of his selves watching the other do nothing. Liza has more freedom. She is another of Dostoevsky's virtuous victims, representing the values which all flawed-victim novels, in their own way, seek to advance.

The problem of clarity, then, like the problem of hope, does not leave writers defenseless, but the problems remain despite the defenses. Like the opposite risks of the virtuous-victim novel, the risks of excessive pessimism and confusion seem to go with the project of writing a flawed-victim novel. Largely for this reason I think, many writers have rejected its hero, the most oppressed of all victims of society, and taken up instead the pseudo victim. In doing so, they have turned, as we do now, from realism to comedy—and from one set of risks to another.

5

The Pseudo Victim

The good end happily, and the bad unhappily. That is
what fiction is.

—Oscar Wilde

ALL the victims of society so far considered undergo the
pathos characteristic of the tragic hero, and we perceive the injustice against them in the disproportion between
how much they suffer and how little they deserve to. What
are we to think, however, when suffering as well as deserv-
ing to is minimized—when it is trivialized to pseudo pathos?
In Kingsley Amis's *Lucky Jim* the hero suffers primarily from
such experiences as making love to an unattractive, bespec-
tacled academic woman and having to endure the boredom
of pretentious scholarship, Welsh culture, and amateur re-
corder concerts. In William Faulkner's *Wild Palms* a Missis-
sippi flood and other natural catastrophes frustrate a convict
desperately trying to get back to the comfort and security of
prison. In Evelyn Waugh's *Handful of Dust* Tony Last has to
establish his legal infidelity so that his adulterous wife can
divorce him. To pretend to be caught by photographers *in
actu flagrante,* he takes a prostitute for a weekend excursion
and much of the time finds underfoot her daughter, whom
she has brought along to enjoy a holiday. The novel ends
with Tony trapped deep in the Amazonian jungle with an
illiterate Bozolater named Todd, in the pseudo pathos of having to read Dickens novels aloud.

133

The privileged mode for presenting the pseudo victim is, of course, comedy. Whatever else it may entail it subverts real pathos by some sort of slippage between conditions and consequences, a slippage manifested by arbitrariness, improbability, and odd juxtapositions. We have seen leaps of faith in both positive and negative conversions. We have seen motivational gaps at key moments in the flawed victim's story and assessed them as signs of individual freedom or of the heterogeneity of social conditions. In the pseudo-victim novel such slippage is much more thoroughgoing—insisted upon as a part of the basic vision of the work, rather than sporadic or partly concealed by a barrage of motives. We can take it also as a sign of the hero's freedom or of contradictions in the social milieu, but these alternatives somehow do not seem to exhaust the possibilities. The gaps have a way of remaining gaps, unless we resort to such explanations as Meredith's Comic Spirit.

Invulnerability makes the pseudo victim a close relative of the innocent victim, the oddly resilient hero with whom we started. From comic romance we have come full circle to comedy proper. In doing so we have seen that each type of victim offsets some disadvantages of other types while incurring risks of its own. We can see in the pseudo victim now an attempt to offset the risks of the flawed victim by giving up realism for the comedy which underlies much modernism. Assessing its risks should help put those of other types in better perspective.

The victim-of-society novels considered so far have presented injustice largely as an ethical matter. In the pseudo-victim novel it is an intellectual one. Comedy subverts the cause-and-effect relationships on which the idea of suffering depends. Impeding pathos, it also impedes empathy, calling us to neither pity nor terror. By doing so, it urges us to think rather than feel. This subversion of cause and effect has a curious result on the pseudo-victim novel. In the constant denial that power of any kind works in a straightforward way, what might seem a mere comic technique becomes thematized. Political power becomes as problematic as any other.

As a result the privileged subject of the pseudo-victim novel becomes power. What *is* comes to have an authority of its own, as opposed to what *ought* to be. The actual in its own right is valorized at some expense to the ideal or the expected. But in the comic vision of what actually is, we should not be surprised to discover some surprises.

Pseudo victims have such a strange relationship to the conditions under which they live that character loses its psychological coherence. It may have the rigidity which many have associated with comic character, or it may disintegrate into various characteristics not in harmony with each other. In spite of this fact, however, pseudo-victim novels support F. M. Cornford's view that character rather than plot is primary in comedy.[1] The similarity of other victim-of-society novels to tragedy justifies seeking their thematic or intellectual center in their motivation and arrangement of incident, or plot. Because purpose creates structure, structure reveals purpose, and structure can be roughly identified with plot. In presentations of the pseudo victim, however, motivation is often perfunctory, and the arrangement of incident is so arbitrary that large chunks of narrative can be excised or transposed with little loss. The structure or rhetorical composition is more spatial than temporal—an arrangement not so much of incidents as of characters. Choices about character may or may not affect plot, but they are of first importance in themselves.

The structure of character in the pseudo-victim novel depends greatly on whether the protagonist is one of the fools or not. If not, he may be a wit who unmasks the pretensions of fools around him, from whom his antagonists are drawn. This is the *eiron* unmasking the *alazon*, in the terms that Northrop Frye appropriated from Aristotle. The unfoolish pseudo victim may also be, again according to Frye, one of those bland, uninteresting young lovers whose desire is frustrated by the fools around him.[2] In any case, the unfoolish pseudo victim serves as some sort of norm or standard against which the foolishness of antagonists is measured. Often, however, the pseudo victim is also a fool. He too is

135

likely to be surrounded by fools, but the threat of pathos or pseudo pathos comes partly from within. To some degree he incorporates also the antagonist function, and the norm or standard is implicit rather than explicit. The distinction between the unfoolish pseudo victim and the foolish one thus correlates loosely with that between the virtuous victim and the flawed.

As far as there is a standard plot in the pseudo-victim novel, its action may be described as the escape from suffering, whether pathos or pseudo pathos. At the end, the hero's enemies do their best to do their worst, but it is not good enough. By remaining unscathed, the hero shows the antagonist's ineptitude or impotence. This is the principal advantage of the pseudo victim for the novelist protesting injustice: both the triviality of the suffering and the escape from it show the vulnerability of oppression. Only the choice of a virtuous victim affords a comparable opportunity for treating victimizers at length without imputing great power to them and using the pseudo victim may impute even less. Antagonists come to be seen as more ludicrous than evil, and readers are not likely to associate power with the ludicrous. If we remember the end of Norman Mailer's *Naked and the Dead*, we can see this attraction very clearly. After taking Croft and Cummings seriously as villains, we suddenly find Mailer turning them into figures of farce, and their ineptness quickly diminishes the sense of their power.

The trivializing or distancing of the protagonists' sufferings underlies our taking them as pseudo victims, but it does not always continue to the end. Just as Aristotle considers the unfortunate ending as the natural ending for tragedy while recognizing the fortunate ending as a variant plot, so we may see the escape from suffering as the natural plot for the pseudo-victim novel while recognizing a variant plot in which the heroes' invulnerability clearly deserts them and they end in real pathos.

Since there are two types of plot and two types of hero, and since plot and character do not determine each other to the extent they do in other types, there are four main hypothetical structures or compositional options for the writer presenting a pseudo victim. This chapter will explore each, using Heller's *Catch-22*, Voinovich's *Life and Extraordinary Adventures of Private Ivan Chonkin*, Kesey's *One Flew over the Cuckoo's Nest*, and Caldwell's *Tobacco Road*. Afterwards, the possibilities of comedy for political expression are explored by seeing how the pseudo-victim novel copes with the problems of clarity and hope.

Yossarian, the *miles ungloriosus* of Joseph Heller's *Catch-22*, is an unfoolish pseudo victim who ends fortunately. Although Heller presents many unavoidable anomalies of life which must be tolerated as the result of cosmic oversight or human undersight, he also presents many avoidable anomalies. Distinguishing the two is fundamental to the victim-of-society novel, but because they may be very similar formally, the temperament or philosophic orientation of the observer is crucial. *Catch-22* is designed to help direct or educate readers to laugh at what cannot be avoided and to withhold laughter at avoidable injustice. By the end of the novel, they, like Yossarian, should be capable of the distinction suggested when Heller writes, "there was a humorless irony in the ludicrous panic of the man screaming for help to the police while policemen were all around him."[3]

If accepting all anomalies is nihilistic and accepting none idealistic, Yossarian is a pseudo victim surrounded by both nihilistic and idealistic fools. In the contrasts between his character and theirs we see the standard against which their foolishness is measured. His claim to be a "sensible young gentleman" (p. 21), living amid contagious insanity, is pretty much true at the beginning when he makes it, and it becomes even more evidently so as the novel progresses. His claim to be a victim of injustice is also pretty much true. He has flown more than his share of missions. His protest has been rendered more difficult by his adversaries' subverting of reason with absurd rationalization and by their appropriating the language of idealism for their own purposes. Nevertheless, much of his suffering consists of witnessing that of others, much is recounted briefly or in flashbacks to experiences we know he has survived, and much is pseudo pathetic.

Among the fools around him, one idealist is Clevinger, who is a fool because "there were many principles in which Clevinger believed passionately" (p. 17). Since the importance he attaches to principles is often disputed by Yossarian, we may fall into the error of thinking Yossarian opposed to principle until we look more closely at the point in dispute. When Yossarian claims that "they" are trying to kill him, giving as evidence that the Germans shoot at him on every mission, Clevinger objects that they are shooting at everyone. When Yossarian gives as evidence that his food was twice poisoned, Clevinger objects similarly that poison was put into everyone's food. For Clevinger then, believing in principles seems to entail believing that "everyone" contains no individuals. He has "lots of intelligence and no brains" (p. 70), because he thinks the public world operates according to the civilized rationality which he imputes to academic politics. He has a naive belief in human reason and consequently fails to see that political decisions are reached not so much by a process of reasoning about relevant principles, but by a series of accommodations with conflicting interests and powers. Unlike Yossarian, he is incapable of paranoia, however well justified, because he cannot conceive that some people simply take a dislike to others. Even when a victim himself, he cannot see that some make the legal system serve themselves rather than justice. In short, he underestimates evil in men, power in the world, and the extent to which both have neutralized or co-opted reason. By disputing with him Yossarian is not rejecting goodness, reason, or principles, but the degree of efficacy which Clevinger attributes to them.

"Clevinger was dead. That was the basic flaw in his philosophy" (p. 107). Yossarian's opposition to Clevinger is partly based upon a commitment to survival, a value currently subverting all others. It is hard not to view this as Clevinger does, as something shameful and egoistic, and hard also to keep from associating Yossarian with the *élan vital* and quoting a battery of theorists to the effect that the hero of comedy is always on the side of life. Nevertheless, we must try to see Yossarian's commitment to his own life as an ordinary, healthy instinct which every ordinary, healthy human being has and to see this as a value without making an absolute out of it. To help us do so, Heller has provided another fool for a foil to Yossarian. Not many pages after telling us that Yossarian "had decided to live forever or die in the attempt," making that "his only mission each time he went up" (p. 30), he provides us with the foolish version of such a commitment. Dunbar, who also wants to keep himself alive, tries to make his life pass as slowly as possible by doing things he hates. To the question of why anyone would want such a life, he can only ask, "What else is there" (p. 40)? Like those who would defend democracy by abolishing it, or villages by destroying them, Dunbar would make life his only value by emptying it of value. For Yossarian there is something more important than life, even his own, as we can see later when, like Uncle Tom, he turns down an opportunity to preserve his life because it entails helping the establishment exploit the lives of others.

Contrasts with other fools further establish what Yossarian's character is, and the fact that it is a standard. His friend Nately is another idealist. Unlike Clevinger he is an aristocratic and chivalric one rather than an academic and rationalistic one. While Yossarian seeks to stop flying missions, Nately flies even more than required in order to stay in Europe near the woman whose love he finally wins, only to bring her to grief at his death. Doc Daneeka, "a warm, compassionate man who never stopped feeling sorry for himself" (p. 35), is another fool, one who imagines himself a victim of injustice only because his army service keeps him from making big money back home. Through him we notice that Yossarian protests his legitimate grievances with much less self pity. We see that Yossarian is not the antisocial person Clevinger thinks he is by contrasting him with Major Major, who is a "flagrant nonconformist" (p. 88) because he really believes all the copybook maxims he has been taught. Despite his elaborate schemes for maintaining his own isolation, even Major Major is not really antisocial, but too frantically in need of friendship to be given any.

Yossarian is contrasted with more nihilists than idealists, because keeping him distinct from them is more difficult and important. Aarfy, "a lead navigator who had never been able to find himself since leaving college" (p. 269), laughs at everything, especially the suffering of others, for the same reason that the devil traditionally does—because his lack of values keeps him from taking anything seriously. A similar figure is the old man in the Roman bordello, another fool bent only on survival. He has opportunistically supported Mussolini, the Nazis, then the Americans—whoever is in power. He dies fittingly because of Catch-22, which may be the Absurd, but certainly embodies the principle that might makes right. His philosophy has the same flaw as Clevinger's, as Yossarian helps us to see: "It was logical and true: once again the old man had marched along with the majority" (p. 417).

Milo Minderbinder, believing only in money, expresses righteous indignation at any opposition to his amassing it. Unable to persuade Yossarian to join him in black marketeering, Milo reluctantly concludes that he is simply honest, because "anyone who would not steal from the country he loved would not steal from anybody" (p. 64). When using the squadron's planes for his purposes, he paints over their idealistic emblems of "Courage, Might, Justice, Truth, Liberty, Love, Honor, and Patriotism" (p. 259) with his own sign, so that we are not surprised when Yossarian is unable to persuade him of his moral responsibility for the deaths he has caused. Yossarian represents a minority attitude toward Milo. After being "caught red-handed in the act of plundering his countrymen," "his stock had never been higher" (p. 378), because everyone, including the Germans, has a share in his enterprise.

Unlike his friends, Yossarian's adversaries are all nihilistic fools. The insecure psychiatrist will not ground him despite finding him a bundle of neuroses: "You're antagonistic

140

to the idea of being robbed, exploited, degraded, humiliated or deceived. Misery depresses you. Ignorance depresses you. Persecution depresses you. Violence depresses you. Slums depress you. Greed depresses you. Crime depresses you. Corruption depresses you. You know, it wouldn't surprise me if you're a manic-depressive!" (p. 312) Colonel Cathcart, a firm believer in the merit system, operates on a degraded utilitarian calculus of the good impressions and bad impressions that he believes he is making on superiors who are actually paying no attention to him. He "was impervious to absolutes. He could measure his progress only in relationship to others" (p. 192). Yossarian, on the other hand, is no calculator and is free from the gospel of success. Colonel Korn shares Cathcart's aspiration and his willingness to achieve it through the death of other people: "What else have we got to do? Everyone teaches us to aspire to higher things. A general is higher than a colonel, and a colonel is higher than a lieutenant colonel. So we're both aspiring" (p. 435). He is so cynical that he is sure Yossarian can be bought off, but he is right, even if lying, when he says, "You're an intelligent person of great moral character who has taken a very courageous stand. I'm an intelligent person with no moral character at all, so I'm in an ideal position to appreciate it" (p. 432).

When Yossarian openly revolts and refuses to fly any more missions, he becomes an even more responsible person, but this is by no means a complete turnabout. The decision gives both the resolution of the plot conflict and the solution to the problem it presents—civil disobedience. The novel ends with Yossarian swimming out to sea to escape the army. We cannot worry about his safety. Amid a great deal of suffering, he has proven invulnerable, threatened personally with only a slipshod nemesis. Like other pseudo victims, he is protected by a comic compact between writer and reader that his invulnerability will continue. Like all conventions, it can be broken, as we will see, but not without notifying the reader. This invulnerability establishes the vulnerability of his antagonists. Cathcart and Korn hate each other, and both are extremely sensitive to public opinion because they cannot attempt to use it for their own ends without overvaluing it. Yossarian's revolt is likely to prove contagious, as they can readily see in the hope it has inspired in other victims, and they would not be trying to win his love and buy him off if they were in a stronger position. Although they deny that he has them over a barrel, everything they do indicates that he does. The chain of command works backwards as well as forwards. Yossarian's pseudo victimage shows their pseudo power.

There are many ways to make the pseudo victim a fool, but weak-mindedness is one of the best. The more stupid he is, the more ludicrous the system which cannot cope with him. His final escape from the threat of suffering must therefore be explained by the vulnerability of oppression, perhaps together with the protection traditionally accorded to fools by God or fate. The foolish pseudo victim in the fortunate plot could be illustrated by the hero of Jaroslav Hašek's *Good Soldier Schweik*, were it not for the fact that some readers, finding him both cunning and successful, attribute the latter to the former and therefore ignore his idiocy. Let us turn instead to another soldier, in Vladimir Voinovich's *Life and Extraordinary Adventures of Private Ivan Chonkin*.

Chonkin is very decent and likable, but a fool nevertheless because of his ignorance and stupidity.

> All sorts of thoughts would visit Chonkin. From his close observation of life and his fathoming of life's laws, Chonkin had understood that it is usually warm in the summer and cold in the winter. But if it was the other way around, he thought, cold in the summer and warm in the winter, then summer would be called winter and winter would be called summer. Then a second, even more serious and interesting thought came into Chonkin's head, but it slipped his mind immediately and he couldn't recall it for the life of him. To know that he had lost a thought grieved Chonkin sorely.[4]

His ineptness as a soldier—his inability to dress, march, or salute properly—has caused him to be assigned to the stable, to company he really prefers. When someone is needed to guard a plane forced to crash-land in a village not far away, he is readily considered expendable. He wants to do a good job and stand by his post until properly relieved, but when Germany invades Russia, his superiors have no time to send for him or to countermand his orders.

Chonkin is surrounded by others as foolish as he, though not all as ignorant. Golubev, the tippling *kolkhoz* chairman, thinks that every stranger who turns up in town, including Chonkin, is a secret inspector. He expects the lies with which he is forced to fill his reports to be exposed soon, bringing an end to his career of pretending to be busy and trying to squeeze work out of an uncooperative force of women, old men, and cripples. He welcomes the war as an alternative to the threat of prison camp or execution: "The war will write everything off. The main thing's to get to the front as fast as possible; there either you get a chest full of medals or a head full of bullets, but either way, at least you can live like an honest man" (p. 116). Gladishev, the rationalist and amateur scientist, is a parody of Lysenko. He is trying to develop a plant giving potatoes below the ground and tomatoes above. Seeing the food chain as a long and inefficient process, he fills his house with shit, which he is trying to make edible. Captain Milyaga, of the secret police, has devoted his life to badgering suspects as inconspicuously as possible because of the occasional triumph of legality and the much less occasional triumph of illegality over its own cat's-paws.

When Gladishev sends an anonymous letter to Milyaga denouncing Chonkin as a deserter, a chain of incidents begins which demonstrates even further the ineptness of Chonkin's adversaries. Milyaga and his seven men are captured by Chonkin because they have brought no authorization to relieve him of his sentry duty. When the capture is reported as the work of "Chonkin and his girl," the message is misunderstood as "Chonkin and his gang," partly because of a faulty telephone connection but mostly because of unwillingness to attribute to so few the capture of so many. The district authorities go to the provincial authorities, who go to the military authorities, and Chonkin's gang becomes inflated to a behind-the-lines group of German paratroopers commanded by the "so-called Chonkin." When an infantry regiment is sent to subdue him, Chonkin mistakes them for Germans because they are wearing winter uniforms. They capture Milyaga. Sublieutenant Bukashov, who has studied a little German, is assigned to interrogate him. Addressed in German, Milyaga thinks he has been captured by Germans, declares himself a member of the Russian equivalent of the Gestapo, offers to work for the Germans, praises Hitler, and is shot. Bukashov, believing himself about to go into battle against Germans and still feeling the humiliation of his father's death as a traitor to Stalin, writes a notice that if he is killed, he wishes to be considered a communist. When the battle begins, the soldiers forget to pull the pins on the grenades, and Chonkin holds them off for some time with the guns of the plane. When he does get captured, the general gives him a medal for valor to still the laughter resulting from one man's holding off a regiment, only to rescind the order on finding Chonkin charged with being a traitor.

Because of his foolishness Chonkin is part of the problem, but because of his adversaries' foolishness, he is only a small part. He mistakes friendly forces for the enemy, but such mistakes are rife throughout the novel, in war or peace. Suspicion is in the air, and the ineptness of those in power has not prevented them from making real victims. Government, like the secret police, "operates on the principle of 'beat your own so that outsiders will fear you'" (p. 169), and people are afraid, including those who administer the government. As the inflation of the Chonkin threat shows, the bureaucracy consistently overestimates the power of the enemy in order to justify itself, much as American bureaucracies manipulate crime statistics and estimates of the Russian military threat. Curiously, the enemy threat is not only maximized but minimized, and Chonkin is not the only fool when we see him responding to Stalin's radio speech saying that the Germans are advancing despite the destruction of their best divisions: "Chonkin listened to the words spoken with the noticeable Georgian accent, and believed in them implicitly, but there still were certain things he could not understand. If the enemy's best divisions and the best units of his air force had been smashed and had found their graves, what was there worth getting so upset about? It'd be even easier to smash his weaker units and divisions" (pp. 159–60). The government, like the critics of social injustice we have seen, has to argue that its opposition is both strong and weak. The very measures and rhetoric by which it would strengthen itself reveal its own awareness that its power is very limited. The paradox of reform is a paradox of government too.

Chonkin's stupidity is part of a very widespread problem. Born the by-blow of a Russian prince during the Civil War, later deprived of his guardians by the massacre of *kulaks*, he is an ignorant peasant, created by political convulsions. He represents elements of Russian society which have proved intractable to the Communist leadership. The government has created even more stupidity by inhibiting the right to think. One of Stalin's defenders asks sympathy for him, because "it's so hard for him right now. Having to think for us all by himself" (p. 143). When circumstances demand some initiative by individuals, they are like Golubev, "oppressed by freedom of choice" (p. 49), and anyone who seems to have an idea is immediately presumed to have got it from the top, the only permitted source of ideas. Voinovich presents this epidemic of stupidity as a dehumanization bringing people close to animals. When Gladishev tells Chonkin that man evolved from a monkey because monkeys work hard, Chonkin disturbs his convictions by wondering why man did not evolve from horses, which work much harder. Gladishev dreams that the horse Osoaviakhim becomes a human being and complains of having been gelded. The novel ends as he wanders over the battlefield and discovers the body of Osoaviakhim with a scrap of paper beneath his hoof: "In spite of the gathering dusk and his none-too-sharp eyesight, the born breeder was able to make out the large wavering script beneath the caked-on mud and bloodstains: 'If I perish, I ask to be considered a Communist'" (pp. 276–77).

If the invulnerability of pseudo victims shows a limit to the power of oppression and creates the expectation that they will ultimately be delivered, denying that expectation and invulnerability by departing from the usual comic ending reasserts the power of injustice. Just as using the pseudo victim can be seen as an attempt to correct the view of the antagonist implied by the flawed victim, the variant comic plot can be seen as correcting the comic vision itself. Having minimized the power of injustice, the writer wakes his readers from the dream he has spun to show them that such power need not be total to be a menace. When the foolish pseudo victim ends by suffering seriously, his foolishness turns from a shield against suffering to an instrument of it—one fashioned, like the flaws of flawed victims, partly by society itself. When the unfoolish hero ends by suffering seriously, oppression is not mediated through his character and therefore must be presented more directly. The result is a confrontation between protagonist and antagonist in which the relative power of each can be assessed with some precision, as Ken Kesey displays in *One Flew over the Cuckoo's Nest*.

Like Yossarian, Randle Patrick McMurphy is no fool, but he is far from perfect. A con man and poker hustler, he is cruel at times and even more often insensitive. In the psychiatric ward, which he has talked his way into to escape the dull routine of a prison work farm, he sees the Big Nurse and the blacks who run it only as oppressors and not as themselves oppressed. Like Yossarian, he too uses laughter as a weapon to attack the foolishness he is surrounded by. More than foolishness surrounds them, however. Just as Heller has Yossarian find, particularly on his walk through Rome late in the novel, that injustice often displays the form of the comic without its substance, Kesey is concerned also with inhibiting a comic response to the fundamentally serious. The ward is "like a cartoon world, where the figures are flat and outlined in black, jerking through some kind of goofy story that might be real funny if it weren't for the cartoon figures being real guys."[5] In *One Flew over the Cuckoo's Nest*, however, the caution against laughing at victims becomes less important than teaching the victims to laugh.

Just as Dickens envisions creating a community by opposing the fecundity of evil with the fecundity of duty, Kesey shows one formed by opposing contagious fear with contagious laughter. McMurphy finds the patients "even scared to open up and *laugh*. You know that's the first thing that got me about this place, that there wasn't anybody laughing. I haven't heard a real laugh since I came through that door, do you know that? Man, when you lose your laugh you lose your *footing*" (p. 68). He finds the only community in being is the "Therapeutic Community." In group therapy the patients are urged to expose their own weaknesses and to criticize each other for failures to adjust. They spy on one another, reporting any embarrassing self-revelations which others let slip, so that these can be discussed during therapy sessions. McMurphy quickly stops the spying, encourages them to respect themselves and others, and starts turning them into a community of laughers. Only then does a real community form, "because he knows you have to laugh at the things that hurt you just to keep yourself in balance, just to keep the world from running you plumb crazy. He knows there's a painful side . . . but he won't let the pain blot out the humor no more'n he'll let the humor blot out the pain" (pp. 237–38). Though thought antisocial, McMurphy brings an alternative society into being and thus illustrates Henri Bergson's remark that "laughter always implies a kind of secret freemasonry, or even complicity, with other laughers."[6]

Since laughter creates a community, it also creates power, even if directed against an oppression even more powerful. McMurphy radiates power from the moment he walks in. The attendants who are so fearsome to the other patients chase him around in vain with a rectal thermometer in mock homosexual rape, as he contests for power among the patients. Like a Western hero coming into a strange saloon or a saga hero into a strange meadhall, he wants to establish his eminence and insists on becoming the "bull goose loony" of the place. Chief Bromden, the narrator, feels an infusion of power from McMurphy's handshake, and Nurse Ratched sees him immediately as a threat to her dreams of ordering ward and world according to army discipline.

The source of McMurphy's power is a firm grasp on the real and complete possession of himself. He gets the patients to play basketball outside and to go on a fishing trip, to remind them of a whole world which they have forgotten. He shows them how to be more than Nurse Ratched would make them, exercising the freedom no one denies them to sing in the shower, and making the pretended democracy of the group meeting into a more real one. Unlike the patients, who have wives or mothers outside to worry about, he has the invulnerability of the pseudo victim because he has "no one to *care* about him" (p. 89). But this very source of his power becomes threatened by his increasing commitment to the men in the ward. Encouraging them to stop playing safe, he must become more and more vulnerable himself, because "as soon as a man goes to help somebody, he leaves himself wide open" (p. 131).

By temperament, McMurphy is no Christ, but he undergoes a passion nevertheless, because he sees no other way to keep hope alive among the men. He exposes himself to the power of the adversary quite literally, by undergoing shock treatments rather than breaking faith with the men and leaving their small resistance movement with no leader.

> We couldn't stop him because we were the ones making him do it. It wasn't the nurse that was forcing him, it was our need that was making him push himself slowly up from sitting, his big hands driving down on the leather chair arms, pushing him up, rising and standing like one of those moving-picture zombies, obeying orders beamed at him from forty masters. It was us that had been making him go on for weeks, keeping him standing long after his feet and legs had given out, weeks of making him wink and grin and laugh and go on with his act long after his humor had been parched dry between two electrodes (pp. 304–5).

Though for a time he has enough strength to pretend he has more, he proves by no means invulnerable in the end. He refuses to escape when he has the chance, and after eventually undergoing a lobotomy, he is killed by Chief Bromden because "he wouldn't have left something like that sit there in the day room with his name tacked on it for twenty or thirty years so the Big Nurse could use it as an example of what can happen if you buck the system" (p. 308).

At the end the Big Nurse is defeated, but at considerable cost. Men who had remained voluntarily in the ward, thinking its regimen would improve them, return to the outside no longer ashamed of being different, and ward policies change as patients insist on their rights. There is no illusion of any final or permanent victory, but rather a conviction that even partial and temporary victory, desirable as it may be, requires an unending series of sacrifices. No utopia is promised, partly because injustice remains powerful and partly because the novel makes the wholesome admission that people do not suffer solely because of defects in the organization of society. If the victim-of-society novel at its best tempers both optimism and pessimism, basing itself on a realistic appraisal of the power both of the oppressed and the oppressor, *One Flew over the Cuckoo's Nest*, despite its many flaws, deserves to rank high.

Erskine Caldwell's *Tobacco Road* resembles other comic presentations of poverty such as Steinbeck's *Tortilla Flat*, but it ends with serious suffering. In the final chapter Jeeter Lester, its foolish pseudo victim, dies with his wife when his shack catches fire. The ending is prepared for, but surprising nonetheless, and it forces us to see that the novel has been dealing with serious suffering all along, although quite literally diverting us at the same time. When the diversion stops, we are forced to re-evaluate what we have read, without the consolation of laughter, as a presentation of suffering and injustice.

To get an idea of how Caldwell prepares this trap, we

can look closely at the opening chapters of the novel. First, we see Lov Bensley going home with a sack of turnips and the Lesters watching him approach, determined to have his turnips. This absurd conflict, over what many think inedible, provides the main suspense. With our attention thus fixed, Caldwell, in the manner of a hypnotist, begins to develop, a little at a time, the serious plight of the Lesters. First he presents the very unserious plight of Lov, who has come to Jeeter for help, knowing well the threat the Lesters pose to his turnips. Lov has married Jeeter's twelve-year-old daughter Pearl, who has insisted on sleeping alone on a pallet, ignoring her wifely duties and Lov. In connection with this problem, we are told that Jeeter's wife, Ada, used to be as uncommunicative, though not as sexually uncooperative, as Pearl, but that "hunger had loosened her tongue, and she had been complaining every since."[7] Here we get the first mention of the Lesters' suffering, though it is only a partial revelation. In this reference to a past hunger which may no longer exist we see only Ada's part, buried in an expository passage really devoted to Lov and Pearl, and from that part we are diverted by the standard joke that when uncommunicative people do start talking, others may wish they hadn't.

During the expository passage showing Lov's concern over Pearl, the Lesters have been watching only the turnips, which therefore receive much of the reader's attention. When attention shifts to the Lesters, we are told that "there had been very little in the house again that day to eat" (p. 11). But we can hardly sympathize with them when we are told at the same time that they shoved away their own grandmother—with whom we also can't sympathize very well because this is the first we've heard of her. Moreover, Caldwell quickly diverts our attention to the stationing of other Lesters in the scene. Ellie May, a daughter, is trying to attract Lov's attention, for purposes we can only wonder about. Dude, a son, is bouncing a baseball off the house. Jeeter is trying to patch an inner tube. While they maintain these stations, Lov tries to talk about Pearl, and Jeeter about the turnips, the latter with an eye to negotiating a trade. As the first chapter ends, Jeeter is launching into a plaint to which he will return whenever possible. We can hardly sympathize, however, since the burden of his song is largely to the effect that some day God, who "knows best about turnips," will "bust loose with a heap of bounty" (p. 14).

As the Lesters, now complete with Ada and the grandmother, closely watch Lov eating one of his turnips, the negotiation continues. Only on the second page of chapter two are we told of the increasing poverty of the Lesters: "they had been living off of fat-back rinds several days already, and after they were gone, there would be nothing for them to eat" (p. 16). The grandmother is "frantic with hunger" at seeing Lov's turnip sack. Almost immediately, however, we are diverted by Ellie May's beginning to move "closer and closer to Lov, sliding herself over the hard white sand" (p. 18). As Lov continues his pitch, Jeeter his plaint, and Dude his ball throwing, she moves closer until she begins to get Lov's attention, and much of our own. Then we find out that she has a harelip and that her designs are apparently on Lov's person rather than on his turnips.

In chapter 3 Ellie May gets within reach of Lov, and we have been drawn even further into the question of what will happen to him, as well as his turnips. In Jeeter's plaint, which continues along with the nonsense he has begun to talk about Ellie May, we discover that whenever he does manage to sell a load of wood he gets a dozen jars of snuff so that he and Ada won't feel hungry. With this information, we may not feel their hunger either. As Ellie May tousles Lov's hair several yards from his turnips, we discover that Ada has been ill with pellagra for several years. In the next sentence, however, Dude says that Lov is going to "big" Ellie May, and he stops chunking his ball to watch. A group of passing blacks stops to speak to Lov, who isn't interested in chatting with them at the moment. In chapter 4 Jeeter finally grabs the turnip sack and Ellie May grabs Lov, as the chorus of blacks laughs.

Other diversions from serious suffering continue throughout the novel. We are not encouraged to laugh at what the novel takes to be serious, which is the Lesters' suffering, brought about by their being unable to obtain capital for working their land. Instead, Caldwell prestidigitates, insinuating but de-emphasizing the serious. By the end he has, as it were, written two novels. Then he takes the comic one away and leaves the serious one standing. Jeeter and Ada die because the fire he sets to burn over their land works its way back to their shack during the night. Jeeter's ignorance, shown in this antiquated practice, eventually proves fatal.

The idea that comedy favors Tories has become almost proverbial. Nevertheless, many have challenged it. Stendhal found in the comedy of real social life "something of the spirit of opposition."[8] James R. Kincaid has argued that Trollope expressed his conservatism in comedy only by subverting its natural tendency.[9] Turning from literary criticism to social and political history, we find still more doubt that comedy is conservative. Crane Brinton has shown how Beaumarchais' *Marriage of Figaro* undermined the *ancien régime*.[10] Lyford P. Edwards has made the more general claim that ridicule hastened many revolutions: "The condition of repression which exists in any society before a great revolution really is stupid and silly when looked at rationally, just as it is tyrannical and unjust when regarded emotionally. Nothing undermines authority so completely as making it ridiculous—particularly to itself."[11] Turning from the history of politics to establishment politicians themselves, we find little faith in the conservatism of comedy. The Union of Soviet Writers expelled Vladimir Voinovich, and James Ngugi languished in a Kenyan prison not for his serious and tragic novels, but, as far as Amnesty International could judge, for a comic play. Comic writers, to be sure, are often conservative, but for comedy, no less than for other literary forms, claims of inherent political bias tend to cancel each other out. A writer of any persuasion or none may use it. As Wylie Sypher has said in a short treatment of the social meanings of comedy, "The ambivalence of comedy reappears in its social meanings, for comedy is both hatred and revel, rebellion

and defense, attack and escape. It is revolutionary and conservative. Socially, it is both sympathy and persecution."[12]

To some extent, the capabilities and limitations of the
pseudo-victim novel depend on the hero it uses. The loose
correlation of the unfoolish hero with the virtuous victim
gives rise to similar implications. McMurphy and Yossarian
are as clearly distinguished from Nurse Ratched and Colonel
Cathcart as are Jean Valjean and Uncle Tom from their antagonists. In the contrast of the unfoolish hero with his foolish
antagonists, comedy creates a melodrama of its own, generating a similar conceptual clarity and paying for the advantage by the risk of falling into manichaeism. The unfoolish
hero also shares with the virtuous victim a freedom from
oppressive conditions suggesting that something can be done
about injustice, and writers pay for this advantage by risking
excessive optimism. The foolish pseudo victim, on the other
hand, gives rise to implications similar to those of the flawed
victim. Chonkin and Jeeter Lester, like Clyde Griffiths and
Bigger Thomas, show the complexity which real people have
as a result of sharing some characteristics with their oppressors, and their complexity too risks confusing the reader. The
foolish hero also shares with the flawed victim more subjection to oppression, suggesting strongly that something needs
to be done, but risking excessive pessimism.

More important than these correlations, however, comedy
provides its own intellectual thrust within the pseudo-victim
novel. As a result it resembles the virtuous-victim novel with
respect to the problem of hope, although having different
resources for qualifying its optimism. With respect to the
problem of clarity, it resembles the flawed-victim novel, although demonstrating a very different complexity. Like both
of them, its limitations derive from the same source as its
strength.

Insofar as the pseudo-victim novel foregoes real pathos
and maximizes the hero's invulnerability, it tends toward optimism. No action may seem needed to help real people.
Certainly they have few problems if they resemble the hero,
because being lucky solves everything. The establishment's

vice may lose half its evil by losing all its power. Even if some action seems needed, no sense of urgency may appear. Moreover, in refusing emotional appeals to sympathy, the pseudo-victim novel may gain intellectual ends but ignore the principal spring of action in its readers. The strong sense of moral conviction and passionate self-righteousness of do-gooders may have their drawbacks, as many people keep reminding us, but where would resistance to injustice be without do-gooders?

Despite whatever optimism derives from the hero's invulnerability, the pseudo-victim novel has considerable resources for flexibility in whatever hopes it seeks to inspire. Being able to choose a foolish or unfoolish hero and a fortunate or unfortunate ending—or indeed some midpoint between them such as the partly foolish Tony Last's ending in pseudo pathos—the novelist can vary over a wide range the hero's subjection to injustice. As a result we get something of a graded series, from the relatively hopeful to the relatively unhopeful, a series ordered much like the sequence in which we have examined pseudo-victim novels. Yossarian combines the lack of subjection of the unfoolish hero with that implied by the fortunate ending. If any of these novels is excessively optimistic, therefore, it ought to be *Catch-22*, but Heller compensates by showing plenty of real suffering. Chonkin, as a foolish hero, is more subjected—to the systematic stupidification Voinovich sees his country as undergoing—but his stupidity also provides him with some protection from suffering and leads to some sort of triumph. McMurphy, although no fool and thus fairly exempt from the effects of the psychic management going on around him, eventually succumbs to it. In this way Kesey qualifies both optimism and pessimism. Jeeter Lester, as a fool whose foolishness eventually kills him, seems to give a more decidedly pessimistic view than any of the other novels considered. His invulnerability is fragile from the start, and neither the Lesters nor their situation provides much footing for hope, In fairness to Caldwell, however, one might plausibly argue that the need for readers to help people like his characters should become all the more urgent as their incapacity for helping themselves becomes more evident.

With regard to the problem of clarity in the pseudo-victim novel, we might expect a similarly graded series. To some extent we get it. Unfoolish heroes such as Yossarian and McMurphy, like virtuous victims, make the line distinct between the values of protagonists and antagonists. Foolish heroes such as Jeeter or Chonkin, like flawed victims, obscure it somewhat. But comedy itself provides a far more important influence.

Comedy obtains a certain amount of intellectual clarity by avoiding the confusions emotions can cause. The fact is, however, that the pseudo-victim novel offers at least as many interpretational problems as does the flawed-victim novel. We may recall that innocent and virtuous victims are used to protest such evils as the Poor Law, the Fugitive Slave Law, and the lawlessness of some political regimes. Readers who are persuaded can state quite definitely what they are persuaded *of* and what action they might take in consequence: harboring runaway slaves, agitation for repeal of an unjust law, or opposition to Tsarism or Stalinism. The flawed victim promotes a cultural protest against widespread false consciousness. Those it persuades know what beliefs they should reject and encourage others to reject as inauthentic, even if they cannot readily identify oppressors. The pseudo-victim novel may make an even less clearly targeted protest. If it persuades readers, what does it persuade them *of*? What might they do as a result? Novels such as *Catch-22*, *The Life and Extraordinary Adventures of Private Ivan Chonkin*, and *The Good Soldier Schweik* are often described as antiwar novels. If so, that is clear enough, and readers ought to be able to figure out what to do in order to oppose war, or perhaps some particular war. But are they antiwar novels? Perhaps so, perhaps not. *One Flew over the Cuckoo's Nest* attacks the way mental hospitals can undermine the dignity of patients, but should the readers it persuades also oppose the much more widespread therapeutic community that some professions are promoting? Or should they see a larger target in "the Combine," the object of Chief Bromden's fears? That would seem to depend on what mixture of comic paranoia and justifiable apprehension they find in those fears. What do readers laugh at when they laugh at the stupidity of Chonkin or Jeeter Lester? If they see it as socially conditioned, is it still funny? If not, is it relevant to any social issues? In the case of un-foolish heroes, how easy are readers at laughing with them instead of at them? Since Yossarian and McMurphy are both blind to their own oppressive attitudes toward others, just how loose is the correlation between them and virtuous victims? What is the precise nature of the norm, standard, or ideal they represent?

If the case against their confusion were put harshly, one might say that pseudo-victim novels merely exploit social issues, promoting a commitment so vague as to have all the advantages of noncommitment, that they respond to an apparently widespread cultural need for a confusion strong enough to ward off any sense of responsibility. It is no accident that this harsh case has some of the earmarks of Lukács' attack on the ideology of modernism.[13] I think it too harsh, however. The uncertainties in the pseudo-victim novel are simply the price it pays for its strength, placing a salutary emphasis on the complexity of social problems. If, like the flawed-victim novel, it risks some confusion, its complexity is no less valuable and is not readily available without using the special angle of vision it enjoys.

The complexity of the pseudo-victim novel reverses that of the flawed-victim novel. Instead of, or in addition to, seeing that oppression can reach down to the lowest of the low and corrupt even its own victims, we see that the lowest of the low can reach up to the oppressive system and play havoc with it. If the flawed victim interiorizes the false values of the establishment, the establishment also interiorizes the human limitations of its victims. If the flawed victim has a divided consciousness, that of the establishment can also become divided and fractured. We see in power a feedback principle. Yossarian, Chonkin, and Schweik may be victims of the army, but the army is emphatically their victim. The establishment must depend on the people it exploits, and they make mistakes. They forget to pull pins on grenades. They show up for inspection nude. They use the freedom provided by the contradictions of a system which wants the oppressed smart enough to serve it capably and dumb enough to accept their own exploitation. If the victims are like Chonkin, zealously accepting the values of the establishment, the damage may be even greater than that done by its opponents. In the other novels we have seen, the establishment occupies a position analogous to that of nemesis or fate in Greek tragedy. In the pseudo-victim novel the establishment too becomes subject to fate. It too becomes a victim, sometimes much more evidently so than the hero does. The high man on the organization chart becomes the low man on the totem pole.

The pseudo-victim novel, like the other types we have seen, derives its strength from the same source as it does its weakness. By challenging the necessity between condition and consequence, it does obscure its target and therefore its remedy. Utilitarians and Marxists have been criticized for their necessitarianism on the ground that it assigns no role to our freedom to promote greater justice. However that may be, one purpose of their necessitarianism is to forestall the objection that a change in social conditions may not bring more justice. It enables them to answer, as Zola does, that changing the right conditions must necessarily bring more just consequences. The pseudo-victim novel forfeits such an argument and leaves the reader in some wonderment, not only about what the unjust conditions are but also about whether changing anything will have beneficial effects. But if it robs possible remedies of their necessity, it also robs injustice of its necessity. The facade of omnipotence and rationality—the entire effort of entrenched power to make itself look natural and legitimate—comes tumbling down. We see instead jerrybuilt gimcrackery and constant improvisation. To mystification the pseudo-victim novel opposes mystery itself.

6

Permutations and Combinations of Victims

Let us teach them both that they are victims and that
they are responsible for everything.

—Sartre

THE preceding chapters have treated types of victims
somewhat as parts of speech isolated from morphology
or syntax. Now it should be possible to make some observations on the permutation of types within single protagonists
and the combination of types which can result from multiplying protagonists.

The first of these subjects need not detain us long, because the various conversions already examined are in fact
permutations of type: Clyde Griffiths develops from innocent
to flawed victim, for example. What remains to be done is to
look at some rudimentary principles or morphological rules
which seem to govern such transformations. Some caution
is in order, however. First, the rules proposed here make no
claims about real victimage. Second, they are tentative, based
on the preceding, somewhat macrotextual, study. Last, they
are even less prescriptive than are those of even the most
tolerant grammarians of language.

The first rule is that the innocent victim is the starting
point for all permutation of types. As far as the past of vir-

tuous or flawed victims is indicated, they can be seen to have developed through innocent victimage, motivated in part by their dissatisfactions with it. It is thus the first step beyond not being a victim at all.

Other types of victims do not develop *into* innocent victims. In real life the virtuous or the flawed may suffer fates having little or nothing to do with their character. In victim-of-society novels, once readers start accounting for the hero's suffering by some virtue or flaw, it is difficult or perhaps pointless to send them a signal that they should stop doing so. The only violation of this rule I can recall occurs in Alberto Moravia's *Conformist*. After becoming a flawed victim early in the novel partly because he thinks he has killed a man, the hero ultimately discovers the man to be alive, so that the possibility of canceling his initial conversion is suggested. Soon afterward he is killed, randomly, by an enemy warplane. Since rules are usually violated in order to conform to other, sometimes superordinate, rules, I take it that Moravia wanted to stimulate his readers to look for one, to see the hero as a victim of more than society.

If the innocent victim is the starting point for development and not a type which others develop to, the virtuous victim is an ending point, a type which does not develop into any other. In real life this rule too does not apply. Political prisoners have suffered heroically for their beliefs, only to capitulate at last. Although it is difficult to imagine a novelist engaged in social protest presenting such an experience, one might argue that Arthur Koestler does so in *Darkness at Noon*. In general, however, the reasons for creating virtuous victims in the first place tend to preclude taking them down from their pedestals. Though tempted to change, Uncle Tom and Jean Valjean keep up their heroic resistance.

If these rules are valid, it follows that the flawed victim can develop only from the innocent and to the virtuous victim. In Jean Valjean we can see at least in outline the whole story of the victim of society, made up of the whole stories of innocent, flawed, and virtuous victims.

Since flawed and virtuous victims correlate roughly with

the different types of pseudo victims, we might expect foolish heroes to develop sometimes into unfoolish ones, but not the reverse. This is the case. Such a rule, I suspect, applies beyond victim-of-society novels to comic characters in general, although they often fail to develop at all.

Changing anything to anything else implies that it has to begin with some potential for becoming what it isn't. That potential, in literary characters designed to undergo change, must exist actively as an alien part in an otherwise coherent character. In Jean Valjean the very possibility of being converted with the help of Bishop Myriel, created partly by the bread-stealing episode in his past, tempers the image of the flawed victim at the beginning. After Jean Valjean's conversion, the old rebel within him tempers the virtuous victim for the remainder of the novel. Permutation, though temporal, can be seen untemporally as a combination of types within a single character.

If so, what are we to make of a character like Harry Wilbourne in Faulkner's *Wild Palms*? He seems to be an innocent, virtuous, *and* flawed victim simultaneously. He may simply indicate an inadequacy in the scheme of classification. This is to be expected at some point or another, since no matter how comprehensive a scheme or how mutually exclusive its categories, reality often refuses to cooperate. Such straddling of categories, however, does not necessarily indicate any inadequacy, either in categories or the categorized. If the permutation of types of victims within a single character can be seen untemporally as combination, combination itself may be viewed as an immanent form of permutation, much in the way that we have already seen in Ivan Denisovich and other characters. If not, perhaps combinations of types should be seen in the way that V. L. Propp sees compounds such as the helper-donor.[1] Just as we understand the helper-donor by understanding helpers and donors, so any understanding of Harry Wilbourne which resulted from the scheme of classification used here would come simply from knowing the elements compounded.

However this may be, let us turn now to the far simpler

matter of combining types not within single protagonists, but in groups of them. Since it uses a combination of dissimilar types, Dickens' *Bleak House* will illustrate what is now called a polyphonic novel. Steinbeck's *Grapes of Wrath* and Silone's *Fontamara*, which combine similar types, will illustrate two different options for the collective novel. Then Kazantzakis' *Fratricides* will illustrate a common pattern derived by multiplying antagonists rather than protagonists.

The risks of presenting a single type of victim often lead, as we have occasionally noticed, to balancing the protagonist with other types of victims as minor characters. In *Ivan Denisovich* the innocent victim protagonist contrasts with the Captain, a virtuous victim made to suffer because of his resistance. In *Les Misérables* the virtuous victim contrasts with many innocent victims, including Fantine. In *Under Western Eyes* the flawed victim contrasts with Natalia Haldin, a virtuous victim. Such contrasts extend the range of social portrayal, and, taken with other contrasts involving characters who are not victims, they help to create what Lukács calls totality in the presentation of society. Here, however, let us see them as part of the novelist's strategy for controlling meaning.

Having large meanings and ponderous implications is no problem at all. A single sentence or word may have vast implications. The problem in fiction as in other discourse, largely boils down to inhibiting undesired implication in order to leave desired implication standing. Just as in driving cars we can adopt the tactical paranoia that everyone else on the highway is trying to kill us, we can assume in writing that readers have certain misconceptions which they will foist on our text if we do not forestall them. Harriet Beecher Stowe, for example, anticipated many of the dodges which would have occurred to readers of *Uncle Tom's Cabin*. Those who thought that only slaves suffered from slavery were shown victimage among the owners. Those who wanted to think the system could be made tolerable were shown the failures of Mrs. Shelby's kindness and of St. Clare's leniency. Those who thought the masters' self-interest would make them take care of their living property were shown Simon Legree, who could not even take care of himself. Those who thought slavery a Southern problem were shown generous Southerners and racist Yankees. Those who thought suffering ennobled people were shown Prue, who responded to beatings with drunkenness. Those who thought slaves irretrievably brutalized were shown the response of Topsy to kindness. Those who thought slavery would always continue were shown the opposition of slaves, masters, and children of masters. Those who thought slaves unable or unwilling to improve themselves or to resist were shown George Harris and his escape. Those who thought slaves naturally subservient were shown in Uncle Tom a martyr who strongly encouraged other slaves to escape rather than to submit.

From controlling unwanted implication by contrasting minor characters, it is only a step to dispensing with a principal protagonist and multiplying protagonists of equal or nearly equal stature. There may be two, as in Dreiser's *Sister Carrie*, in which Carrie's rise is made to look very ambiguous by the correlative fall of Hurstwood, creating what E. M. Forster called an "hour-glass" pattern.[2] More commonly, protagonists can be multiplied yet further in a polyphonic novel such as Solzhenitsyn's *First Circle*. Lukács has discussed its form as a sort of compounded novella, sacrificing unity of plot in order to discriminate different human responses to a similar situation: "The 'settings' that ask questions of the characters" help to create "the most important narrative and descriptive consistency of the 'totality of objects', namely the totality of human reactions to them."[3] Lukács conceives such settings narrowly, having in mind the sanatorium of *The Magic Mountain* and the research-institute prison of *The First Circle*, but in fact there are characters outside the prison who must also respond to similar questions because Solzhenitsyn sees them too as in some sense imprisoned by a similar situation. To establish a broader conception we could say simply that various characters are responding variously to a fairly homogeneous political, social and cultural atmosphere. In Dos

Passos' *USA* the settings proper are various, but the pressure at any given time, say the depression, does ask similar questions of all the characters. They respond, many of them, by becoming various kinds of victims of society.

Dickens' *Bleak House* can illustrate the multiple protagonist victim-of-society novel devoted primarily to different responses to a similar situation. It is a good, rich novel, neither better nor worse for being woven more tightly than *USA* and more loosely than *The First Circle*, and a consideration of it should diminish the impression of formal novelty these works have presented.

Bleak House opens with an extended evocation of an atmosphere unifying its various settings and calling forth responses discriminating its characters. These responses, in turn, further define the atmosphere and justify Dickens' claim for its wide provenance. Mud, fog, and gas are everywhere, and "at the heart of the fog" is the Court of Chancery, which "gives to monied might, the means abundantly of wearying out the right."[4] The atmosphere is murky and uncertain, and at its center injustice masquerades as justice, mystification as mystery, humbug as the human condition, and precedent as the pillar of state. "The forensic wisdom of the ages has interposed a million obstacles to the transaction of the commonest business of life" (p. 124), not because justice requires complexity but because injustice abhors simplicity. In its "full dress and ceremony" the highest court presents merely a "polite show" with "no reality in the whole scene" except the suffering of its victims (p. 317). Law has become bureaucratized, serving only its practitioners: "The one great principle of English law is, to make business for itself. There is no other principle distinctly, certainly, and consistently maintained through all its narrow turnings. Viewed by this light it becomes a coherent scheme, and not the mysterious maze the laity are apt to think it" (p. 503).

Like the pervasive atmosphere, the looseness of plot in *Bleak House* has long been noted. It has suspense and development, but not consecutive narration, and it ends, like the case on which much of it centers, when it has exhausted its subject. Dickens defines its characters in relation to a rather uniform set of values, all connected with injustice and its mystifications. Some characters have a penchant for mystery and secrecy rather than openness and candor. Some prefer eloquence to plain speaking. Some are indifferent rather than earnest or passionate. Some are parasites rather than producers. And some live in the past or future rather than the present.

In general, Dickens condemns the first in each of these sets of opposites and upholds the second. However, these defining values are being themselves defined in relation to each other, so that most are subject to important qualifications. Mystification is not always bad, because we can see Bagnet's fiction of masculine supremacy and the hiding of their good deeds by Jarndyce and Snagsby. Nor is its opposite always good, because we can see Vholes' apparent and Skimpole's real openness as self-serving. Similarly, eloquence is not bad in Boythorn's angry denunciations, nor is Tulkinghorn's plain speaking admirable. Indifference is not bad in George Rouncewell, who is "a vagabond of the harum-scarum order, and not of the mean sort" (p. 781), nor are the passion and earnestness of Mrs. Snagsby and Mlle. Hortense good. Living in the past or future does not distract Boythorn, Esther, and Mrs. Rouncewell, or Jarndyce and Mr. Rouncewell, from living in the present—which is not altogether good, as we can see in Skimpole. Among these values, only parasitism remains an unqualified evil and productiveness (not present-day "productivity") an unqualified good.

The victims presented in *Bleak House* similarly advance and qualify its implications. Since they come from every social class, the reader is restrained from thinking that injustice afflicts only the poor. Lady Dedlock, despite her station or because of it, suffers from her own mystifications and those of others. She harbors a secret past which brings her suffering even before it is disclosed. With her pride of manner she screens it from her fashionable world, so that psychologically she is a solitary. Like other flawed victims she suffers most because of the isolation she imposes on herself, the estrange-

ment from both her old and her new social class. But everyone in her fashionable world is alienated by an indifference
setting reality at a distance and confusing essential distinctions, and Dickens' call for earnestness and passion will seem
merely quaint unless these qualities are recognized as anti-
thetical to the indifference which destroys both the soul and
society: "But so long accustomed to suppress emotion, and
keep down reality; so long schooled for her own purposes,
in that destructive school which shuts up the natural feelings
of the heart, like flies in amber, and spreads one uniform and
dreary gloss over the good and bad, the feeling and the un-
feeling, the sensible and the senseless; she had subdued even
her wonder until now" (p. 694). The presence of Lady Dedlock in the novel also restrains the reader from thinking that
organized institutions such as Chancery are the only source
of mystification, injustice, and suffering. The fashionable
world, like Chancery, is a thing of "precedent and usage" (p.
7), ruled by the past rather than by reason—by the need to
keep busy rather than to be productive.

Richard Carstone is a flawed victim who plays by the
rules: "the uncertainties and delays of the Chancery suit had
imparted to his nature something of the careless spirit of a
gamester, who felt he was part of a great gambling system"
(p. 209). Like Clyde Giffiths he suspects the system is unjust
and hopes for a break, for he too "had been educated in no
habits of application and concentration" (p. 208). He is also
a dreamer with no "now" (p. 480), living for the future when
he is to be rich, and trying to influence that future by im-
mersing himself in the misty past of *Jarndyce v. Jarndyce*. Such
single-mindedness might resemble earnestness or passion,
but Dickens carefully rejects it as an obsession, the result of
an almost hypnotic attraction, "postponing his best truth and
earnestness, in this as in all things, until Jarndyce and Jarndyce should be off his mind" (p. 479). His indifference resembles Lady Dedlock's in its leveling of differences, and is
expressed in the fashionable ungrammaticality of "it don't
matter! It'll do as well as anything else" (p. 212). In vain
Esther Summerson remonstrates, "this is an objection to all
kinds of application—to life itself" (p. 213).

The next victim down on the social ladder is Gridley, the Shropshireman who was a farmer before becoming a full-time Chancery suitor. Unlike Lady Dedlock and Richard Carstone, he is a virtuous rather than a flawed victim. His resistance permits Dickens not only to take up this important subject but to correct or complement his narrator's presentation of what is amiss socially. Gridley insists on seeing the system very concretely: "The system! I am told, on all hands, it's the system. I mustn't look to individuals. It's the system. . . . I mustn't go to Mr. Tulkinghorn, the solicitor in Lincoln's Inn Fields, and say to him when he makes me furious, by being so cool and satisfied—as they all do; for I know they gain by it while I lose, don't I?—I mustn't say to him, I will have something out of some one for my ruin, by fair means or foul! *He* is not responsible. It's the system" (p. 198). As we have seen, Dickens' use of atmosphere presents what is wrong as pervasive and invites us to see Chancery at its heart. The cost of doing so, however, is to render the role of Chancery ambiguous. We cannot tell whether it is cause or symptom of injustice. Undoubtedly, Dickens wants us to see it both ways, in which case its bureaucrats are and are not responsible. To some degree they too are victims of something impersonal or suprapersonal. Dickens' presentation of injustice as systematic, then, can be achieved only through the deflection and diffusion of individual blame. Gridley, however, helps to establish that the systematic nature of social injustice does not preclude individual responsibility. Dickens does not hold up as a model Gridley's espousal of violence, but neither does he repudiate it entirely. What is wrong with Gridley's resistance is not so much the threat of violence it represents, but its futility. To fight the system through its individuals, in the final analysis, comes to little more than playing games with Inspector Bucket and others so subordinate that it is hard to attach much blame to them. Regardless of tactics or outcome, this fight cannot touch what is fundamentally wrong.

Lowest on the social scale are Jo, Guster, Jenny, and Liz, innocent victims designed to keep the reader from thinking that the poor are few, lazy, unwilling to help each other, picturesque, or amiable. Living outside hope and sometimes envying the dead, they display little of that resilience which many have objected to in Oliver Twist. As a not-quite-nameless few living among great numbers of the anonymous, they are instances of those "dying thus around us every day" (p. 596). To their situations they respond predictably, having little choice; but how they respond to each other and how others respond to them guide the reader's own responses. For the grasping Chadband, Jo is being justly punished for lacking religion, on the supposition that the godly are rewarded in this world. For Skimpole, more attuned to secular grace, Jo does not have the touching pathos that the fictions of poetry have. To each other, however, they respond as individuals, and they are respected as such by Esther, Snagsby, Allan Woodcourt, and those who themselves must be respected by the reader.

Other victims, at least for a time, are Snagsby, Jellyby, George Rouncewell, and the children of Neckett, Mrs. Jellyby, Mrs. Pardiggle, and Turveydrop. These permit Dickens to make discriminations which anticipate still more evasions readers might make. They establish, for example, that the root problem is injustice itself—man's inhumanity to man—not poverty or even mystification, which must be seen as consequences of injustice simply because not all victims suffer from them. The range of these characters also permits Dickens to warn the reader about possible solutions. The fact that some people, like Charley Neckett and George Rouncewell, cease being victims suggests that solutions exist for those who can command love. Some characters, however, are victims of purported solutions. The family can hardly be thought a solution when husbands beat wives, wives reduce husbands to ciphers, or their children suffer more than orphans. Philanthropy, both religious and secular, cannot be considered a solution—despite the example of Jarndyce—because many of the victims are children of philanthropists.

Those who inflict suffering are almost as numerous as the victims. Indeed, some victims are also victimizers, illustrating Esther's maxim "injustice breeds injustice" (p. 510).

Lady Dedlock, Richard Carstone, and even Gridley have their own victims, and the destitute bricklayers try to forget their suffering in drinking up their meager wages and beating their wives. Krook is a victim who seeks to victimize others. His spectacular end is not Dickens' solution to the problem of social injustice, but his vision of nature's solution—the backlash of dehumanization on those who dehumanize others. It alerts us to look in other victimizers for some sign of their own victimage, and we will always find it in their stunted characters. Spontaneous combustion, if we recall *A Tale of Two Cities*, would aptly describe Dickens' Carlylean view of revolution, and *Bleak House* contains many oblique references to revolution which make it tempting to put that construction on it here. But only in the case of Krook does it reach its destined end, and the Chancery Court with which he identifies because of his muddle must necessarily be left standing at the end of the novel despite Dickens' suggestion of its impending disintegration. Dickens thus avoids, better than some other social analysts, suggesting that his readers may leave the fight against injustice to impersonal and inevitable social forces, but he recognizes that such forces exist.

Many victimizers in *Bleak House* are lawyers, none betraying much concern for justice. In Tulkinghorn, Kenge, Vholes, and Guppy the principal constants are professionalism and mystification, which Dickens thus invites us to connect. Tulkinghorn has no personal relations or even personal conversation. Kenge uses eloquence, standard letters, and elaborately polite forms to keep others at a distance. Vholes claims to have personal ties with his daughters and father, but they are never seen. Guppy is becoming a lawyer and well on his way. He has a sporadic heart entirely disconnected from his head except when he borrows the rhetoric of calculation. The lack of personal relations causes lawyers to live entirely in an atmosphere of distrust for others, for as Vholes says, "the confiding eye of affection is not the distrustful eye of business" (p. 505). It also causes them to find the language of ordinary morality an embarrassment. Vholes uses *immoral* and *unlawful* as synonyms, and Kenge speaks of treading "in the paths of virtue and honour, and—the—a—so forth" (p. 20). Professionalism is simply another manifestation of the indifference which not only brings about injustice but stands in the way of alleviating it. By cutting away the ordinary and subverting belief in common sense, it creates mystification, serving only to shield its bureaucracy and inner workings from lay scrutiny.

In Mrs. Jellyby and Mrs. Pardiggle, Dickens presents two philanthropists who oppress their own children. They organize to do charity wholesale by having meetings, appointing committees, soliciting subscriptions, arranging testimonials, and giving to the poor only their advice. In contrast to Gridley, they treat injustice only as systematic, and to it they oppose nothing but system. Their organizing promotes and reflects indifference by transferring attention from immediate needs to bureaucracy, from the near to the far away. Like the lawyers, Mrs. Jellyby distances reality, "seeming to look a long way off" (p. 34), and we are invited to see this as a concomitant of the fact that she "devotes herself entirely to the public" (p. 31).

Lawyers and philanthropists produce empty words, but some victimizers produce even less. Turveydrop and Smallweed are old, stupid, and physically incomplete parasites—one having nothing but manners and the other having no manners at all. Harold Skimpole, however, brings to parasitism the full resources of mind and art. Dickens has taken the response he does not want readers to make to injustice and presented it within the novel through this thoroughly selfish trifler. In his sophistication, Skimpole sees Gridley's suffering as occupying his combativeness well, the Neckett children as charming in their social virtues, American slaves as compensated by the poetry they inspire in him, Jo as too unpoetic to become interesting through crime, and Richard as happy enough in his delusions. In short, all suffering serves some agreeable purpose: "It might be in the scheme of things that A should squint to make B happier in looking straight; or that C should carry a wooden leg, to make D better satisfied with his flesh and blood in a silk stocking" (p. 478). Though often congratulating himself on his sympathy and sensitivity, Skimpole is the most indifferent person in the novel, and its only artist. He should make it impossible for any reader to believe that poetry will save us.

Among those who are neither victims nor victimizers Dickens embodies his solution to the injustice he presents, and it is drawn largely from Carlyle's secularization of the New Testament. If indifference results from seeing at a distance, the solution is attending to those who are near, being a good neighbor. In Esther Summerson's words, cited earlier, "I thought it best to be as useful as I could, and to render what kind services I could, to those immediately about me; and to try to let that circle of duty gradually and naturally expand itself" (p. 96). If "injustice breeds injustice," duty also breeds duty. This injunction to work for others, without organizing or theorizing, should not lead people to expect others to work for them, however. Jarndyce urges, "Trust in nothing but Providence and your own efforts" (p. 165).

Among those suggesting solutions we should also count a group of characters who might be called code heroes: The Bagnets, Mrs. Rouncewell, George Rouncewell, and Phil Squod. They have a soldierly or feudal aspect to them, not because Dickens admires the medieval or the military, but because they show the doing of duty and the social ties resulting from personal loyalties. Their characteristic action is work, a virtue which Dickens does not see as merely bourgeois. The bourgeoisie proper is represented by Mr. Rouncewell, the captain of industry. He is clearly becoming a greater social force while Sir Leicester Dedlock is becoming a lesser one. Since Dickens presents injustice so often as the dead hand of the past, and in Krook's death sees its disintegration, perhaps we should see the forward-looking industrialist as a regenerative force, at least until Dickens' presentation of another captain of industry in *Hard Times* shows him disabused of such hopes. We might better say, however, that productiveness is the solution for parasitism, for another character who certainly embodies Dickens' solution is Boythorn, who could have served as the model for Thomas Mann's Mynheer

Peeperkorn: "He lived in a pretty house, formerly the Parsonage-house, with a lawn in front, a bright flower-garden at the side, and a well-stocked orchard and kitchen-garden in the rear, enclosed with a venerable wall that had of itself a ripened ruddy look. But, indeed, everything about the place wore an aspect of maturity and abundance" (p. 227). In his house and his association with producing, Boythorn contrasts strongly with Tulkinghorn, who is a misogynist living in quarters formerly occupied by the state. Just as Tulkinghorn seems a successor to government, exercising a power which the novel denies the state, Boythorn exercises a love which the novel denies the church.

Bleak House and other polyphonic victim-of-society novels show society as a whole by presenting different responses to the conditions defining it. The victims are related—to each other, their victimizers, their benefactors, and even apparent bystanders—but they need not know one another. Lady Dedlock never meets Richard Carstone, who never meets Jo, who never meets Gridley, who never meets Lady Dedlock. Protagonists can be multiplied, however, primarily to develop their similarities rather than their differences and to show that they form a group or community of victims within society as a whole. They remain different, and society as a whole remains a matter of interest. But differences become important more for their effect or lack of effect on group cohesion, and those who are not victims often recede well into the background. Instead of using the polyphonic novel to present multiple victims of society, then, writers can use the collective novel, as they have so often been urged.

In the thirties many Marxist critics recommended the collective novel. Malcolm Cowley, for example, saw Dos Passos' *USA* as a collective novel which had realized one of his hopes.

The real hero of *The 42nd Parallel* and *1919* is society itself, American society as embodied in forty or fifty representative characters who drift along with it, struggle to change its course or merely to find a secure footing—perhaps they build a raft of wreckage, grow fat on the refuse floating about them; perhaps they go under in some obscure eddy—while the current sweeps them onward toward new social horizons. In this sense, Dos Passos has written the first American collective novel.[5]

More commonly the collective novel was urged as a means of presenting the struggle of the masses or proletariat against wealth or capitalism. Henri Barbusse, who had written a collective novel himself, urged, "Today we must enter into the collective drama! It is even more stirring than the drama of the individual, and it does not end in death. We must raise on stage a new protagonist, the most imposing of all: the masses."[6] Granville Hicks even more closely linked the collective novel with the presentation of a group as protagonist: "On the one hand, the author must fully convey his sense of the group's unity in feeling action and his recognition that it is more important than the individuals who compose it. On the other hand, he must make the reader feel that the group is made up of comprehensible human beings, and he must differentiate individuals insofar as they have separate parts to play."[7]

Insofar as the group is an innocent, virtuous, flawed, or pseudo victim, the possibilities for the collective novel should accord fairly well with those of novels already discussed. Barbusse's poilus in *Under Fire* are innocent victims, Jorge Icaza's Indians in *Huasipungo* pass from innocent to virtuous victims, and Zola's miners in *Germinal* are flawed victims. Viewed in this way, collective novels offer few advantages. They do show directly that the suffering they present is not isolated, and they do, as Barbusse says, show a hero with a good claim to immortality, so that no tragedy is final. These advantages, however, have been readily gained by the novelists we have already seen, focusing on single protagonists. We must look elsewhere for the peculiar strengths of the collective novel. Its privileged subject is a collective consciousness, its center of interest the cohesion among its members. It seeks to discover what causes unity and disunity, which differences are healthy in a group and which fatal, and why some groups resist oppression and others do not. In exploring these questions it does not prejudice its conclusions by focusing unduly on leaders. On the contrary, it makes the very idea of leadership problematic.

The search for the sources of group resistance may be carried out by presenting a group which does not resist or one which does. The lack of group resistance may be seen in Barbusse's *Under Fire*, but I shall examine it in Steinbeck's *Grapes of Wrath*. Resistance may be seen in *Huasipungo*, Norris' *Octopus*, or Cantwell's *Land of Plenty*, but I shall examine it in Silone's *Fontamara*. Because making these choices leaves certain matters out of account, I want to mention two of them here.

Some novels, such as Victor Serge's *Birth of Our Power*, deal with successful group resistance, showing the emergence of a new or improved social order and commemorating those who suffered to bring it about. Despite their worthy purpose, I omit these novels because, as a rule, they celebrate the end of social victimage rather than protesting its continuance. In treating strike novels, Walter Rideout has wondered why, during a period in which American labor was going from one success to another, the writers of strike novels kept dealing with strikes which failed.[8] The reason, I suggest, is primarily that the writers wished to produce social criticism. The second matter, which I shall less justifiably omit developing, is a frequent concern of novels depicting group resistance which fails—the reasons for failure. In *Huasipungo*, for example, despite our admiration for the Indians' resistance, we must finally see it as a jacquerie which could have achieved little. Their cohesion, when it comes, leads only to their death with dignity. To have any chance of success, it needed to be greater, submitting itself to the advantages and perhaps also the disadvantages of organization.

In *Grapes of Wrath* Steinbeck mentions so often the desirability and imminence of group resistance that we can easily forget how little he shows. The Joads are an extended family sharing with and helping others, the ancient image of the community of man. When they meet in a "congress" or "family government," "they seemed to be part of an organization of the unconscious."⁹ As we can see from the way in which members take their places, it is hierarchically arranged from Grandpa, the titular head, through Pa and Uncle John, the adult men, the women, then the children. When asked for her advice about taking in Jim Casy, however, Ma shows a power belying her station. The family has lost its land and sold most of its belongings to go to California, and their story is a catalog of attrition and disintegration. Successively, they lose the dog, Grandpa, Noah, Connie, Grandma, Jim Casy, Tom, and Al, until at the end the group is reduced to Pa, Ma, Rose of Sharon, two smaller children, and Uncle John, who continually wants to go away. As a group the Joad family is an innocent victim throughout the novel, showing, like many other innocent victims, considerable resiliency and a dignity still alive under the pressures of degradation. Yet, like the thousands of other Okies and mankind itself, they endure. "Ever'thing we do—seems to me is aimed right at goin' on" (p. 577).

Struggling against this disintegration and recording the pain it entails is Ma. Even at the start she is a product of transcendence: "Her hazel eyes seemed to have experienced all possible tragedy and to have mounted pain and suffering like steps into a high calm and a superhuman understanding" (p. 100). Losing house and land has hardened her and made her dream of organized resistance—"if we was all mad the same way" (p. 104)—but Ma's resistance is almost wholly to the oppression, not to the oppressors. It manifests itself in opposing those whose desire to leave threatens group solidarity and in opposing her son Tom when he wants to strike out at the oppressors. Her own power in the family, to her way of thinking, is itself a sign of its disintegration, the fallen hierarchy resulting when the breadwinner no longer wins bread. By the end of the novel she is readily consenting to the departures she had resisted and pronouncing the elegy over the family's disintegration: "Use' ta be the fambly was fust. It ain't so now. It's anybody" (p. 606). She has concluded, so that the reader can too, that the family is not a unit of resistance, but at best of endurance.

The family has its own divisions—some of no moment, some quite necessary, and some regrettable. The very old fight each other as do the very young, some young adults want to leave to have their own families, and some loners want out, either for their good or the family's. As a group, moreover, it must inevitably be divided from those outside it. Ma's principle of sharing with others receives a severe jolt when she prepares a scant meal for the family and insists that they eat it in the tent to avoid the gaze of a number of hungry children outside. Social conditions force them as a group to compete with others for work, wages, and good picking. Hunger pits them against others in their situation, just as it causes the defection from their class of strikebreakers, police rowdies, orchard guards, and the man who runs the company store. Oppression brings about some solidarity among the oppressed, but this solidarity is limited by the disintegration and dissension which it also fosters.

For the image of resistance in *The Grapes of Wrath* we must turn away from the family and the sprawl of the dispossessed, to organization. In the camps of migrants along the way community arises spontaneously, establishing rights and rules, and automatically turning to the most wise for leadership (chap. 17). But this spontaneous community, though a good foundation, is not enough, and in the federal camp we see it developing into the formal organization of elected committees and a leadership which can resist the forces trying to destroy it. It is modeled, as Steinbeck has one character observe, on a union: "Fella organizin' for the union was a-talkin' out on the road. He says we could do that any place. Jus' stick together. They ain't raisin' hell with no two hunderd men" (p. 488). If the solution is organization, so too is the enemy. When dispossessed of their land, those who want to resist don't know whom to shoot. Banks and businesses are impersonal organizations, as is the economic system which destroys needed food to keep prices up.

At the same time the Joad family is disintegrating, and in part contributing to that disintegration, Jim Casy and Tom Joad are developing as leaders in the struggle to organize the workers. In the beginning Jim Casy is a leader with no place to lead people to, a preacher whose Christianity has turned to the humanitarian pantheism of believing only that men must stick together for the sake of the one soul they share. He finds a new vocation when he joins Tom Joad's impromptu resistance to a deputy who is trying to kill a worker, and then goes to jail claiming to have been the only person who interfered. When we see him next, he has met a union organizer in jail and become one himself. He cannot persuade Tom Joad to organize his family and the other workers to support the strike, but when thugs come in and kill him, Tom avenges him and then devotes himself to Casy's work. Presumably he will continue to warn the oppressed against self-pity and self-reproach, and like Jim dissuade them from useless violence.

In *The Grapes of Wrath* oppression does bring about some degree of solidarity: the Okies find their identity in the epithet of their enemies. But the novel does not demonstrate Steinbeck's second historical law, that "when a majority of the people are hungry and cold they will take by force what they need." Rather, it illustrates the third: "repression works only to strengthen and knit the repressed" (p. 324). Oppression is aimed at people, and as we have seen, its effects are mixed. Repression is aimed at organization, and its effect in the novel is to create one leader from the people, then another to replace him when he falls. To the conundrum of whether the leader produces the resistance or the resistance the leader, Steinbeck suggests that both are true.

Steinbeck's Okies share many attitudes with the *cafoni* of Ignazio Silone's *Fontamara*. Both believe that working on land must underlie any valid claim to owning it, and both are fundamentally conservative, responding to the disruption and dislocation caused by capitalistic control of agriculture and of the forces of law and order. They see themselves as victims of a colonialism of the rich over the poor—embodied primarily in banks. To them, writing is a sign of the legalized theft of their labor, and their exchange of oral anecdote is fundamental to building the solidarity they so much need. Under such circumstances, to resist requires committing crime. If we see these resemblances mainly as signs of Silone's literary influence, however, we will miss the most important likeness between the two novels, the similarity of two groups struggling against similar economic conditions. As Silone says, "all poor farmers are alike in every country. They are men who cause the earth to bear fruit; they suffer from hunger; and whether they are called fellahs, coolies, peons, muzhiks, or *cafoni*, they form their own nation, their own race and their own church all over the world, even though no two are exactly alike."[10]

Nevertheless, the differences between these two novels must receive our attention. Steinbeck's narrative voice is impersonal, but very poetic. Without loss of concreteness it presents the Joads as merely one of thousands of dispossessed groups of Okies. Silone's narrative voice is the voice of the people themselves. Thematically, and often grammatically, the subject is "we," as a father tells what he did with the other men, his wife what she did with the other women, and their son what he did with other young people. The reader has direct access to the group's consciousness and sees it develop toward greater solidarity. The language of both groups seems to express more than they know, but Steinbeck usually achieves this effect through pathos and Silone through humor. Most important to our purposes, however, is the way in which leadership is presented, signalized by the different Christian analogues each makes. In *The Grapes of Wrath* Jim Casy's death is obviously a new crucifixion. In *Fontamara* the group itself is crucified. Underlying this difference is the fact that Silone shows considerably more group resistance.

The relationship of the leader to the group in *Fontamara* will not be clear without some textual considerations. Silone published the novel first in 1930 while in exile, and revised it for its first publication in Italy in 1945. The original edition was translated into English by Michael Wharf and the revised edition by Harvey Fergusson II. In a foreword to the latter, Malcolm Cowley has written,

Chiefly his revisions consist in omitting several passages—among them one long episode—and in telling us more about the life of Berardo Viola, but still their effect is decisive. In the new version, as translated by Harvey Fergusson II, the community recedes into the background—much as in *Man's Fate*—and Berardo comes forward as the hero and dying god. We still have the sense of hearing a medieval legend, rough-hewn and angular, reduced to its essential outlines as if by generations of storytellers in the village marketplace, but it is no longer a *fabliau* about peasants and the Devil. Instead it becomes a golden legend about Christ reborn, tempted in the wilderness, and crucified in Jerusalem—or is Berardo rather John Baptist, who prophesies the coming of the Solitary Stranger? (p. 7).

I regret differing from a fine critic who can speak much more authoritatively than I of the collective novel—but let us look at some of the revisions.

The omitted long episode to which Cowley refers is the delightful story told by Peppino Goriano, who went to Rome to find work, and after spending time as a pimp, thief, and convict, earned his living as a political thug (ch. 6). After his return to Fontamara he continues to be an important character. By omitting this passage and other signs of him, Silone removed the only character with a stature comparable to Berardo Viola's, and this did indeed make Berardo stand out more, an effect enhanced by touching up somewhat the character of the shoemaker, Baldissera, whose commitment to the past makes him a foil to Berardo. Silone gives very little additional space to Berardo. He does, however, add to the revised edition several references to the "Via Crucis" of the villagers themselves, so that if we want to see Berardo as Christ, we must see him as one among many. He also has the villagers refer several times to the local capitalist as the Devil, so that we see the struggle in the novel as primarily their struggle. He also deletes from Berardo's last words an appeal to the villagers to keep unified, for, as we will see, the villagers are unified well before Berardo joins their cause. For either edition, R. W. B. Lewis's description of *Fontamara* is true: "For two-thirds of the novel Fontamara is itself the hero, the village and the villagers taken en masse."[11] We can add, furthermore, that Berardo's sacrifice is the prelude to that of the villagers which ends the novel.

Unlike *The Grapes of Wrath*, *Fontamara* does not permit us to separate the development of the group from that of the leader, and Silone is even more equivocal about who is leading whom. At the beginning the villagers are torn by dissension. As in *Bleak House*, the proliferation of laws and lawyers has brought about a weakening of the social bonds, and as far as their means permit, the people engage in suit and countersuit. When the stream which waters their farms is diverted, they fear getting involved. The women make their protest only to prevent two outcast whores from being the only ones who do, and it is marked by quarrels about precedence among themselves. Like the whores, Berardo is an individualist held in some awe because he is outspoken even with the authorities, a leader with or without followers. Since he owns no land, he has nothing to lose, and very early he tries to bring peace among the other peasants quarreling over what little is left of the water. He is an exceptional peasant, whose mother keeps reminding everyone that the Violas are different, more likely to die on the gallows than in bed.

As a result of their protest the villagers become thought of as subversive by the authorities, who fear them. Despite their claim that they never talk about politics—only about prices, salaries, taxes, laws, licenses, war, and emigration—they find that these are political and forbidden topics. Berardo is delighted. He has always argued against arguments because they lead to the villagers' accepting every injustice and has recommended direct reprisals against their oppressors. When the Fascists come to shoot up the place and intimidate them, the villagers fear Berardo will compromise them with violence. But he amuses himself "by suggesting impudent answers to the boys in his group, all of which involved being against and not for something" (p. 139). The villagers' disarray is contrasted with the Fascists' strength.

Any one of us could beat up three of them. But at this moment what did we have in common with one another, all of us who had been born in Fontamara, as we had? Nothing—except that we were at the same place at the same time! Beyond this, everyone thought of his own affairs. Everyone was trying to think of his own way to get out of the formation of armed men and to leave the others in. Everyone was the head of a family and was thinking of his family. Maybe Berardo was thinking of something else, but he had no land and no wife (p. 135).

At this point the villagers have the kind of unity which Steinbeck's Okies achieve. They see themselves as a group which is oppressed as a group, and their enemies fear a unity which has not at all emerged.

Immediately afterwards Silone starts to reverse the relation between the leader and the group. Berardo becomes engaged to marry Elvira, and he devotes himself entirely to earning the money needed for buying the land he sees as necessary to his self-respect as a husband: "He was no longer the man he had once been. He didn't joke or laugh and he avoided company" (p. 148). At the same time the villagers become more united. When the loss of their water kills their crops and threatens a foodless winter, they are ready to resist. As a group, they believe themselves to have been treated so as to abrogate the social contract with the state.

"When the laws of the government aren't any good any more and when the ones who should enforce them are the first to break them, then we go back to the law of the people," replied Baldissera indignantly.
"What is the law of the people?" someone asked him.
"God helps those who help themselves!" said Baldissera, who had ended up by embracing Berardo Viola's bitter doctrine (p. 173).

Here again we have the hourglass pattern, the villagers ready to resist and Berardo ready merely to mind his own business:

"When the whole village had ended up thinking as he formerly did, Berardo had changed his way of thinking" (p. 179).

Berardo tries to get work in Rome but cannot do so because the village's conduct has been reported to the police. He is thrown into jail with a group of men on suspicion of being the Solitary Stranger who is active in clandestine newspapers urging resistance against the Fascists. In the cell with him is the Solitary Stranger himself, with whom he argues politics until resistance is reborn in him and "he was his old self again" (p. 206). To the police he pretends to be the Solitary Stranger and maintains the pretense under torture until his new friend has been released. When he retracts his confession so that he too can be released, he is killed. With the help of the Solitary Stranger, the villagers, together now and able to resist, print a newspaper to try reaching peasants in nearby villages, and the Fascists respond by killing as many of them as possible.

As a group the villagers begin by becoming innocent victims, suffering not because of their character but because a wealthy and powerful man wants their water. They end as virtuous victims, suffering because they resisted. They begin by fighting among themselves and end by banding together. In between, they undergo as a group a conversion similar to Pelagueya Vlasov's. We don't so much see new hope created as old hopes destroyed—the hope of muddling through, of saving oneself amid the general ruin, or of seeking protection in the legal system. Indeed, the law no longer protects them, and their loss of hope in the aptly named Don Circostanza is later matched by Berardo's loss of hope in Don Pazienza.

This negative moment of conversion does not suffice, however. To resist, the villagers must grasp an alternative, or the possibility of one, some source of order contrasting with the lawless oppression they reject. This is the ordinary function of ideology, but for them ideology is not abstract. They can remember the time before the Fascists came and even the earlier time when law was simple, and their resistance takes the form of seeking alternatives by asking the question Lenin appropriated from Chernyshevsky, "What can we do?" Just as Jean Valjean's alternative is embodied in Bishop Myriel and Pelagueya's in her son's little group of socialists living the future, their alternatives are embodied in Berardo, a model representing yet another way of concretizing ideology. He is an exemplar and helper in their conversion, but he is not their leader because their conversion occurs at a time when he no longer resists, when they see him as confused. By the time they actually do resist, moreover, he is dead, and only his example of self-sacrifice can affect them. We are not dealing, then, with leadership, at least in any ordinary sense, and we do well to recall that when Silone was first writing, *Il Duce* meant Mussolini.

Just as Berardo serves as the villagers' model or helper, the Solitary Stranger serves as Berardo's. If we ask simple, obvious questions such as who the Solitary Stranger is and what he does, we run headlong into mysteries serving little other purpose than preventing us from viewing him simply. We cannot even be clear that the man from Avezzano is the only Solitary Stranger, since "those who are found with illegal printed material always confess that they got it from the Solitary Stranger," and "on the same day he is discovered in several different provinces and even at the frontier" (p. 201). As to what he does, Silone made a revealing textual revision when he deleted the first of the following two sentences in revising the novel: "Wherever he turns up the farmers start rioting. Wherever the farmers start rioting he turns up."[12] Clearly, the peasants to some extent lead the Solitary Stranger, whatever he does. If we look to his one clearly ascertained act with the peasants, it consists of providing them with a simple duplicating machine on which they can print their paper, then leaving before they decide what they will say in it. He can seem to be in different places at the same time because he provides channels of communication, vehicles for community. When he converts Berardo, he creates not a follower but a friend. Berardo does not do what the Solitary Stranger wishes, return to Fontamara to lead the peasants, but what the Solitary Stranger himself does. In the language of later revolutionaries, he takes credit—and therefore blame—for resistance. Like Christ, to whom he has been compared, he tries to deflect guilt from others, but unlike Christ he shares it with the community, something few leaders have done, at least willingly.

Another configuration can result from multiplying and differentiating antagonists rather than protagonists. In its purest form, which may be illustrated by Ralph Ellison's *Invisible Man*, it has a plot in which the protagonist is first victimized by establishment power, then, after joining its opponents, is also victimized by them. More loosely, it is the situation of a character caught between at least two powerful and opposed political groups, such as we find in Norman Mailer's *Barbary Shore*. For convenience protagonists in such situations may be called double victims, but they represent no new addition to the types already elaborated, all of which may serve as double victims. In Walter Scott's *Old Mortality* Henry Morton is an innocent victim caught between Burley's extremist Scottish covenanters on the one hand, and Claverhouse's Royalists loyal to England on the other. In Victor Hugo's *Ninety-Three*, Gauvin is a virtuous victim caught between Royalists and the Republicans fighting in the Vendée. In Conrad's *Under Western Eyes* Razumov is a flawed victim caught between the lawlessness of autocracy and the lawlessness of revolution. In Biely's *St. Petersburg* Nikolai is a pseudo victim caught in the same bind. Malraux's *Man's Fate* is a collective novel in which Kyo and his comrades are virtuous victims fighting against those both outside and inside their own revolutionary organization.

As these illustrations may suggest, double victims and double-victim novels are extremely common. From a purely literary point of view the attraction seems to be the intensification of dilemma. From a representational point of view it seems to be the opportunity to present both sides in a conflict. Walter Scott, who may be credited with inventing the double victim, has explained the "insipidity" of his heroes and the "twists and turns" in their stories as an attempt to produce some immediate and perhaps temporary effect. This could hardly be done without representing the principal character either as inconsistent or flexible in his principles. The ease with which Waverley adopts, and afterwards forsakes the Jacobite party in 1745, is a good example of what we mean. Had he been painted as a steady character, his conduct would have been improbable. The author was aware of this; and yet unwilling to relinquish an opportunity of introducing the interior of the Chevalier's military court, the circumstances of the battle of Preston-pans, and so forth, he hesitates not to sacrifice poor Waverley, and to represent him as a reed blown about at the pleasure of every breeze.[13]

Also from a representational point of view, the double victim facilitates the portrayal of modern man as the object of contention in mass politics, where, according to Jacques Ellul, "the individual is seized, manipulated, attacked from every side: the combatants of two propaganda systems do not fight each other, but try to capture *him*."[14]

As a target for competing propaganda, the double victim has another attraction closer to our concern with rhetoric and poetics. All novels may be dialectical, but the double-victim novel is particularly so. Since the two contending sides are negated by the unjust suffering they impose on the double victim, sometimes the result is little more than the protagonist's and presumably the reader's rejection of both. On the other hand, the result may go well beyond, but we should not allow our hopes to get too high for that. Just as Noam Chomsky has found that in linguistics "combinations of systems rarely have interesting properties,"[15] and R. S. Crane has been similarly skeptical about mixing systems of literary criticism,[16] we may not find blends of political theories attractive, at least in the abstract. Furthermore, we should resist the automatic awe which dialectic so often inspires, and adopt a show-me attitude toward the alluring prospects which it holds out.

Even when the dialectic simply calls down a plague on both houses, some sort of synthesis, no matter how rudimentary, will be embodied in, and probably expressed by, the protagonist. If, as is usually the case, the opposed positions are the status quo and the radical or revolutionary assault upon it, positioning the protagonists somewhere between the two will favor some sort of moderate change. The beliefs of many double victims resemble Razumov's rejection of revolution for evolution in *Under Western Eyes*. Even if the protagonists are revolutionaries of sorts, as in Styron's *Confessions of Nat Turner*, Bontemps' *Black Thunder*, and Bellamy's *Duke of Stockbridge*, they are still moderate relative to some other characters, usually the extremists among their own followers.

Such moderation can be very attractive, favoring both justice and peace as it usually does, but it often appears insufficiently political to not-so-moderate readers. Resting on the rejection of political alternatives backed by organized constituencies—sometimes both inside and outside the novel—it may have a breadth of appeal unmatched by the depth necessary to organized political activity. Indeed, many novels accused of being apolitical or antipolitical turn out on inspection to advocate moderation through double victims. Raymond Williams has found apolitical Kingsley's *Alton Locke* and Dickens' *Hard Times*, in the latter of which Stephen Blackpool is a double victim.[17] Irving Howe has similarly criticized *Under Western Eyes* and Silone's *Bread and Wine*.[18] Significantly, Williams is attracted by Robert Tressel's *Ragged-Trousered Philanthropists*, which makes its double victim a socialist who rejects both the bourgeois employers and their oppressed but apolitical employees.[19]

I see more value in apoliticism than do Williams and Howe. The rejection of both sides, particularly when politics has become extremely polarized, may be the only way of carrying out a commitment to humane politics. Anarchists have argued that apoliticism can be beneficially subversive. Certainly it can be constructive and healing at times. Many historical novels present double victims longing for that peace and freedom from politics that the reader already enjoys. James Ngugi's *Grain of Wheat* and Mikhail Sholokov's *Silent Don*, appearing shortly after the Kenyan and Russian revolutions, presented heroes weary of the whole business and appealed to the common humanity of former adversaries.

Less predictable and more interesting dialectically are novels that drop the status quo as one term and attempt a synthesis of positions that can be opposed both to it and to each other. The dialectic is, as it were, displaced from the antagonists between whom the double victim suffers, and the point at issue shifts accordingly. In *Man's Fate*, Kyo and his comrades are double victims who suffer the gunfire of both the warlord establishment and the Kuomintang opposing it, but the dialectic, as Murray Krieger observed, is "between the inhuman discipline of the Party apparatus, most purely symbolized by Vologin, and the all-too-human private fanaticism of the terrorist Ch'en."[20] In *Invisible Man*, similarly, the protagonist suffers both because of the establishment, represented in part by Bledsoe, and the Party, represented by Jack, who has him charged with political deviation. But the dialectic is between the political discipline of the Party and the apparently unpolitical and certainly undisciplined alienation of Rinehart and, eventually, Tod Clifton. For both novels the key terms in opposition are power and freedom. In Silone's *Bread and Wine*, the action of which is completed only in *The Seed Beneath the Snow*, Pietro Spina is caught between Fascism and his fading Communism, but the dialectic is between socialism and Christianity.

Similarly, Father Yanaros, in Nikos Kazantzakis' *Fratricides*, suffers from both the Communists and the Truman-supported "blackhoods" whom they are trying to overthrow, but the dialectic is between Communism and Christianity. The novel would have been very timely had it been published in 1949, when Kazantzakis pronounced it finished, but he kept working on it from time to time until his death in 1959. Thus it might have benefited from his feeling in 1950 that his "old antinomies [were] beginning to become organized into an organic synthesis."[21]

Father Yanaros is the pastor in the village of Castello, held by the blackhoods but periodically attacked by the red-hoods camped in the nearby mountains. He strongly condemns both sides for their killing of each other and of un-armed villagers. During Easter week he refuses to hold the Resurrection service, arguing that Christ continues to be crucified. When he beseeches God to let him know which side to support, he is told that God gave man freedom and will not intervene for either side. He decides to surrender the village to Drakos, his reprobate son and the captain of the reds, on condition that they respect property and harm no one in the town. After he and his followers manage, peacefully and somewhat miraculously, to disarm the black garrison, he sees the people as having risen, providing Christ with an apt resurrection. The reds come in and break their promise, executing all the able-bodied who refuse to fight for them. Father Yanaros asks to be executed too, and when he announces that he intends to go from village to village seeking to organize men to fight against both sides, he is shot.

As we might expect, the synthesis of Communism and Christianity in Father Yanaros consists largely of his embodying their common values. Both are international. Both deny that the earth can really belong to any individual. Both urge the brotherhood of man. Both want to help widows, orphans, the poor, and the downtrodden. Both want to make people more human through sharing. The materialism of Communism is assimilated to a theology heavily stressing incarnation and the redeeming of man and all creation from the groans of bondage. The Christ who drove the money changers from the Temple is invoked as consistent with Marx, and the Christ whose kingdom was not of this world is unmentioned. Significantly, the main feature common to both, yet ignored, is their institutionalization in church and party. In place of institutions we have, as in many double-victim novels, the people. We are invited to hope that they might somehow function in a spontaneous way, as if they were organized without really being organized. Such a hope is not as odd as it may sound and does indeed form part of both Christianity and Communism in the form of providence and history, but it is an article of belief hard to realize, even imaginatively.

The failure of Father Yanaros' Christian pacifism occasions the final step in Kazantzakis' dialectic. Early in the novel we find, "In this world, he thought, you're either a lamb or a wolf. If you're a lamb, you're eaten up; if you're a wolf, you do the eating. My God, is there no third animal, a stronger, kinder one?"[22] After the debacle, Father Yanaros finds this third term, when he resolves, "I am going to preach about the new Christ, the armed Christ" (p. 252)! In the process he has moved from the Miltonic position—that God permits evil so that man can be free—to the position with which John Stuart Mill thought the best of thinkers solved the problem of evil—that God is good, but not omnipotent: "so freedom is not almighty, it is not immortal, it, too, is the child of man and it needs him!" (p. 250).

Here the Christian will likely see bad theology, resulting from making Christianity into a political philosophy, and the Marxist a bad political philosophy resulting from making Communism a religion, but the dialectic has forfeited their approval from the start. It cannot be judged within the framework of either. Nevertheless, whether right or wrong, practical or impractical, it is hardly dazzling, new, or profound. It justifies us, I think, in restraining our expectations about literary dialectic. It makes the somewhat less dialectical novels with which we have been concerned look much better. And perhaps it should suggest too that if we are to see literature as fundamentally dialectical, at least in this manner, we have good reason to moderate rather than inflate our claims for it.

7

Conclusion: Literary Form and Political Implication

By now, any answers this book provides to the questions it addresses should be evident, but some overview of the argument and comment on the conclusions is in order.

In treating its privileged subject of oppression, the innocent-victim novel handles fairly well the problems of hope and clarity, but its privileged form, comic romance, forfeits organic plot.

In treating its privileged subject of political repression, the virtuous-victim novel runs the risk of excessive optimism and a clarity which can oversimplify. Its privileged form, tragic romance, allows an organic plot and a good look at both the unjust institution and the community of those resisting it.

In treating its privileged subject of false consciousness, the flawed-victim novel runs the opposite risks of excessive pessimism and an unclear presentation of the target it attacks, but its privileged form, realism, allows an organic plot and a good look at the psychological disasters caused by a powerful and manipulable culture.

In treating its privileged subject of power, the pseudo-victim novel runs the risks of too much optimism and too little clarity, but its privileged form, comedy, allows it to capitalize on its lack of organic plot by unmasking the pretensions to rationality and inevitability that entrenched institutions make.

In treating the different responses that different types of victims make to injustice, the polyphonic novel undercuts the risks of presenting only one type and achieves considerable comprehensiveness, at some sacrifice of plot. In treating group cohesion, the collective novel, on the other hand, tends to multiply victims of the same type, thus running the same risks as novels with single protagonists. In treating political dialectic, the double-victim novel usually presents two antagonists opposed not only to the protagonist, but to each other, and its limitations seem to be those of dialectic or mediation itself.

Each of these forms has certain tendencies which make it more suitable for some purposes than for others, and each runs some risk, so that none is ideal. Nevertheless, these risks usually derive from corresponding strengths, and they do not doom the victim-of-society novel to misfire. Long ago, when beginning research on this book, I suspected otherwise. I tended to accept the view that every major literary form is inherently conservative. By their considerable resourcefulness, however, novelists showed me that they can cope very well with the constraints within which they operate, often turning risks into advantages. They persuaded me that fiction, comedy, tragedy, romance, and realism are not so limited in their potentials as to allow us to speak meaningfully of inherent generic biases.

If this is the case, why have so many people thought otherwise? Why has unintended conservatism been so often found in victim-of-society novels?

Part of the reason is political. The normal and healthy inertia which keeps human beings from being blown about by every wind can be called conservatism, and in this sense most people, fortunately, are conservatives. However, if we conflate this conservatism with the extremely narrow variety which rejects all claims to justice as threats to order, conservatism becomes a vast cosmic trap, in which the victim-of-society novel is only one of many casualties. If we do not, such novels may be fundamentally conservative, but in no very disturbing sense. The same is true of other fundamental conservatisms. All sensory perception depends on the distortion of a present image toward memories of past images. All thinking depends on fitting previously derived categories in very approximate ways to new experience and thus making mistakes. All argument depends on finding common ground and ignoring the fact that logical objections can be made to it. All action takes place in given, not ideal, situations, thus producing feedback and side effects. All interaction depends on taking people as we find them and to a great extent leaving them that way. We're limited creatures, living with the weight of the past upon us. Nevertheless, we still perceive, think, argue, act, and interact. Whatever theories we spin—imperfectly, of course—we still live by Chesterton's maxim that anything really worth doing is worth doing badly.

Another political reason that any victim-of-society novel can be charged with insufficient radicalism or liberalism is that any political policy, principle, or value can be. The same is true when insufficient conservatism is the issue. In Thomas Mann's *Dr. Faustus* there is a character who makes a game of such charges. Faced with self-styled conservatives, he knows that they must want to perpetuate some past political settlement once achieved by radicalism or liberalism. It is child's play for him to point out their bad faith and then fetch his own conservative credentials from a dim prehistory which no one can challenge. Similarly, some radicals keep upping the ante for radicalism until it becomes a party of one. That too is child's play. Thus we should expect to find some conservatism in novels protesting against social injustice because we can find some in any political stance. It is usually a sign that the writer is dealing with reality, not that literary form has frustrated political expression.

Victim-of-society novels have also been accused of misfiring or failing to harmonize political and literary values because, as we have seen, some principles of literary criticism operate as covert political censorship. The insistence that all tragedy be Aristotelian or that all comedy show the social integration of the hero makes any particular tragedy or comedy either bad art or conservative. A tension theory of literature, if pushed far enough, would have us see any value in a literary work as negated by its opposite, so that nothing is really championed. The rejection of melodrama can make suspect any conceptual clarity. The rejection of sentimentality in the name of tough-mindedness can insist on a hardheartedness which makes tolerable any injustice to others. The insistence on art for art's sake, pure poetry, the autonomy of literature, or formalism—the name of the product keeps changing—does not exclude content or convictions from literary works, but only content or convictions seeking to affect the world outside the individual. Such principles are not the neutral underpinnings of an objective, disciplined, or scientific literary criticism, but masks for ideology. Nor do they facilitate our understanding even of literary works relatively unconcerned with social protest.

The victim-of-society novel is only one of many literary forms which deal with social and political issues. For this reason, any conclusions a study of it can make about political expression in general must be limited. Like those above, they can simply challenge broad principles that others have adopted. Briefly stated, the conclusion of this book as to political expression in general is simply that the resistance which literature makes to it has often been exaggerated. Either political or literary aims, when taken separately, show many paradoxes and incompatibilities which ought not to be attributed to their combination, and some literary and political aims are quite compatible. If we do not expect from those who have taken up the pen the attitudes of those who have taken up the sword, and if we do not invoke principles of literary evaluation which are routinely violated by acknowledged masterpieces not intent on social protest, we can reasonably expect what indeed we find, that many committed works deserve considerable esteem on both political and lit-

erary grounds. We can also expect, of course, to be challenged in the name of "higher" political or literary standards,
or both, because it is easy to conceive either literature or
politics in such a way as to insure their incompatibility.

Whatever the precise contours of political expression in
literature as a whole, such a conclusion carries two note-
worthy consequences. First, it is no unmixed blessing that
some literary works can be used for political expression without significant misfiring. Belief in autonomy theories is, after
all, reassuring, because although literature may not do us
much good politically, it at least should do no great harm.
However, if literature can promote justice, it can also promote injustice. Since we live in a culture more saturated with
"literature" than any in the history of mankind—lyrics on
the radio, drama on television, and best-seller fiction in su-
permarkets—it is disquieting to give up the belief that something in the nature of literature is protecting society automatically from baneful political influence. Moreover, if our
search for political content in literary works is a search for
conservatism or liberalism or radicalism, we may miss it altogether, for, as we have seen, political tendencies do not
always align in this way. For example, much of the drama on
television promotes consumption and attacks self-denial, just
as the advertisements do, and similar content may be found
also in "high" or "serious" literature, which must compete
with other media. Is this conservative, liberal, or radical? I
don't know, but it is dangerous.

Second, the prescriptive literary criticism which has
sought some literary form to recommend to politically committed writers is a very questionable enterprise. All the forms
we have seen are open to political expression, but all have
constraints suggesting that there is unlikely to be any ideal
form which ought to be promoted on political grounds.
Therefore, although this book has argued that the victim-of-
society novel is still a viable literary form or set of forms, I
do not seek to promote its use. There are likely to be many
other literary forms as good for expressing political commitment, and there are other commitments as important as po-

litical commitment. Indeed, one could argue, probably with the blessing of Marx at least, that writers can best promote an understanding of society merely by writing as well and as truthfully as they can.

Notes

Index

Notes

1. INTRODUCTION: A PROBLEM IN COMPOSITION

1. William Godwin, *The Adventures of Caleb Williams*, ed. George Sherburn (New York: Rinehart, 1960), p. xxiii.

2. Wilbur L. Cross, *The Development of the English Novel* (New York: Macmillan, 1928), p. 91.

3. Malcolm Cowley, "Dos Passos: The Poet and the World," *Think Back on Us . . . A Contemporary Chronicle of the 1930s*, ed. Henry Dan Piper (Carbondale: Southern Illinois Univ. Pr., 1967), p. 213.

4. Harry Levin, *The Gates of Horn: A Study of Five French Realists* (New York: Oxford Univ. Pr., 1966), p. 62.

5. Harry Levin, "Society as Its Own Historian," *Contexts of Criticism* (New York: Atheneum, 1963), p. 183.

6. R. S. Crane makes imitative and didactic works mutually exclusive groups in *The Languages of Criticism and the Structure of Poetry* (Toronto: Univ. of Toronto Pr., 1953), pp. 156–58. Sheldon Sacks claims that satires, apologues, and novels are mutually exclusive in *Fiction and the Shape of Belief* (Berkeley: Univ. of Calif. Pr., 1964), pp. 26, 46. John Reichert argues persuasively that any really mutually exclusive genres would be trivial or empty of interpretive implication in "More than Kin and Less than Kind: The Limits of Genre Theory," *Theories of Literary Genre*, Yearbook of Comparative Criticism, vol. 8, ed. Joseph P. Strelka (University Park: Pennsylvania State Univ. Pr., 1978), pp. 60–66. Todorov sees genres as not mutually exclusive in *The Fantastic: A Structural Approach to a*

Literary Genre, trans. Richard Howard (Ithaca, NY: Cornell Univ. Pr., 1975), pp. 21–22.

7. René Wellek and Austin Warren, *Theory of Literature* (New York: Harcourt, 1956), p. 221.

8. *Sir Walter Scott, On Novelists and Fiction*, ed. Ioan Williams (London: Routledge and Kegan Paul, 1968), p. 193.

9. G. Jean-Aubry, *Joseph Conrad: Life and Letters* (Garden City, NY: Doubleday, 1927), vol. 2, p. 81 (hereafter cited parenthetically in the text).

10. Donald B. Gibson, "Ralph Ellison and James Baldwin," *The Politics of Twentieth-Century Novelists*, ed. George A. Panichas (New York: Hawthorn, 1971), p. 309; on Malraux and Silone, see Murray Krieger, *The Tragic Vision: Variations on a Theme in Literary Interpretation* (Chicago: Univ. of Chicago Pr., 1960), pp. 52, 77; Irving Howe, *Politics and the Novel* (Cleveland: World, 1957), p. 23; David Caute, *The Illusion: An Essay on Politics, Theatre and the Novel* (New York: Harper, 1971), p. 67; James Baldwin, *Notes of a Native Son* (New York: Bantam, 1968), p. 14; Leon Trotsky, *Literature and Revolution* (Ann Arbor: Univ. of Michigan Pr., 1960), p. 70.

11. George Steiner, *The Death of Tragedy* (London: Faber and Faber, 1963), p. 125.

12. Sigmund Freud, *Civilization and Its Discontents*, trans. James Strachey (New York: Norton, 1961), p. 33.

13. H. D. F. Kitto, *Greek Tragedy: A Literary Study* (Garden City, NY: Doubleday, 1955), p. 118; René Girard, *Violence and the Sacred*, trans. Patrick Gregory (Baltimore: Johns Hopkins Univ. Pr., 1977), pp. 76–78.

14. *The Complete Works of William Hazlitt*, ed. P. P. Howe (London: Dent, 1932), vol. 11, p. 24.

15. André Malraux, *Days of Wrath*, trans. Haakon M. Chevalier (New York: Random House, 1936), p. 4.

16. T. W. Adorno, "Society," trans. Fredric R. Jameson, *Salmagundi*, nos. 10–11 (Fall 1969–Winter 1970), p. 144.

17. G. K. Chesterton, *Charles Dickens* (London: Methuen, 1913), pp. 269–70.

18. For this reason I am puzzled by Marvin T. Herrick's seeing rhetoric as a part of poetics in his excellent article,

"Rhetoric and Poetics," *Princeton Encyclopedia of Poetry and Poetics*, ed. Alex Preminger (Princeton: Princeton Univ. Pr., 1974), p. 702.

19. Tzvetan Todorov, *Introduction to Poetics*, trans. Richard Howard, Theory and History of Literature, (Minneapolis: Univ. of Minnesota Pr., 1981), vol. 1, p. 6; Wayne Booth, Preface to *The Rhetoric of Fiction* (Chicago: Univ. of Chicago Pr., 1961).

20. R. S. Crane, *Critical and Historical Principles of Literary History* (Chicago: Univ. of Chicago Pr., 1971), p. 11.

21. E. D. Hirsch, Jr., *Validity in Interpretation* (New Haven: Yale Univ. Pr., 1974).

22. Kenneth Burke, "*Coriolanus*—and the Delights of Faction," *Language as Symbolic Action: Essays on Life, Literature, and Method* (Berkeley: Univ. of Calif. Pr., 1966), p. 83 (hereafter cited parenthetically in the text).

23. Kenneth Burke, *The Rhetoric of Religion: Studies in Logology* (Berkeley: Univ. of Calif. Pr., 1970), p. 221.

24. Burke, *Language as Symbolic Action*, p. 498.

25. John Reichert, *Theories of Literary Genre*, p. 77.

26. Kenneth Burke, *The Philosophy of Literary Form: Studies in Symbolic Action* (New York: Vintage, 1957), p. 262.

27. Richard Ohmann, "Literature as Act," *Approaches to Poetics*, ed. Seymour Chatman, Selected Papers from the English Institute (New York: Columbia Univ. Pr., 1973), p. 96. Fredric Jameson objects to the concept of "strategy," one of Burke's favorite terms for dealing with purpose: "The problem is that this concept, which so boldly proclaims itself a praxis-word, tends, by focusing our attention on the inner mechanisms of the symbolic act in question, to end up bracketing the act itself and to suspend any interrogation of what constitutes it as an act in the first place, namely its social and ideological purpose." From "The Symbolic Inference; or Kenneth Burke and Ideological Analysis," *Critical Inquiry*, vol. 4 (1978), p. 514.

28. S. I. Hayakawa, *Language in Thought and Action*, 3rd ed. (originally published 1939; New York: Harcourt, 1975), p. 130n.

2. THE INNOCENT VICTIM

1. Elizabeth Gaskell, *Mary Barton*, ed. Myron F. Brightfield (New York: Norton, 1958), pp. 56–57.

2. Pierre Legouis, for example, has argued from Moll Flanders' evident lack of innocence that she is not a victim of society at all. "Marion Flanders est-elle une victime de la Société?" *Revue de l'Enseignement des Langues Vivantes*, vol. 48 (1931), pp. 289–99.

3. Edgar Johnson, "General Introduction," *Dombey and Son*, by Charles Dickens (New York: Dell, 1963), p. 19.

4. Kitto, *Greek Tragedy*, pp. 264, 133, 281.

5. Northrop Frye, *The Secular Scripture: A Study of the Structure of Romance* (Cambridge: Harvard Univ. Pr., 1976), p. 54 (hereafter cited parenthetically in the text).

6. Stephen Crane, *Maggie: A Girl of the Streets*, ed., Thomas A. Gullason (New York: Norton, 1979), p. 132 (hereafter cited parenthetically in the text).

7. Charles Child Walcutt, *American Literary Naturalism, A Divided Stream* (Minneapolis: Univ. of Minnesota Pr., 1956), p. 122.

8. Preface to the third edition, *Oliver Twist* (originally published 1837–38; New York: New American Library, 1961), p. vi (hereafter cited parenthetically in the text).

9. Humphrey House, *The Dickens World* (London: Oxford Univ. Pr., 1960), p. 220.

10. Chesterton, *Charles Dickens*, p. 278.

11. George Orwell, *A Collection of Essays* (Garden City, NY: Doubleday, 1954), p. 93.

12. Frank Kermode, *The Sense of an Ending: Studies in the Theory of Fiction* (New York: Oxford Univ. Pr., 1967), p. 30.

13. J. Hillis Miller, *Charles Dickens: The World of His Novels* (Bloomington: Indiana Univ. Pr., 1969), p. 42.

14. Patrick Brantlinger, *The Spirit of Reform: British Literature and Politics, 1832–1867* (Cambridge, MA: Harvard Univ. Pr., 1977), pp. 48–55.

15. Charles Dickens, *Bleak House* (London: Dent, 1956), p. 96.

16. House, *Dickens World*, pp. 92–100.

17. Frye, *The Secular Scripture*, p. 164.

18. Preface to the Charles Dickens Edition, 1867, *Oliver Twist*, pp. xvii–xviii.

19. For the influence of Carlyle's anti-utilitarianism on Dickens, see Michael Goldberg, *Carlyle and Dickens* (Athens: Univ. of Georgia Pr., 1972).

20. Kenneth Burke, *A Rhetoric of Motives* (Berkeley: Univ. of California Pr., 1974), pp. 298–301.

21. E. M. Forster, *Aspects of the Novel* (London: Edward Arnold, 1953), pp. 91–92.

22. René Girard, *Deceit, Desire, and the Novel: Self and Other in Literary Structure*, trans. Yvonne Freccero (Baltimore: Johns Hopkins Univ. Pr., 1965), pp. 307, 300.

23. Aleksandr Solzhenitsyn, *One Day in the Life of Ivan Denisovich*, trans. Max Hayward and Ronald Hingley (Originally published 1962; New York: Bantam, 1970), p. 178 (hereafter cited parenthetically in the text).

24. Kermode, *Sense of an Ending*, p. 138.

25. *The New York Review of Books* (4 Oct. 1973), vol. 20, p. 14. The development of this idea in Solzhenitsyn's writings is treated briefly by Francis Barker, *Solzhenitsyn: Politics and Form* (London: Macmillan, 1977), pp. 10–13.

26. Freud, *Civilization and Its Discontents*, p. 25.

27. Barker, *Solzhenitsyn*, p. 25.

28. "The Concept of Plot and the Plot of *Tom Jones*," *Critics and Criticism*, ed., R. S. Crane, abridged ed. (Chicago: Univ. of Chicago Pr., 1957), p. 67.

29. Edwin Muir, *The Structure of the Novel* (London: Hogarth, 1954), p. 24.

30. Georg Lukács, *Solzhenitsyn*, trans., William David Graf (Cambridge: MIT Pr., 1971), p. 22.

31. Harriette Arnow, *The Dollmaker* (New York: Avon, 1974). This edition reprints Joyce Carol Oates' essay as an afterword (hereafter cited parenthetically in the text).

32. Frye, *The Secular Scripture*, pp. 77, 57.

33. Northrop Frye, *Anatomy of Criticism: Four Essays* (Princeton: Princeton Univ. Pr., 1957), p. 186.

34. Raymond Williams, *Culture and Society: 1780–1950* (London: Chatto and Windus, 1959), pp. 87–109; *The English Novel: From Dickens to Lawrence* (New York: Oxford Univ. Pr., 1970), pp. 48–50.

35. Especially in his treatment of Ernst Bloch, Fredric Jameson ably defends utopianism in *Marxism and Form: Twentieth-Century Dialectical Theories of Literature* (Princeton: Princeton Univ. Pr., 1971).

36. *Complete Works of William Hazlitt*, vol. 11, pp. 64–68.

3. THE VIRTUOUS VICTIM

1. In Theodore Ziolkowski's *Fictional Transformations of Jesus*, see especially chap. 3, "The Christian Socialist Jesus," and chap. 6, "Comrade Jesus" (Princeton: Princeton Univ. Pr., 1972); R. W. B. Lewis, *The Picaresque Saint: Representative Figures in Contemporary Fiction* (Philadelphia: Lippincott, 1959). Some cases of virtuous victims, but many more of victims who happen to be virtuous, are discussed in R. F. Brissenden's *Virtue in Distress: Studies in the Novel of Sentiment from Richardson to Sade* (London: Macmillan, 1974), which is fully aware of social implications.

2. Gerald F. Else, *Aristotle's Poetics: The Argument* (Cambridge, MA: Harvard Univ. Pr., 1957), pp. 364, 367.

3. *The Ethics of Aristotle*, trans. J. A. K. Thomson (Baltimore: Penquin, 1962), p. 31.

4. *Aristotle's Poetics: A Translation and Commentary for Students of Literature*, trans. Leon Golden (Englewood Cliffs, NJ: Prentice-Hall, 1968), p. 176f.

5. Augusto Boal, *Theater of the Oppressed*, trans. Charles A. and Maria-Odilia Leal McBride (New York: Urizen, 1979), p. 44.

6. Frye, *The Secular Scripture*, p. 154.

7. Walter B. Rideout, *The Radical Novel in the United States, 1900–1954: Some Interrelations of Literature and Society* (New York: Hill and Wang, 1966), p. 180.

8. Jerome Hamilton Buckley, *Season of Youth: The Bil-*

dungsroman from Dickens to Golding (Cambridge: Harvard Univ. Pr., 1974), pp. 17–18.

9. René Girard, *Deceit, Desire, and the Novel,* pp. 294–314.

10. Kenneth Burke, *Permanence and Change: An Anatomy of Purpose* (Indianapolis: Bobbs-Merrill, 1977), p. 142.

11. Thomas S. Kuhn, *The Structure of Scientific Revolutions* (Chicago: Univ. of Chicago Pr., 1970), pp. 151, 148, 158.

12. Leo Tolstoy, *Resurrection,* trans. Louise Maude (New York: Norton, 1966), p. 244.

13. *Les Misérables,* trans., Charles E. Wilbour (Originally published 1862; New York: Modern Library, n.d.), p. 77 (hereafter cited parenthetically in the text).

14. Georges Piroué, *Victor Hugo Romancier: ou les Dessus de L'Inconnu* (Paris: Éditions Denoël, 1964), p. 50.

15. André Brochu, *Hugo, Amour/Crime/Révolution: Essai sur les Misérables* (Montréal: Les Presses de l'Université de Montréal, 1974), p. 241.

16. Crane Brinton, *The Anatomy of Revolution* (New York: Random House, 1965), pp. 39–50, 69–86.

17. Herman Melville, *Billy Budd, Sailor,* ed. Harrison Hayford and Merton M. Sealts, Jr. (Chicago: Univ. of Chicago Pr., 1962), p. 78 (hereafter cited parenthetically in the text).

18. Hayford and Sealts survey the criticism, pp. 24f. Any collection of criticism of the novel is likely to contain some of the debate about Vere. *Melville's "Billy Budd" and the Critics,* ed. William T. Stafford (Belmont, CA: Wadsworth, 1962) contains defenses of Vere by Milton R. Stearns and E. L. Grant Watson, and attacks by Phil Withim and Leonard Casper. Perhaps I might do well to bury in this footnote the confession that I have lived under too many Navy captains to be an impartial observer of Captain Vere.

19. Herman Melville, *White-Jacket, or The World in a Man-of-War,* ed. Hennig Cohen (Originally published 1850; New York: Holt, 1967), p. 137 (hereafter cited parenthetically in the text).

20. *The Confessions of Jean Jacques Rousseau* (New York: Modern Library, n.d.), p. 336.

21. Graham Greene, *The Lawless Roads* (London: Heinemann, 1955), p. 129.

22. Graham Greene, *The Power and the Glory* (Originally published 1940; New York: Penguin, 1977), p. 23 (hereafter cited parenthetically in the text).

23. Alexander Welsh, "Opening and Closing *Les Misérables*," *NCF*, vol. 33 (1978), pp. 20–21.

24. Harriet Beecher Stowe, *Uncle Tom's Cabin* (Originally published 1852; New York: Harper, 1965), pp. xviii–xix (hereafter cited parenthetically in the text).

25. Moody Prior cites many such accusations against the novel and defends it well in "Mrs. Stowe's Uncle Tom," *Critical Inquiry*, vol. 5 (1979), pp. 635–50.

26. Edmund Wilson, *Patriotic Gore: Studies in the Literature of the American Civil War* (New York: Oxford Univ. Pr., 1969), p. 6.

27. Richard Chase, *The American Novel and Its Tradition* (Garden City, NY: Doubleday-Anchor, 1957), p. 38.

28. Eric Bentley, *The Life of the Drama* (New York: Atheneum, 1964), pp. 203–4, 210–15. See also Robert Bechtold Heilman, *Tragedy and Melodrama: Versions of Experience* (Seattle: Univ. of Washington Pr., 1968).

29. Frye, *The Secular Scripture*, p. 50; Bentley, *Life of the Drama*, p. 202; Peter Brooks, *The Melodramatic Imagination: Balzac, Henry James, Melodrama, and the Mode of Excess* (New Haven: Yale Univ. Pr., 1976), p. 4.

30. James L. Rosenberg, "Melodrama" and Wylie Sypher, "Aesthetic of Revolution: The Marxist Melodrama," *Tragedy: Vision and Form*, ed. Robert W. Corrigan (San Francisco: Chandler, 1965), pp. 243, 267; Brooks, *Melodramatic Imagination*, p. 15; Chase, *American Novel and Its Tradition*, p. 38.

31. George Worth, *Dickensian Melodrama: A Reading of the Novels*, Univ. of Kansas Humanistic Series, no. 50 (Lawrence: Univ. of Kansas, 1978), p. 20.

32. Alan Swingewood, *The Novel and Revolution* (London: Macmillan, 1975), p. 61.

33. Brian Wilkie, "What is Sentimentality?" *College English*, vol. 28 (1967), p. 570.

34. Kitto, *Greek Tragedy*, p. 57.
35. Steiner, *Death of Tragedy*, pp. 7–9.
36. Burke, *Philsophy of Literary Form*, pp. 83–84. The point is also developed in Burke's *Rhetoric of Religion*, pp. 229–30.

4. THE FLAWED VICTIM

1. Richard Bjornson, *The Picaresque Hero in European Fiction* (Madison: Univ. of Wisconsin Pr., 1977), p. 11.
2. John Orr, *Tragic Realism and Modern Society: Studies in the Sociology of the Modern Novel* (London: Macmillan, 1977).
3. Theodore Dreiser, *An American Tragedy* (Originally published 1925; New York: Dell, 1959), pp. 188, 22 (hereafter cited parenthetically in the text).
4. F. O. Matthiessen, *Theodore Dreiser* (New York: William Sloane, 1951), p. 191.
5. Willard Motley's *Knock on Any Door* (New York: Appleton-Century-Crofts, 1947), for example, begins the story of Nick Romano, who will eventually be executed for murder, by showing him happily discharging his duties as an altar boy. The son of a prosperous grocer, he lives in the right part of the city, attends a good school, enjoys a loving atmosphere, and dreams of the day when he can become a priest. His father's business failure throws him out of this desired world and into a bad neighborhood and a bad school. He soon participates marginally in petty crime, but is sent to reform school for a bicycle theft he did not commit. There the brutality helps turn him from a very shy boy to a rebel, capable of human relationships only within the subculture of Skid Row, where he takes to more serious crime. This novel may suggest a good reason for not starting the flawed victim's story so far back. Motley's real subject, the social deformation of his hero and its results, leads him to extreme compression in presenting the process of innocent victimage. He devotes but a few pages to it, in contrast with the hundred or so pages which Harriette Arnow devotes to the Kentucky

idyll of *The Dollmaker*. As a result, the desirability of the desired world cannot be as convincing as it should be.

6. Theodore Dreiser, "Background for *An American Tragedy*," *Esquire*, vol. 50 (Oct. 1958), p. 157.

7. Ellen Moers, *Two Dreisers* (New York: Viking, 1969), p. 275.

8. Donald Pizer, *The Novels of Theodore Dreiser: A Critical Study* (Minneapolis: Univ. of Minnesota Pr., 1976), p. 240.

9. Claudio Guillén, *Literature as System: Essays toward the Theory of Literary History* (Princeton: Princeton Univ. Pr., 1971), p. 80.

10. Matthew Josephson, *Zola and His Time* (New York: Macaulay, 1928), pp. 529–30, 533.

11. Levin, *The Gates of Horn*, pp. 336–37.

12. F. W. J. Hemmings, *Emile Zola* (Oxford: Clarendon Pr., 1966), p. 119.

13. Emile Zola, *L'Assommoir*, trans. Atwood H. Townsend (Originally published 1877; New York: New American Library, 1962), p. 44 (hereafter cited parenthetically in the text).

14. Richard Lehan, *Theodore Dreiser: His World and His Novels* (Carbondale: Southern Illinois Univ. Pr., 1969), pp. 157–69.

15. Buckley, *Season of Youth*, p. 17.

16. Richard Wright, *Native Son* (Originally published 1940; New York: Harper, 1966), p. xxvi (hereafter cited parenthetically in the text).

17. Baldwin, *Notes*, pp. 26–27.

18. Ralph Ellison, "Richard Wright's Blues" and "The World and the Jug," *Shadow and Act* (New York: New American Library, 1966).

19. Baldwin, *Notes*, p. 27.

20. Baldwin, *Notes*, p. 24; Ellison, *Shadow and Act*, pp. 7, 136.

21. Stendhal, *Memoirs of an Egotist*, trans. T. W. Earp (New York: Noonday, 1958), p. 83.

22. Stendhal, *Red and Black*, trans. Robert M. Adams

(Originally published 1831; New York: Norton, 1969), p. 359 (hereafter cited parenthetically in the text).

23. Michael Wood, *Stendhal* (Ithaca: Cornell Univ. Pr., 1971), p. 89.

24. *Selected Journalism from the English Reviews by Stendhal with Translations of Other Critical Writings*, ed. Geoffrey Strickland (New York: Grove, 1959), pp. 152–53. See also p. 178.

25. Leon Blum, "A Theoretical Outline of 'Beylism'," *Stendhal: A Collection of Critical Essays*, ed. Victor Brombert (Englewood Cliffs, NJ: Prentice-Hall, 1962), p. 107.

26. Wood, *Stendhal*, p. 91.

27. John Stuart Mill, *Autobiography* (Oxford: Oxford Univ. Pr., 1955), p. 120.

28. Josephson, *Zola and His Time*, p. 528.

29. Hemmings, *Emile Zola*, p. 124.

30. Erich Auerbach, *Mimesis: The Representation of Reality in Western Literature*, trans. Willard Trask (Garden City, NY: Doubleday-Anchor, 1957), p. 408.

31. René Wellek, "The Concept of Realism in Literary Scholarship," *Concepts of Criticism*, ed. Stephen G. Nichols, Jr. (New Haven: Yale Univ. Pr., 1965), pp. 240–41.

32. George Levine, *The Realistic Imagination: English Fiction from Frankenstein to Lady Chatterley* (Chicago: Univ. of Chicago Pr., 1981), p. 56.

33. Levin, *The Gates of Horn*, pp. 60–62.

34. Wellek, *Concepts of Criticism*, p. 241.

35. Levin, *The Gates of Horn*, p. 66.

36. Readers wishing to follow the debate on the political implications of realism may find many references in George Levine's recent book on realism, cited above. For the work of those participants mentioned in the text and not previously cited bibliographically, see the following: Bertolt Brecht, "Against Georg Lukács," trans. Stuart Hood, *New Left Review*, no. 84 (March-April 1974), pp. 39–53; *Brecht on Theatre: The Development of an Aesthetic*, trans. John Willett (New York: Hill and Wang, 1964); Georg Lukács, *The Meaning of Contemporary Realism*, trans. John and Necke Mander (London: Mer-

lin, 1969); Roland Barthes, *Writing Degree Zero and Elements of Semiology*, trans. Annette Lavers and Colin Smith (Boston: Beacon, 1970); Alain Robbe-Grillet, *For a New Novel: Essays on Fiction*, trans. Richard Howard (New York: Grove, 1965); Terry Eagleton, *Marxism and Literary Criticism* (Berkeley: Univ. of Calif. Pr., 1976); Leo Bersani, *A Future for Astyanax: Character and Desire in Literature* (Boston: Little, Brown, 1976); and Gerald Graff, *Literature Against Itself: Literary Ideas in Modern Society* (Chicago: Univ. of Chicago Pr., 1979). Of those contributing to this debate but rejecting any need for categorical choice between realism and modernism, perhaps the most notable is Fredric Jameson, in *The Political Unconscious: Narrative as Socially Symbolic Act* (Ithaca, NY: Cornell Univ. Pr., 1981).

37. Terry Eagleton, *Walter Benjamin, Or Towards a Revolutionary Criticism* (London: Verso, 1981), pp. 157–59.

38. Lionel Trilling, *Beyond Culture: Essays on Literature and Learning* (New York: Viking, 1968), pp. 76–77.

39. Burke, *The Philosophy of Literary Form*, pp. 277–78.

40. Georg Lukács, "The Intellectual Physiognomy of Literary Characters," *Radical Perspectives in the Arts*, ed. Lee Baxandall (Baltimore: Penguin, 1972), pp. 106–7.

41. Hemmings, *Emile Zola*, p. 116.

42. Robert M. Adams, "Liking Julien Sorel", *Red and Black*, trans. Robert H. Adams (New York: Norton, 1969).

43. Budd Schulberg, *What Makes Sammy Run?* (New York: Penguin, 1978), p. 252.

44. Caute, *The Illusion*, p. 262. Ian Watt is sometimes cited as believing in the novel's bias toward individualism, but he may be speaking rather of a bias in eighteenth-century culture. See *The Rise of the Novel: Studies in Defoe, Richardson and Fielding* (Berkeley: Univ. of Calf. Pr., 1964), pp. 60–92, 198.

45. Michel Butor, "Thoughts on the Novel: The Individual and the Group," *Perspectives on Fiction*, ed. James L. Calderwood and Harold E. Toliver (New York: Oxford Univ. Pr., 1968), pp. 169–82.

46. Ernest Hemingway, *To Have and Have Not* (New York: Scribner's, 1970), p. 98.

47. Meir Sternberg, *Expositional Modes and Temporal Ordering in Fiction* (Baltimore: Johns Hopkins Univ. Pr., 1978), pp. 99–102.

48. Fyodor Dostoevsky, *Notes from Underground*, trans. Mirra Ginsburg (New York: Bantam, 1974), pp. 77–78 (hereafter cited parenthetically in the text).

5. THE PSEUDO VICTIM

1. Francis Macdonald Cornford, *The Origin of Attic Comedy*, ed. Theodore H. Gaster (Garden City, NY: Doubleday-Anchor, 1961), p. 172.

2. Frye, *Anatomy of Criticism*, pp. 172–74. Frye's distinctions are more complex than my own.

3. Joseph Heller, *Catch-22* (Originally published 1961; New York: Dell, 1970), p. 425 (hereafter cited parenthetically in the text).

4. Valdimir Voinovich, *The Life and Extraordinary Adventures of Private Ivan Chonkin*, trans. Richard Lourie (Originally published 1969, 1975; New York: Bantam, 1979), p. 22 (hereafter cited parenthetically in the text).

5. Ken Kesey, *One Flew over the Cuckoo's Nest* (Originally published 1962; New York: Viking, 1970), p. 31 (hereafter cited parenthetically in the text).

6. Henri Bergson, "Laughter," *Comedy*, ed. Wylie Sypher (Garden City, NY: Doubleday-Anchor, 1956), p. 64.

7. Erskine Caldwell, *Tobacco Road* (Originally published 1932; New York: New American Library, n.d.), p. 8 (hereafter cited parenthetically in the text).

8. Stendhal, *Selected Journalism*, p. 171.

9. James R. Kincaid, *The Novels of Anthony Trollope* (Oxford: Oxford Univ. Pr., 1977), p. 102.

10. Brinton, *Anatomy of Revolution*, pp. 67–68.

11. Lyford P. Edwards, *The Natural History of Revolution* (Chicago, Univ. of Chicago Pr., 1970), p. 64.

12. Sypher, "The Meanings of Comedy," *Comedy* p. 242.

13. Lukács, *The Meaning of Contemporary Realism*, p. 17.

6. PERMUTATIONS AND COMBINATIONS

1. V. L. Propp, *Morphology of the Folk Tale*, trans. Laurence Scott (Austin: Univ. of Texas Pr., 1968), pp. 80–81.

2. Forster, *Aspects of the Novel*, pp. 137–38.

3. Lukács, *Solzhenitsyn*, pp. 49, 31. Lukács' account of the character contrasts in *The First Circle* may well be supplemented by Alan Swingewood's in *The Novel and Revolution*, pp. 229–46.

4. Charles Dickens, *Bleak House* (Originally published 1852–53; London: Dent, 1907), pp. 2–3 (hereafter cited parenthetically in the text).

5. Cowley, *Think Back on Us*, p. 216.

6. Henri Barbusse, "Writing and War," *New Masses: An Anthology of the Rebel Thirties*, ed. Joseph North (New York: International, 1969), p. 214.

7. Quoted by Jack Conroy, "Robert Cantwell's *Land of Plenty*," *Proletarian Writers of the Thirties*, ed. David Madden (Carbondale: Southern Illinois Univ. Pr., 1968), pp. 78–79. Originally published in *The Anvil*, Sept.-Oct. 1933.

8. Rideout, *The Radical Novel*, pp. 178–80.

9. John Steinbeck, *The Grapes of Wrath* (Originally published 1939; New York: Viking, 1971), p. 135 (hereafter cited parenthetically in the text).

10. Ignazio Silone, *Fontamara*, trans. Harvey Fergusson II (Originally published 1930, revised 1945; New York: Dell, 1961), p. 14 (hereafter cited parenthetically in the text).

11. Lewis, *The Picaresque Saint*, p. 146.

12. Ignazio Silone, *Fontamara*, trans. Michael Wharf (New York: Modern Age, 1938), p. 129. In Fergusson's translation of the revised edition, the passage is on p. 201.

13. *Sir Walter Scott, On Novelists and Fiction*, pp. 240–41. John P. Farrell has elaborated on some of the themes which result from using such heroes in *Revolution as Tragedy: The Dilemma of the Moderate from Scott to Arnold* (Ithaca, NY: Cornell Univ. Pr., 1980).

14. Jacques Ellul, *Propaganda: The Formation of Men's At-*

titudes, trans. Konrad Kellen and Jean Lerner (New York: Knopf, 1968), p. 254.

15. Noam Chomsky, *Language and Responsibility*, trans. John Viertel (New York: Pantheon, 1979), p. 56.

16. Crane, *The Languages of Criticism*, pp. 28–29.

17. Williams, *Culture and Society*, pp. 94–118.

18. Howe, *Politics and the Novel*, pp. 92, 222.

19. Williams, *The English Novel from Dickens to Lawrence*, pp. 155–56.

20. Krieger, *Tragic Vision*, p. 51.

21. Helen Kazantzakis, *Nikos Kazantzakis: A Biography Based on His Letters*, trans. Amy Mims (New York: Simon and Schuster, 1968), pp. 480, 549.

22. *The Fratricides*, trans. Athena Gianakas Dallas (Originally published 1963; Oxford: Bruno Cassirer, 1964), p. 86 (hereafter cited parenthetically in the text).

Index

215

George Goodin is Associate Professor of English at Southern Illinois University, where he has taught since 1966. He received his bachelor's degree from Marquette University and his doctorate from the University of Illinois. He has published articles on Sterne, Conrad, Scott, and discourse analysis, and edited *The English Novel in the Nineteenth Century* (1972).